The Poverty Problem

To Yvonne: Without you, none of this is possible.

The Poverty Problem

How Education Can Promote Resilience and Counter Poverty's Impact on Brain Development and Functioning

Horacio Sanchez

FOR INFORMATION:

Corwin

A SAGE Company

2455 Teller Road

Thousand Oaks, California 91320

(800) 233-9936

www.corwin.com

SAGE Publications Ltd.

1 Oliver's Yard

55 City Road

London EC1Y 1SP

United Kingdom

SAGE Publications India Pvt. Ltd.

B 1/I 1 Mohan Cooperative Industrial Area

Mathura Road, New Delhi 110 044

India

SAGE Publications Asia-Pacific Pte. Ltd.

18 Cross Street #10-10/11/12

China Square Central

Singapore 048423

Publisher: Jessica Allan

Senior Associate Content
  Development Editor: Lucas Schleicher

Associate Content
  Development Editor: Mia Rodriguez

Production Editor: Astha Jaiswal

Copy Editor: Patrice Sutton

Typesetter: C&M Digitals (P) Ltd.

Proofreader: Lawrence W. Baker

Indexer: Integra

Cover Designer: Candice Harman

Marketing Manager: Olivia Bartlett

Library of Congress Cataloging-in-Publication Data

Names: Sanchez, Horacio, author.

Title: The poverty problem: how education can promote resilience and counter poverty's impact on brain development and functioning/Horacio Sanchez.

Description: Thousand Oaks, California: Corwin, 2021. | Series: Corwin teaching essentials | Includes bibliographical references and index. | Summary: "There is no greater challenge facing education right now than poverty. It impacts everything, including access to technology and racial disparities. *The Poverty Problem* describes how brains change and adapt due to low SES and its ramifications on learning and behavior. It presents findings from both neuroscience and resiliency research and explains how the research relates to school environments. The book also shows solutions rather than merely explaining the problems. This focus on solutions is critical because it reduces the misapplication of the findings. Each chapter presents concrete strategies to help educators counteract, minimize, and in some cases, reverse the impact poverty is having on the child and adolescent brain. Topics include the lack of culturally competent instruction and its impact on students of color, poverty's effect on language development and how it can be influenced, the importance of reading, and how to counteract the effects of stress which are so endemic in lower SES environments. This is an important book, and though it tackles difficult topics, its message of hopefulness is apparent"— Provided by publisher.

Identifiers: LCCN 2020045065 | ISBN 9781071842928 (paperback) | ISBN 9781071842935 (epub) | ISBN 9781071842942 (epub) | ISBN 9781071842959 (pdf)

Subjects: LCSH: Children with social disabilities—Education—United States. | Poor children—Education—United States. | Poverty—United States. | Poverty—Psychological aspects. | Brain—Growth. | Cognitive learning. | Cognitive neuroscience.

Classification: LCC LC4091 .S26 2021 | DDC 371.826/940973—dc23

LC record available at https://lccn.loc.gov/2020045065

This book is printed on acid-free paper.

21 22 23 24 25 10 9 8 7 6 5 4 3 2 1

Contents

How a strange sequence of events and one individual's arbitrary decision shaped a nation's thinking and behavior toward poverty.

Why the lack of cultural competent instruction on poverty contributes to the poor self-image of students of color.

Poverty compromises the capacity of the prefrontal cortex, limiting the brain's ability to focus, analyze, and plan. The loss of capacity causes our mental processor to slow, prohibiting full mental function. The outcome is poverty's cognitive load compromises decision-making regardless of intellect.

The stress related to poverty is so unique that it dramatically affects infant brain development during the first two years of life. The ramification of this type of stress inhibits infant-mother attachment and certain executive brain functions. The stress problems related to low SES are evident even in the most positive low-income homes and seem to intensify in cases of generational poverty. The result is a higher pattern of stress-related issues in low-income Black families due to their overrepresentation in persistent poverty.

Chapter 4: Speechless 49

Poverty diminishes language development and expressive language, altering academic achievement, social growth, and emotional stability. Because of these limitations, low SES has acted as a gag on the voices of the poor. Poverty reflects a perception that causes those who are socially advantaged to dismiss poor people as unintelligent.

Chapter 5: You've Lost That Loving Feeling 67

The emphasis on self, which is common to an individualist culture, coupled with access to information, negatively impacts the self-esteem of people living in poverty and is contributing to a drop in empathy.

Chapter 6: See No Evil, Hear No Evil, and Speak No Evil 79

Neuroscience has established that culture can alter brain function and can even produce brain mutations. In the same manner, poverty can modify certain hardwired brain functions that produce social bias. Much of a child's intuitive understanding of the social world is a product of how humans have evolved to notice facial, hand, posture, and voice tone cues. Under normal circumstances, our focus on these cues creates instantaneous biases concerning others. The purpose is to help us identify individuals who are safe and avoid people who are threatening. However, under the stress of poverty, our abilities to read and appropriately respond to these hardwired cues can be compromised and negatively influence social behavior.

Chapter 7: Poverty Is a Story of Risk 95

Poverty and resiliency are so closely correlated that poverty usually predicts poor resiliency, and poor resiliency often predicts poverty. Socioeconomic status is not an organism that can interact directly with people's brains and bodies. It is the predictable risk factors that usually occur with economic hardship that produce the outcomes commonly associated with poverty. Resiliency studies identified the specific risk factors associated with failed life outcomes. Unfortunately, the majority of the risk factors found in resiliency studies are associated with poverty.

Chapter 8: Principles of Good Instruction for Students from Low SES

This chapter seeks to highlight the validated principles of good instruction that have success with students from low SES across the globe. Neuroscience research supports these evidence-based principles. When teachers have confidence that instructional strategies will work, it increases perseverance and certainty, which positively affects outcomes.

Chapter 9: The Only Academic Protective Factor

Reading is the only academic protective factor identified in resiliency research. One reason might be that the ability to read is not only reflective of a healthy brain but also a student's ability to maintain grade-level reading milestones signifies normative brain development. The process the brain uses to read changes as we age. Perhaps reading is the most crucial academic skill primary school students should master because if reading lags, the brain begins to produce alternative pathways to compensate for the brain regions not performing efficiently. Once the brain develops alternative pathways, it becomes difficult to correct as children age. However, if a struggling reader can attain and maintain reading on grade level, it improves the structure and functioning of many regions of the brain, providing a wide range of unrelated benefits.

Chapter 10: Promoting Resiliency

This chapter details how schools can successfully promote protective factors so that students can become more resilient. The ability to develop protective factors is a strength-based approach to combating the adverse effects of poverty. For schools with a high concentration of students from low SES, building protective factors is a proactive approach for addressing expected academic, behavioral, and mental health issues students will face.

Preface

The first draft of this book was completed just as the pandemic and racial unrest of 2020 began in America. It is likely that the conditions created by the pandemic produced a unique set of circumstances that caused the nation to not only notice but also pay attention to one particular atrocity that became the catalyst for racial change. As the nation, states, institutions, and individuals seek solutions to complex racial issues, policies and initiatives will be quickly implemented that, in the long run, might prove ineffective. Historically, a desire to respond quickly can set into motion solutions that are well intentioned and seem rational but produce unintended consequences that give rise to a new set of issues.

As fate would have it, *The Poverty Problem* identifies the historical events that created many of the implicit biases Blacks face today in America. Unfortunately, implicit biases are not as easily corrected as people think. There are a thousand milliseconds in one second, and most of the things we see that bias our opinions of another person occur before 400 milliseconds have elapsed. The result is that the subconscious brain influences one's thoughts before they consciously begin to form. The only solution for combating implicit bias is to first learn how it occurs in the brain, so you can become more cognizant of what is happening. This book also identifies a new bias people of color face in America due to their overrepresentation in the ranks of poverty. Racism differs from implicit bias because it is conscious rather than subconscious. Several neuroimaging studies have concluded that racism is associated with overreaction, rooted in fear, in the emotional brain (amygdala). However, both bias and racism can be reduced by strategies designed to lower the overreaction of the amygdala.

This book offers solutions for many of the issues related to race and poverty that schools and the nation face. The solutions offered are based on sound neuroscience. Simply put, the solutions are designed to change minds, attitudes, and behaviors. Solutions that do not take into account how the brain develops also don't account for how problems develop between people of different races and how the brain will react to the solution. Brain-compatible solutions are trending in many diverse disciplines, as people begin to see the wisdom in aligning our strategies with what we know about the brain. I firmly believe that *The Poverty Problem* is written for such a time as this.

Summary

America is a country that implements some of the most advanced metrics for calculating what the nation values. There are advanced metrics for predicting how each stock on the New York Stock Exchange will perform. Every professional sport in America has advanced metrics for predicting how well an amateur athlete will perform in the professional ranks. There are advanced metrics for predicting political races, weather, and even things as trivial as which television shows will succeed. That is why it is so telling that no advance metric is used in determining when an individual is living in poverty.

One of the truths concerning the human brain is that it is driven by self-interest. As a result, humans are more prone to take action when something concerns them. If we experience someone in the service industry who fails to provide adequate service or acts rudely, it motivates us to write a scathing review and post it on social media. Hardwired functions of the brain influence us to focus on our interests; our eyes, for instance, possess a feature that continually scans the environment on the lookout for things we desire or that support our beliefs, which is why we are more likely to be attracted to people who not only look like us but also share our opinions. Another truth is that whatever the brain values will prompt action. If we value homes or cars, it drives us to find ways of obtaining the object of our desire. If we value politics, it motivates us to get involved in campaigning or voter drives. The need to defend or obtain what we value can lead to emotional outbursts when people contradict our beliefs or irrational spending to purchase the object we delude ourselves into thinking will bring us joy. Our actions provide an accurate measure of self-interests and personal values. It is time to confess that as a nation we neither have interest in nor value the poor. As a nation, our values seem to be shifting from all for one to none for all. The majority do not emotionally defend the poor, nor are they compelled to take action to end the war on poverty. If Nelson Mandela was living in the United States today, he might say that there is no keener revelation of a society's soul than how they treat their poor.

A familiar pattern in the United States is to notice a trend that could have devastating repercussions and not sound an alarm until it has reached a tipping point. Consider the obesity crisis that was identified as a potential issue over forty years ago. Every ten years in America, the rate of obesity climbed, and the warning signs were ignored. Over that time frame, every related medical condition associated with being overweight soared. Financial health experts identified obesity as the root cause of soaring medical costs. Almost every industry involved in food sales sought to capitalize on our increasing addiction to food. The obesity problem finally became a crisis, and medical professionals sounded the alarm. In 2018, the prevalence of obesity among adults was 42.4%, and for children and adolescents was 18.5% (13.7 million), and based on historic trend data, all indications point that this percentage will continue to climb without significant change in behaviors (Hales et al., 2018). Our response to the warnings related to obesity came much too late. Let us not continue the pattern of ignoring an emerging and evident issue. It is now time to sound the alarm concerning poverty before the figures reach a crisis point. Poverty is transforming the brains of children and adults at an alarming rate and with devastating results. The issues are exponentially compounded with generational poverty. Cognitive and psychological problems are more likely to be present at birth each generation a family remains in poverty. Poverty is becoming a condition that the longer you remain in it, the less capacity you have to escape it. Yet in the face of mounting evidence, most of us will stay virtually silent as long as it does not affect us, and our material desires remain within our reach. Our greatest sin related to the issues of poverty is to ignore it. I am reminded of the words of Reinhold Niebuhr: "All human sin seems so much worse in its consequences than in its intentions" (Niebuhr, 1956, pp. 1–24).

It is impossible not to consider that the lack of concern with the eradication of poverty may be related to its association with people of color. It is a natural product of the human brain to lower empathy toward those in the out-group category. The bias shortcut is so advanced that when we notice someone from an out-group, our brains automatically identify that they are not members of the in-group and reduce our abilities to observe and recall their physical features. When we reduce the ability to notice and recall distinct physical features, we also lower the empathy response. In any individualist culture, the issues of the out-group are more easily dismissed because it involves people who don't look like us. The American Association for the Advancement of Science conference on poverty found that Americans have developed a callousness toward the plight of the poor. Perhaps Edmund Burke was right when he said, "The only thing necessary for the triumph of evil is for good men to do nothing" (Bartlett, 1968, p. 454).

The association of people of color with the negative characteristics associated with poverty is influencing how effectively we educate our poor students. The commonly held biases are undermining teacher attitudes and behaviors. The most devastating fact is that the majority of teachers are unaware of these subconscious positions that most in our society hold. Fermat's Last Theorem, which took mathematicians 358 years to solve, proves one thing: it is easier to create a problem than to solve one. Poverty is a complex problem in which many of the root issues are not only misunderstood but also misdiagnosed. Unless educators understand the neuroscience of poverty, the solution will elude them. Just as in the case of Fermat's theorem, the solution requires an accurate understanding of the problem and a focused effort in resolution. It took Andrew Wiles over six years to solve Fermat's theorem. What enabled Wiles to solve this complex problem is the fact that he was the first mathematician to bring fresh ideas and apply new strategies to an old problem. Education will also need to be creative in solving the poverty issue that consumes many of its institutions. The solution to the problem will require creative new strategies firmly rooted in neuroscience research.

It is in this bleak new reality that public education must not only sound the alarm but take a front line in the fight against poverty as well. It is absurd to think policy makers will suddenly prioritize the war on poverty since they have failed for over fifty years to even address the issue of how poverty is calculated. The greatest weapon education has always wielded is knowledge. However, knowledge is useless unless applied. Education has to have a sound strategy to address poverty that includes modifying school climate, instruction, curriculums, social and emotional training, and support services. Why dedicate so much to this fight? Because poverty will be the biggest challenge facing education for the foreseeable future. If we do not address the unique issues produced by poverty, it will only become more difficult with each subsequent generation. Norman Vincent Peale said, "Understanding can overcome any situation, however mysterious or insurmountable it may appear to be" (BrainyQuote.com, n.d.). However, understanding is insufficient in the war against poverty. The fight requires surgical application of the most effective strategies that not only overcome brain deficits but also improve both brain structures and functions.

About the Author

Horacio Sanchez is a highly sought-after speaker and educational consultant, helping schools learn to apply neuroscience to improve educational outcomes. He presents on diverse topics such as overcoming the impact of poverty, improving school climate, engaging in brain-based instruction, and addressing issues related to implicit bias. He is recognized as one of the nation's leading authorities on resiliency and applied brain science.

Horacio has been a teacher, administrator, clinician, mental health director, and consultant to the Department of Education in North Carolina, Pennsylvania, and other states. His diverse education and background have helped him to merge research, science, and practice. Horacio sits on True Health Initiative Council of Directors, a coalition of more than 250 world-renowned health experts, committed to educating on proven principles of lifestyle as medicine. He has authored several articles and books on the topics of resiliency, closing the achievement gap, and applying neuroscience to improve educational practices and outcomes. He is the author of the best-selling book, The Education Revolution, which applies brain science to improve instruction, behaviors, and school climate.

Learn more at https://resiliencyinc.com or follow Horacio for the latest brain science updates

https://www.facebook.com/Resiliency-Inc-122261404853500/

https://twitter.com/ResiliencyInc

https://www.linkedin.com/in/hsanchezceo

Introduction
The Invisible Line

How a strange sequence of events and one individual's arbitrary decision shaped a nation's thinking and behavior toward poverty.

How Poverty Is Defined in America

Poverty is the single most significant issue impacting public education today. Every year, school districts dedicate resources, draft policies, and create new services to meet the academic and behavioral challenges associated with students coming from poverty. However, the efforts of public education to address disadvantaged students' needs are generally occurring without understanding how poverty transforms the brains of affected pupils. Attempting to address the issues of people who are poor with only partial information is like trying to complete a puzzle with crucial pieces missing. When assembling the puzzle, you can make out the general picture, but many vital details of the image are lost. The brain transformations resulting from being economically disadvantaged speak to the heart of the academic and behavioral issues schools seek to overcome. The neuroscience of poverty provides not only a clear picture of why academic and behavioral problems occur but also how to design a detailed response to best address the issues.

One needs to answer a simple question before diving into the neuroscience of poverty. How did we, as a country, get to the point that being destitute has become far too often a persistent status rather than a temporary condition?

How did we, as a country, get to the point that being destitute has become far too often a persistent status rather than a temporary condition?

For many policymakers, the poverty line is a clear demarcation based on a series of mathematical calculations. You are not considered impoverished if you are above the poverty line, but you are poor if you are below the poverty line. No rational individual should find that concept cogent. What if you are a little above the poverty line? At what level above the poverty line does an individual not have to cope with the issues that plague the disadvantaged? Add to this misguided concept of a poverty line the bizarre manner in which it came into existence, and it becomes surreal.

In 1963, Mollie Orshansky, an employee of the Social Security Administration, was assigned to do an in-house research project on how being destitute affects children in America. At that time, there was no accepted measure of poverty, so she devised her own. To understand how Mollie's past influenced her thinking, one needs only to review her work history. Mollie began her lifelong career as a civil servant in 1939 as a research clerk with the Children's Bureau, where she worked on biometric studies of child health, growth, and nutrition (Fisher, 1992c). She later spent thirteen years at the U.S. Department of Agriculture (USDA) in various roles including family economist, food economist, and director of the Program Statistics Division (Fisher, 1992a). It was there where she became acquainted with the Department of Agriculture's food plans. Food plans were a research service of the USDA designed to help families plan nutritionally adequate meals based on their budgets (no matter how meager). This service was an outcome of the Great Depression, which caused the nation to have a traumatic response to issues related to hunger. As a food economist from 1953 to 1958, Mollie planned and directed the collection and analysis of data on food consumption and expenditures of American households (Orshansky, 1957). She wrote a significant section of a summary report for the USDA's 1955 Household Food Consumption Survey. Therefore, it is not surprising that when Mollie was tasked with devising a definition of poverty, she based it on food consumption.

Mollie used the 1955 Department of Agriculture report, which said that a family of three or more spent on average one-third of their after-tax income on food. She trusted this assertion because she played a pivotal role in drafting the reference document. So she calculated a standard of poverty by multiplying the food plan's low-income household's food budget by three (Gordon, 1992). The logic was simple; if families spend one-third of their budget on food, then multiplying the cheapest of the four plans developed by the Department of Agriculture by three would reflect what a household had to earn to barely survive. The food plan she selected was an emergency plan designed to reflect how a household could still feed a family an adequately healthy diet with severely limited funds. In 1962, it allotted $18.60 a week for a family of four with two school-aged children (Light, 2013). Mollie's calculations would qualify as a family living in need, but could it be used as a threshold for when a family would exit poverty? After all, her assignment was to establish a standard for poverty to estimate the number of children living in difficult economic circumstances. Because of her assignment, Mollie took no care in making sure that her calculations would determine the highest amount a family could earn and still be considered poor. Instead, Mollie's task was to help to determine how many children were living in economically disadvantaged circumstances.

Today, the federal poverty guideline for a family of four is about $26,200 or less, compared to a median income for a household of the same size as $59,039 in 2016. Median income households should sleep soundly knowing that they are so far above the poverty line. However, they should not sleep too soundly, as experts who study the cost of living say that families of four who average $50,000 per year can live adequately only in the least expensive areas in the United States (Gould et al., 2015a).

A Strange Sequence of Events

A strange sequence of events then unfolded. In January 1964, President Lyndon B. Johnson declared a War on Poverty. The president's Council of Economic Advisers had to establish their own measure of poverty. Around this same time, Mollie's supervisors at the Social Security Administration asked her to do an analysis extending her families-with-children low socioeconomic status thresholds to the total population. Mollie completed her analysis by late 1964. The Social Security Bulletin in January 1965 titled *Counting the Poor: Another Look at the Poverty Profile* published her findings (Orshansky, 1965).

Mollie's article came at a time when the Office of Economic Opportunity (OEO) was just established and tasked with leading the War on Poverty. The OEO was under enormous pressure to expedite programs designed to end poverty. OEO officials were exposed to Mollie's analysis because the chief researcher at the OEO, Joseph Kershaw, quoted Mollie's work in one of his reports. By May 1965, due to exposure and expediency, the OEO adopted Mollie's extended thresholds as a working definition of poverty for statistical, planning, and budget purposes. The Office of Economic Opportunity had to get on with the War on Poverty, and Mollie's report had already calculated the scope of the problem. By August 1969, her thresholds became the federal government's official statistical definition of poverty (Gordon, 1992). It is important to note that no review of the validity of the report's assertions was ever conducted. More surprising is the fact that no one observed the subtle difference in the use of her analysis from its original purpose. The original purpose of Mollie's report was to provide a broad estimate as to the number of children who were destitute, not to determine at what cutoff is someone not considered poor. It was an analytical formula already accepted in another branch of government and printed in an official government document; therefore, members of the OEO assumed that it must pass muster.

> The original purpose of Mollie's report was to provide a broad estimate as to the number of children who were destitute, not to determine at what cutoff is someone not considered poor.

Trauma Alters Perception and Logic

One might ask how such an advanced nation settled on such an arbitrary definition of poverty and has based so many policies and programs on this standard? It is essential to understand that the most emotional experiences of our lives shape our views and beliefs and even alter our ability to be logical. Neuroscience determined that as emotions increase, the control functions of the prefrontal cortex diminish, which is critical for rational thinking. Most of the individuals making essential policy decisions at that time grew up during the Great Depression. The impact of the Great Depression cannot be understated. In the 1930s, men were the primary breadwinners. The emotional toll of not providing for their families had a devastating effect on parenting and most marriages. When men lost the ability to provide for their families, they lost their identity and self-worth. Common outcomes included becoming emotionally unfit to parent or completely abandoning the family (Bryson, 2016).

In many cases, multiple families crowded together in a single apartment or home to have shelter. Others would squat in an abandoned building without utilities. Two hundred fifty thousand boys left their homes attempting to unburden their families and hoping to find work or food (Uys, 2003). The nation saw a 50% increase in children entering custodial institutions (Elder, 1974). Food was so scarce that food lines were as long as a city block, and people often fought or even killed for their position in line. Children across the nation suffered from malnutrition, poor living conditions, and emotional trauma. During the Great Depression, food became the most treasured commodity for daily survival. It is not surprising that the children of the Great Depression grew up to equate poverty to the quantity of food available.

Let's look at one of the most significant hunger experiments in history. Toward the end of World War II, thousands across the world were dying of hunger. Thirty-six conscientious objectors at the University of Minnesota volunteered for a study that would bring them to the brink of starvation. Researchers at the university had designed a study in hopes of better understanding the impact of starvation to determine the best course of action to assist the vast number of individuals starved due to the war (Keys et al., 1950).

To replicate the level of starvation seen in most of Europe, the researcher starved the volunteers to the point where their metabolism slowed by 40%; sitting was painful because their muscles had atrophied, and their bellies were bloated because they had filled with liquid. One of the disturbing findings was related to the mental effects of starvation. Although the volunteers had no previous interest in cooking, they became obsessed with cookbooks and cooking recipes. They talked incessantly about every aspect of food. They reported being unable to control their thoughts, spending most waking hours consumed with food. One participant explained it like this, "Food became the one central and only thing really in one's life" (*Christian Advocate*, 1945, pp. 788–790). The study shows how people who have experienced starvation can become consumed with anything to do with food. Therefore, it is not surprising that a nation traumatized by hunger was willing to equate destitution to the ability to procure meals. If your income prevented starvation, life could be considered bearable.

It is not surprising that a nation traumatized by hunger was willing to equate destitution to the ability to procure meals.

Let's look again at Mollie. Historical records identify that she grew up poor, one of seven daughters born to a family of Jewish immigrants living in the South Bronx (Chan, 2006). She often spoke of her experience waiting in food lines with her mother and how her family had to forgo important needs to pay the rent. In 1970, she told the *New York Post*, "If I write about the poor, I don't need a good imagination, I have a good memory" (Eaton, 1970, p. 24). Traumatic experiences alter our brains' ability to process logically topics that provoke high emotion. America was a country biased by the Great Depression and desiring a quick remedy to poverty. Records of the early statements from individuals tasked with ending poverty produce clear evidence that government officials truly believed that they could conquer destitution and prevent anyone from experiencing a similar fate, as what was suffered during the Great Depression. Lyndon B. Johnson's address to Congress in 1964 sums up the position of many politicians and policymakers, "We shall not rest until that war is won. The richest nation on Earth can afford to win it. We cannot afford to lose it" (cited in Peters & Woolley, 1999).

The reason many Americans believed they could end poverty was that they saw being poor as a temporary condition. If individuals worked hard and applied themselves, they could exit the status of poverty and obtain the American dream. Therefore, the logic was simple; temporary government assistance, coupled with the American work ethic, would be a quick formula to end long-term poverty. It is this same thinking that subconsciously biased efforts to revisit Mollie's definition of poverty. Individuals who believe that poverty is only a temporary condition for anyone willing to work hard enough are aided by the brain's tendency to confirm what we believe. This automated bias is referred to as *confirmation bias*, the brain's tendency to notice things in our environment that support existing beliefs, while, without malicious intent, miss contradictory evidence. As a result, if you believe that through hard work anyone can escape poverty, you can reference countless examples of poor individuals who, through hard work, not only escaped poverty but became affluent as well. The belief in the American dream offers a plausible explanation as to why the poverty line was accepted and remained without reexamination until recently. Frankly, it need not be an exact science for what should be only a temporary condition.

Begin with an Erroneous Position

A valid argument is one in which, if the premise is true, then the conclusion must also be correct. However, if the premise is false, then even a valid argument still leads to a wrong conclusion. Economists and social advocacy groups who have recently challenged the poverty line formula focused their concerns on whether food reflects one-third of a family's budget and, if so, does multiplying by three offer an accurate formula for establishing poverty. Most individuals with no economic training would conclude that Mollie's definition of poverty is deeply flawed because it is a one-dimensional assessment of low socioeconomic status (SES). Academics, statisticians, and policy analysts have pointed out numerous issues with the poverty line. The *headcount* approach used in the formula views all individuals as the same, not accounting for economic needs. Food reflects only one item now used to calculate expenses: It excludes taxes, housing expenses, work expenses, medical expenses, and benefits. The poverty line definition is also one-dimensional by not varying the cost of living based on geographic locations; for example, the cost of living in California differs vastly from Wyoming. It has also failed to adjust for changes in the standard of living since its inception. In addition, its definition of the family unit as persons living in the same household who are related by birth, marriage, or adoption does not reflect the 21st-century family unit.

These arguments, although accurate, are clear examples of why logic asserts that when you start with a flawed premise, it focuses the attention on the flaws. The erroneous conclusion shapes the focus and argument. If the goal is to end poverty, should we not focus on the qualities of living absent of poverty rather than attempting to define the income level at which someone is economically disadvantaged? It is this flawed starting point that shaped how low SES is defined in the United States. Despite overwhelming criticism from social advocacy groups, community organizations, economists, and even people within the government, the poverty threshold remains fundamentally unchanged since 1969, with most of the attention on adjusting the existing formula. History forgets that Mollie never set out to establish a poverty line but rather to learn what percentage of children in America lived in dire circumstances.

Why Should Education Care About Poverty?

Besides the families living in poverty, education is the institution most distressed by poverty. Schools serve the fastest-growing poverty group in the United States. Children make up 23% of the U.S. population but account for almost 33% of the people living in poverty (U.S. Census Bureau, 2017). While only a percentage of families with children who are considered low-income qualify for child welfare services, all children in poverty are entitled to a free public education. One in five poor people are children, and 40% of African American children qualify as living in low SES (U.S. Census Bureau, 2017). According to the U.S. Census Bureau, 18% of American children, 13.3 million, lived below the poverty line in 2016 (U.S. Census Bureau, 2017). The result is that one in every four schools is classified as *high-poverty*, meaning that 75% of students attending qualify for free or reduced-price lunch (U.S. Department of Education [DOE], National Center for Education Statistics [NCES], 2012). The problem is only increasing, as there has been a 60% increase in high-poverty schools since 2000 (U.S. DOE, NCES, 2012, 2016a). A more accurate depiction of being disadvantaged is evident in the fact that 20.1 million students qualified for free lunch and two million for reduced lunch in 2016 (Oliveira, 2017). Some would argue that students eligible for reduced lunch can be well above the poverty line. However, eligibility still places families in the category of economically at-risk, meaning they can easily fall into poverty or spend a portion of time living in economic hardship.

> If the goal is to end poverty, should we not focus on the qualities of living absent of poverty rather than attempting to define the income level at which someone is economically disadvantaged?

> There has been a 60% increase in high-poverty schools since 2000.

Researchers have found that the single most potent predictor of gaps in educational achievement is the extent to which students attend schools surrounded by other low-income students. A recent analysis found significant inequities between funding of high-poverty districts and low-poverty districts. The analysis found that the highest poverty districts in our nation receive about $1,200 less per student than districts with the lowest ratio of students in poverty. The disparity grows to roughly $2,000 per student between districts serving mostly students of color when compared to those serving the fewest minority students. Thus, those who need the most services to escape poverty receive the least despite the current initiatives designed to help low-income schools. Educators might not understand that poverty has changed over the past thirty years. The problems of economic hardship combined with issues in our society related to the treatment of the poor have over time produced changes to students' brain structure. These changes dramatically impact learning, behavior, physical health, and emotional stability. Multigenerational poverty is transforming the brain at a genetic level, producing psychological, behavioral, and cognitive issues transmitted to offspring. No institution has dealt with or will continue to confront the impact of the *new poverty* at the level that public education will. The term *new poverty* denotes a clear demarcation of how being poor is impacting children today compared to in the past.

> The single most potent predictor of gaps in educational achievement is the extent to which students attend schools surrounded by other low-income students.

This book helps educators learn how the brain is adapting due to poverty and its ramifications on learning and behavior. It is important to note that regarding low SES, much of the recent neuroscience research is transpiring to find solutions rather than merely understand the problem. For example, Kimberly Noble's work not only identifies the cognitive and neurobiological way in which children acquire reading but also examines how different classroom reading interventions impact identified brain regions (Noble & McCandliss, 2005). The focus on solutions is vital because it reduces the misapplication of the findings. Each chapter will present concrete strategies to help educators counteract, minimize, and in some cases, reverse the impact poverty is having on the child and adolescent brain. The War on Poverty failed at a governmental level. However, education can still fill the gap that policy and government assistance have been unable to do.

The New Deal—
The Old Way

In this chapter: Why the lack of cultural competent instruction on poverty contributes to the poor self-image of students of color.

The Roots of Black Males' Implicit Association with Crime

It wasn't until 1951, almost ninety years after the passage of the Emancipation Proclamation, that Congress passed explicit statutes making any form of slavery a crime. The most common form of slavery after the passing of the Emancipation Proclamation was *convict leasing*. At that time, 90 percent of individuals incarcerated in the South were Black males who were forced into hard labor to replace the workforce loss due to the end of slavery (Blackmon, 2008). The practice of renting prisoners as labor at a fraction of the cost of regular workers is called convict leasing. To achieve this, the South created laws and systems allowing Blacks to be arrested and prosecuted for noncriminal acts. For example, vagrancy statutes made it a crime to be unemployed. Black males would be rounded up and had to show proof of employment at a moment's notice. The enforcement of the law was limited to Black males and sometimes Black females. It was not uncommon to arrest Black males out in public for vagrancy, hold a quick trial, and send them off to prison (Blackmon, 2008). Trial records indicate spikes in arrests during harvest times and whenever any large company needed an influx of workers. The institution of convict leasing created a perfect catch-22;

it reduced Blacks' employment: Why pay more for what you can obtain for a much lower price? It also increased the likelihood of unemployment for Black males, which was then punishable by incarceration. It is important to note that when the Emancipation Proclamation occurred, 92 percent of all Blacks in America lived in the South (Jones, 1985). As late as 1900, approximately 90 percent of Blacks still lived in the South (Jones, 1985). Therefore, the southern Black experience is pervasive in Black culture.

> Convict leasing had devastating effects on the Black family and the psyche of Blacks throughout the South.

Convict leasing had devastating effects on the Black family and the psyche of Blacks throughout the South. It undermined the family structure by removing the male role model from the home. It created a climate where being Black made you a target for incarceration. One detrimental outcome was the persistent association made between Black males and crime. The newspapers, politicians, and ministers throughout the South consistently proclaimed that Blacks should have never been freed because they are inherently prone to criminal behavior (Blackmon, 2008). To justify convict leasing, the southern establishment portrayed Black males as being guilty of a wide range of atrocities. The rhetoric designed to justify the practice of convict leasing over time became a persistent sound bite that turned out to be more believable over the course of the ninety years. Consider children raised in the South hearing consistently from everyone in the community that Black males are imprisoned to keep white women and children safe. Every time you passed farm fields or construction sites, you saw Black males in chains working. One can say that this stereotype created such an overwhelming bias toward Black males that it still exists today. The Harvard bias study found that, regardless of race or gender, most Americans associate Black males with crime and violence (Akalis et al., 2008; Baron & Banaji, 2006; Cunningham et al., 2004; Dunham et al., 2006; Green et al., 2007; Levin & Banaji, 2006; Mazzocco et al., 2006; Sabin et al., 2009; Stanley et al., 2011).

How Teachers Are Influenced by Implicit Bias Toward Black Males

Implicit bias refers to the attitudes or stereotypes that influence our understanding, actions, and decisions in subconscious ways. The manifestation of generalized implicit biases regarding race and criminal behavior may be evident as early as preschool (Eberhardt et al., 2004). The tendency to associate race with the perceived threat of aggression is apparent with Black children as young as age five (Todd, 2016).

The Yale Child Study Center found that early childhood educators expect challenging behaviors from Black male students and, as a result, observe them more closely. The researchers also found that preschool teachers anticipate negative behaviors, even when no such actions are present. They concluded that the anticipation of negative behaviors is evidence of a generalized implicit bias based on the race of the child. Another study demonstrates how behavioral expectations related to race can bias educators' actions. Researchers presented teachers with two fictional male student disciplinary records (Okonofua & Eberhardt, 2015). They placed a stereotypical Black person's name or white person's name on the student records. Both fictional students had engaged in the same minor school violations. Teachers felt more "disturbed" by the offenses of the Black student and recommended severe punishment after the second minor infraction, even though the white student had an identical record.

In both of the above cases, the brain is producing two common phenomena that occur when implicit bias is present. In the first case, the teachers perceived the threat of aggression even when no hostile action is apparent. The human eye has a scanning function called microsaccades that is always active while we are awake. One feature of the scanning movements is to monitor the environment to keep us safe. Once a student is perceived as a threat, the teacher's microsaccades will monitor that student more closely and will tend to catch even minor infractions. As a result, two students can behave in the same manner, and the teacher is more likely to observe the actions of the student who she perceives as a threat. Since this is a subconscious survival function, the teacher does not believe that she is unfairly targeting the student. The Yale Child Center study used eye-tracking instruments and found that Black boys are pre-identified as threats and therefore received most of the teacher's attention. Black boys were monitored 42 percent more closely than the other students, and this equated to 68 percent more monitoring than would occur by chance alone.

In the second case, the teachers acted more callously toward the Black male student who engaged in the same minor infraction as the white student. The second phenomenon that often occurs with implicit racial bias is a reduction in empathy. Empathy is an automated function of the human brain designed to make us acutely aware of how our behaviors influence the feelings of others. There is evidence that empathic responses diminish when the observer is a different race from the observee (Cikara et al., 2011). The drop in empathy suggests that teachers may be less likely to respond with compassion when a child

> The Yale Child Study Center found that early childhood educators expect challenging behaviors from Black male students and, as a result, observe them more closely.

of a different race is exhibiting challenging behaviors. The outcome, in this case, was a higher level of discipline severity administered to one student over another with no awareness of the disparity.

The real-life implications of implicit bias are demonstrated not only in these research studies but also in national school data. School data reveal disproportionate rates of disciplinary referrals and exclusionary practices for Black boys that cannot be accounted for by other factors (Skiba et al., 2011). Black preschoolers are 3.6 times as likely to receive one or more suspensions relative to their white counterparts (U.S. Department of Education [U.S. DOE], Office of Civil Rights [OCR], 2016b). The number of suspensions are of particular concern since Black children compose only 19 percent of preschool enrollment but represent 47 percent of preschoolers suspended one or more times (Gilliam et al., 2016). These data become only more disparaging as Black male students grow older. It is not a leap to think 245 years of viewing Blacks as less than human during slavery and then 90 years of associating Black males with criminal behavior during the period of convict leasing could produce societal bias. The indicators of implicit bias are apparent from the moment Black students enroll in public education. Teachers seeing children as young as age five as threats speak to how strongly we associate Black males with violence in American society.

The Association of Black Individuals with Poverty

During the last seventeen years of convict leasing, the country was at the height of the Great Depression. Unemployment levels in most cities reached staggering levels. President Franklin D. Roosevelt unleashed a series of the most aggressive social and economic programs the country had ever seen:

- The Agricultural Adjustment Act and the National Industrial Recovery Act sought to restore the decimated farming industry and promote industrial expansion.

- The Works Progress Administration (WPA) created jobs for the unemployed.

- The Social Security Act guaranteed pensions to millions of Americans by setting up unemployment insurance.

Until the New Deal, Blacks had been loyal to the party of Abraham Lincoln by voting Republican. However, Black Americans shifted support to the Democratic Party in hopes of jobs and opportunity. Roosevelt's record on civil rights was modest, and to pass New Deal legislation, he needed the support of the southern Democratic Party. The result was that the federal government turned a blind eye to overt exclusion practices toward Blacks in most of the New Deal programs in the South. Discriminatory federal policies no longer limited Jim Crow rules to the South. The National Recovery Administration offered whites the first crack at jobs and authorized separate and lower pay scales for Blacks (Katznelson, 2013). The Federal Housing Authority (FHA) refused to guarantee mortgages for Blacks who tried to buy in white neighborhoods (Katznelson, 2013). The Social Security Act excluded job categories traditionally held by Blacks (Katznelson, 2013).

Unprecedented historical events have led to the implicit bias of associating Blacks with poverty. From the time they first came to America, Black people were slaves and not allowed to have property or earn a wage for their labor. From emancipation to 1951, Blacks in the South were victims of an institutionalized system of slavery through incarceration that disincentivized employment. In reality, convict leasing was worse than slavery because there was no motivation to keep these workers alive and healthy. The common practice was to work Blacks until they dropped dead and then replace them with other Blacks. The undermining and at times outright exclusion of Blacks from New Deal programs created a separation of them from the emerging middle class.

Fast forward to today: The 2017 census data indicate the poverty rate for Blacks and Hispanics is more than double that of whites. Far more telling is that census data over the past twenty-five years reveal that the rate of exiting poverty diminishes over time, and Blacks and Hispanics make up the largest segment of multigenerational poverty. The persistence of people of color being economically disadvantaged in the United States creates a belief that certain minorities are inherently incapable of rising above their circumstances.

Poverty in America correlates with lower academic performance, decision-making skills, and health practices, as well as increased risk of addiction and aggression. Since Blacks and Hispanics are disproportionately poor, the behaviors associated with poverty are becoming assumed attributes of these minority groups. The disproportionate number of minorities of color being economically disadvantaged is how implicit bias occurs. Any association between two distinct things causes the brain subconsciously to put them together. In schools that have a concentration of poor Blacks and/or Hispanics, the observer's brain will begin to associate them with the societal patterns of the poor. Since poverty is already associated with poor academic performance and behavior, the observer's brain will subconsciously ascribe those attributes to students of color. Implicit bias has real-life ramifications. Implicit bias comes out in subtle nonverbal expressions, choice of language, and behaviors. The subtle behavioral cues subconsciously influence the perception of the observer (the recipient) who then sees diminishing academic performance and self-esteem over time. Although these cues are subtle, the brain will notice them and process them even if they are not consciously noticed. As a result, a student can develop a sense that a teacher does not like him without having a rational explanation as to why. The typical response to feeling disliked for no reason is resentment and anger.

A series of school climate studies found that when there is a concentration of poor Black or Hispanic students, evidence of subconscious bias is consistently identified in the majority of school staff regardless of their race or gender (Sanchez, 2010). Implicit bias might begin at the level of subtle cues gradually advancing to actions that, although not consciously racist, can produce a similar outcome, as seen in the studies mentioned above. Societal bias does not discriminate. Consider the words of Jesse Jackson: "There is nothing more painful to me at this stage in my life than to walk down the street and hear footsteps and start thinking about robbery then look around and see somebody white and feel relieved" (Herbert, 1993, pp. 14–15). You might ask why this same bias does not occur when there is a concentration of poor white students? Because the broader pattern is not present. In our society, we do not see a consistent correlation of poverty to whites. Therefore, our brains cannot develop bias without a persistent pattern. However, if there is a white neighborhood of concentrated poverty, over time, teachers might associate the students coming from that community with the behaviors associated with poverty.

Why Culturally Competent Teaching Is Important

Culturally competent teaching attempts to provide (1) a sociopolitical context to help students better understand the world around them, (2) brain-based instruction to help all learners, and (3) a classroom climate that promotes social acceptance. Culturally competent teaching is essential to support students of color with their self-image because it explains their disproportionate representation in the ranks of poverty. By helping students understand that external factors, not internal deficits, are the reasons for their circumstances, it improves self-acceptance and -esteem. The reasons behind the concentration of poverty among Blacks is a matter of historical record; they were victims of unfair practices designed to suppress them economically. Historian Ira Katznelson sums up the era of the New Deal in this brief synopsis:

> If history plays tricks, southern congressional power in the last era of Jim Crow was a big one. The ability of the New Deal to confront the era's most heinous dictatorships by reshaping liberal democracy required accommodating the most violent and illiberal part of the political system, keeping the South inside the game of democracy. While it would be folly to argue that members of the southern wing of the Democratic Party alone determined the choices the New Deal made, their relative cohesion and their assessment of policy choices through the filter of an anxious protection of white supremacy often proved decisive. The triumph, in short, cannot be severed from the sorrow. Liberal democracy prospered as a result of an accommodation with racial humiliation and its system of lawful exclusion and principled terror. (Katznelson, 2013, p. 25)

In other words, the policies passed and enacted through the New Deal institutionalized discriminatory practices not only in the South but also across the nation. In many ways, the New Deal institutionalized the South's mistreatment of Blacks throughout the North, setting back any advancement they may have made. Add to the oppression of Blacks the impact of multigenerational poverty on the brain and one could conclude that escaping poverty for people of color in America is close to a herculean task.

By association, other people of color immigrating to the United States subconsciously receive a similar treatment. Consider this: a poor Black male and poor white male come to America and work hard to achieve the American dream. The white male has a superior chance of escaping poverty because he does not face the effects of subconscious association with failure projected by others. That means the nonverbal behaviors, language, and actions the Black male encounters undermines

Culturally competent teaching is essential to support students of color with their self-image because it explains their disproportionate representation in the ranks of poverty.

his opportunities for success without most people knowing they are engaging in said behaviors. These subtle hurdles seem small compared to some of the practices he will face due to implicit bias. Lending institutions will consider him a greater risk. But there are laws in place to protect the Black male from discrimination! As recent as 2016, the *Wall Street Journal* reported that bank policies still produce a lower number of loans to Blacks and Hispanics who have similar earning power as whites who receive them (Ensign et al., 2016). The reality is, if a Black male does not escape poverty, the risk of his children remaining in poverty is higher. Without culturally competent instruction, students might be unaware of the biases most of us have and how they influence the opportunities of minorities, women, and the poor in America.

RECOMMENDATIONS

Help Students Appropriately Assess Sociopolitical Context

One of the goals of producing independent thinkers is to help them understand and examine the social and political climates that help shape the past as well as their own thinking. The examination of the sociopolitical context requires providing an updated account of historical events often omitted and appropriately assessing its impact on history and the patterns we see today. Some educators wrongly perceive culturally competent teaching as something done to help minorities learn about their past and improve their self-esteem. Self-esteem is not the primary goal of culturally competent teaching; it is to introduce curriculums that provide the social and political events that logically explain the world as it is and in that understanding a logical explanation for the inequalities we see today. It is also creating a climate in which students feel safe enough to identify biases and the reason that they occur. It is this independent, higher-ordered investigation that leads to the self-improvement of all students' understanding of the world around them and of people different from themselves.

Let's look at an example. If students examine the sociopolitical context that created patterns of wealth and poverty that they see today, they might conclude that social climate and political policies created such inequity that, predictably, more Blacks would be destitute. Biases come from patterns, and the human brain seeks to rationalize what it sees.

The attempt to bring meaning void of assessing sociopolitical context to help understand social patterns can produce incorrect conclusions. The evidence of erroneously held findings is clear today when describing the poor: Those people are lazy, lack drive, or do not have the intellectual capacity to help themselves. The institution of education plays a significant role in shaping the process of how students think. Should we teach students to identify only what is evident, or should we teach them to examine why the patterns in our society exist?

What we learn related to any group of people shapes ideology. Curricula today have unwittingly associated the identities of people of color with struggle. Conduct a simple exercise. Have every educator in your school stand and instruct them to remain standing until they hear a name they do not recognize: Harriet Tubman, Dr. Martin Luther King Jr., Rosa Parks, Thurgood Marshall, Ralph Johnson Bunche, Musa Keita I, Dr. Patricia Bath, and Garrett Morgan. Most of the room likely sat down at the mention of Ralph Johnson Bunche or Musa Keita I regardless of their race, culture, or gender. The reason is that the curricula learned related to minorities or people of color are primarily associated with their struggle for land or freedom. The first four names are historical figures because they resisted social and political policies. People of color never learned that Ralph Bunche was the first African American to win the Nobel Peace Prize, that Musa Keita I was a Black emperor who was the wealthiest person who ever lived, that Dr. Patricia Bath was the first African American to complete a residency in ophthalmology and invented a surgical procedure that was the predecessor to Lasik surgery, or that Garrett Morgan designed the prototype for the gas mask.

Studies of countries engaged in long-term civil conflicts reveal that if students' education about the people with whom they identify focuses on conflict, it increases aggression and maladjustment. The length of the conflict and the intensity of the violence is predictive of how extreme a child's ideology and actions will become (Gvirsman et al., 2016). In other words, the more severe the sociopolitical hardship, the higher the propensity to develop a dogmatic ideology and become aggressive. Some would argue that the treatment of certain minorities in America is a far cry from growing up in the Middle East or Somalia. However, many studies discovered that violence in urban neighborhoods resembles war zones and produces many of the same ideological and behavioral outcomes (Bogira, 1987; Dubrow & Garbarino, 1989; Uehara, 1996). Some of these same studies found that when children learn about positive role models that look like them, they are better able to avoid developing extreme ideological positions and better able to

> Should we teach students to identify only what is evident, or should we teach them to examine why the patterns in our society exist?

control feelings of anger and aggression. The ability to not display anger and aggression is especially crucial in a society that associates people of color with violence and has placed an undue hardship on them by limiting upward mobility. Janice Kaplan's study found that male bias accounts for women being excluded from the ranks of genius (Kaplan, 2020). Likely, bias has also excluded most minorities from being recognized in the same elite group. We are all biased by our education, which has consistently identified one profile as comprising 99 percent of all geniuses studied. The result is that minorities and women do not grow up identifying with individuals of extraordinary intellectual prowess.

Ensuring that some aspect of the curriculum addresses the history of minority groups in the United States might have unintended consequences. Sometimes good intentions can be counterproductive when they are not compatible with how the brain processes. The amygdala is the part of the brain that produces emotions and, when triggered, can override the rational part of the brain. Also, the amygdala becomes agitated when focused on the differences between people. Things that are different or unknown place the amygdala in a state of high alertness. Being in a state of readiness too long is agitating to the amygdala. How the amygdala responds to focusing on differences explains why diversity training that focuses primarily on the distinctions between groups often leaves all participants dealing with negative emotions. As a result, there are two inherent problems with how we educate students, concerning the experiences of minorities in America. The first issue is that the curriculum often focuses on the struggles minority groups faced and are facing without ever addressing the contributions its members have made to society at large. The second issue is that schools focus on minority history based on times in the calendar year associated with a specific minority group. Making minority education an isolated section of the curriculum also alerts the amygdala. A brain-compatible approach is to have minority education interwoven in the curriculum holistically. And the curriculum should not focus only on the struggles these groups faced but also on the accomplishments of their members.

It is the job of education to reshape our thinking of the past and to influence our future. It was renowned historian Arthur Schlesinger Jr., who said,

> Conceptions of the past are far from stable. They are perennially revised by the urgencies of the present. When new urgencies arise in our times and lives, the historian's spotlight shifts, probing at last into the darkness, throwing into sharp relief things that were always there but that earlier historians

Things that are different or unknown place the amygdala in a state of high alertness.

had carelessly excised from the collective memory. New
voices ring out of the historical dark and demand to be heard.
(Schlesinger, 2007, p. A19)

Educators should consider how curricula create a collective memory
and have unwittingly biased students. The lessons of the past have
not reshaped our collective consciousness from the biases that plague
American society. If education maintains the status quo, it will pass
on to the next generation a future that perpetuates the past. However,
when we become aware of and bring to light the contributions throughout history of those who have far too long been disenfranchised, we
shape new thoughts and influence new behaviors.

More Than a Lapse in Judgment

In this Chapter: Poverty compromises the capacity of the prefrontal cortex, limiting the brain's ability to focus, analyze, and plan. The loss of capacity causes our mental processor to slow, prohibiting full mental function. The outcome is poverty's cognitive load compromises decision-making regardless of intellect.

The Consuming Experience of Poverty

The terms society uses to describe poverty, such as *low income, economically disadvantaged, impoverished,* and *unprivileged,* are seldom part of the vocabulary of the poor. The terms are innocuous and fail to describe people's daily existence accurately. People who are poor believe that privileged individuals use such terms to avoid the ugliness of poverty. Before we can understand how poverty creates such an overwhelming cognitive load, we must first attempt to appreciate how being poor *feels*. After all, our strongest emotional experiences shape not only how we think but also the structures and functions of our brains. Traumatic experiences influence our responses consciously and subconsciously, especially in times of stress and high emotion.

Poverty is a mindset that is hard to break, even if you are fortunate enough to escape. Anyone who has ever been poor knows that it takes a great deal of time to alter your thinking away from survival. The all-consuming experience of poverty explains why so many individuals

> Poverty is a mindset that is hard to break, even if you are fortunate enough to escape.

who were once destitute and become instantly wealthy continue to engage in actions associated with being economically disadvantaged. Poverty creates a mindset of constant insecurity. You must continually decide between things that the rest of the world takes for granted. Do you purchase medication for your sick son or buy food for the family? Should you let your car insurance lapse, knowing it will add an hour to your commute, or pay the rent? Buy your child the sneakers he had been begging for so he can feel like the other kids at school, or use those funds to purchase enough school clothes not to have to wash them every night?

Poverty is exhausting. Your heart races every time you approach a checkout counter, hoping your bank card has sufficient funds. You fear the embarrassment of the cashier callously saying, "Your card has been declined, do you have another one?" You are always calculating what bills to pay and what can wait until next month, which foods are the cheapest and most filling, how many more minutes are left on your prepaid cell plan. Even with all the calculations, there is never enough, and you always feel like you have let everyone down. Poverty is the feeling when you look into your children's sleepy eyes as you wake them in the middle of the night to pack up and move for the third time in eight months because you cannot pay the back rent. It is when you feel guilty that your kids hate school because they no longer attempt to make friends knowing that if they do, you will move them again.

Poverty tears at the fiber of your character by forcing you to do things you said you would never do to survive: putting a few grocery items into your coat pockets and justifying the behavior by saying to yourself, "the store deserves it because the prices here are higher than in the good neighborhoods"; changing the price tags on items so you can afford them; fabricating stories so you can borrow a few dollars from friends; accepting your son's explanation of how he found a new electronic game, knowing he took it from someone or some store; not using your tax refund to catch up on some bills but making one expensive meal for the kids, knowing the decision will come back to haunt you the moment a more pressing need arises.

In dark moments, you escape in a fog of weed or in the pleasure of casual sex only to return to Earth to find out there is no food in the cupboard, the school has called six times to say pick up your son, and your toothache is worse, but you know you can't afford to go to the dentist. The constant dread of not having enough produces endless exhaustion that cannot be remedied by sleep. You begin to resent anyone who has even a little more than you. The anger envelopes you; you lash out indiscriminately at coworkers, bus drivers, school administrators, and most of all, your kids. Your self-destructive behavior endangers your employment and your relationships with the few people who care about you. As the hope of escaping poverty slowly fades, so does your motivation to try. Life takes on an out-of-body existence—you know you are not dead, but you are sure you are not alive. Poverty places a cognitive load on your shoulders every minute of every day, making you uncertain about even the smallest matter.

The stereotype of the poor being prone to make bad decisions is rooted in constant suggestions that create a subconscious bias. For example, payday loans provide instant high-interest cash on demand, repaid when the borrower gets their next paycheck. The community financial services industry estimates that there are 20,600 payday advance locations across the United States, mostly located in poor neighborhoods (Zampierin, 2013). In Alabama there are four times as many payday lenders as there are McDonald's. Coincidently, Alabama happens to have the nation's third-highest poverty rate. The annual interest rates on most payday loans are 456 percent. During an investigation conducted by the Southern Poverty Law Center, a payday lender in Alabama admitted that he only lends to borrowers whose income makes paying back the full line of credit difficult. The lender said his clients often have to decide between paying rent and paying back the loan. He estimates that 98 percent of his customers don't pay back the loan right away. "I bank on that," he said. "It's put my kids through college. When they come in and say, 'I just want to pay my interest,' yeah, I got them. Once you pay the interest only one time, you're going to be doing it again and again" (Southern Poverty Law Center, 2013, p. 7). He provided an example of a customer who paid $52.50 in interest every two weeks on a $300 loan for two years. This poor woman ended up paying $2,730 in interest alone on a $300 loan. Who else but someone living under the burden of poverty would agree to such predatory terms?

Every time you drive through a poor neighborhood, you are likely to see payday loan centers, pawnshops, and food markets, all advertising terms and prices that a rational person would be unlikely to accept. This constant association between the poor and bad decisions creates a bias: Individuals remain in poverty because they exercise such poor judgment. The association of poverty with poor decisions is the topic of much research. The poor don't have opportunities to take advantage of preventive health care options and are prone to seek medical attention only when situations are dire (Katz & Hofer, 1994). Unwise health care decisions are not limited to preventative care but also include a failure to adhere to medication regimens related to prescribed drugs (DiMatteo et al., 2002). Studies have found a pattern of arriving late or missing appointments prevalent among the poor even when it is not in their best interest (Karter et al., 2004; Neal et al., 2001).

Some studies portray an unflattering picture of the poor by alluding to a lack of character or motivation to help themselves. In 2006, Sorhaindo's research described the work habits of the poor as being less productive than nonpoor workers, jeopardizing vocational advancement and even continued employment (Kim et al., 2006). One of the saddest findings describes the parenting practices of the poor as less attentive and more punitive, hindering brain development and the school readiness of their children (McLoyd, 1998). However, the most pervasive association made concerning the poor is that they are statistically bad at making financial decisions (Barr, 2012; Blank & Barr, 2009; Edin & Lein, 1997). If one considers only the body of research related to the decision-making of the poor, one could wrongly conclude that poverty is the fault of those in it, and they therefore deserve what happens to them. However, recent research concludes just the opposite, that bad decision-making is an outcome of the condition of poverty. Researchers found that the effects of scarcity are so pervasive that they habitually compromise the brain's ability to make a sound decision (Mani et al., 2013). They concluded that the conditions of poverty diminish the decision-making of anyone made economically disadvantaged. The findings of their studies were so compelling that it prompted one of the researchers to say, "If I made you poor tomorrow, you'd probably start behaving in many of the same ways we associate with poor people" (Mani et al., 2013, pp. 976–980).

> However, recent research concludes just the opposite, that bad decision-making is an outcome of the condition of poverty.

Poverty Diminishes Cognitive Load

The poor, including children living in poverty, cannot perform some cognitive-related tasks because poverty imposes such a mental burden on them, reducing attention and effort. Poverty-related concerns drain mental resources, leaving the poor with less mental energy for other activities (Mani et al., 2013). In 2010, Mullainathan and Shafir conducted experiments in a New Jersey mall. They administered the tests used to measure abstract reasoning and fluid intelligence, called Raven's Matrices. Before taking the test a second time, subjects were asked to consider a hypothetical scenario: Imagine you are having car problems and repairs cost $300. Your auto insurance will cover half the cost. You need to decide whether to get the car fixed or take a chance and hope that it lasts for a while longer. How would you make this decision? Financially, would it be an easy or hard decision? Each participant self-reported their household income, allowing researchers to group them based on socioeconomic status. The results of the experiment found no significant difference in the performance based on their socio-economic status on the second administering of the Raven's Matrices after resolving the hypothetical scenario.

However, in the second experiment, the researchers raised the price tag for the repairs to $3,000. Although participants of higher socioeco-nomic status showed no significant difference between their first and second tests, the participants who identified themselves as being at or below the poverty line saw their test scores drop by an equivalent of 14 IQ points. A 14-point drop in IQ is the difference between *superior* intellect and *average* or from *average* intellect to *borderline deficient*. The researchers concluded that merely raising monetary concerns was enough to erode the cognitive performance of the poor. They theorized that people living in poverty facing an unexpected expense would con-front additional real-life stressors such as how will I pay the rent, buy food, and take care of the kids? The mental juggling caused by scarcity depletes the mental bandwidth required to solve problems efficiently. This experiment scientifically explained why the disadvantaged are at higher risk of making poor decisions, such as taking out a payday loan when faced with a financial crisis.

> The mental juggling caused by scarcity depletes the mental bandwidth required to solve problems efficiently.

Immediately after they published the study, some critics questioned whether low-income participants would experience such a significant stress response as to impede cognitive performance if based on a hypo-thetical problem. In response, Mullainathan and Shafir introduced an alternative experiment with Princeton undergraduates, using a high-risk borrowing game designed to simulate the principles of a payday loan. The participants played a version of the popular television game show called *Family Feud*. Contestants had to respond quickly to an array of questions in a time pressure situation. In this experiment, the scarcity was time. They split the contestants randomly into *rich* and *poor* groups. They gave the contestants in the rich group more time to respond to questions, while the poor had less time. All participants had the option to borrow time: Each additional second borrowed would cost them two seconds of *interest* deducted from their total time in later rounds. At first, the poor group performed better than the rich. The initial superior performance of the poor happened because a small amount of stress can improve focus and determination. As the rounds continued, they allowed the subjects with limited time to roll over their loans and repay in subsequent rounds. As a result, the habit of early borrowing created a vicious circle for the poor group; each subsequent round, they were more pressed for time and persistently borrowed. By the final rounds, with most of their time already committed to paying back earlier loans, the poor group's performance diminished, widening the margin of victory by the rich group.

These highly intelligent Princeton students were randomly assigned to a group with a scarcity of resources. The study demonstrated that scarcity over time intensifies cognitive load and increases the risk of making poor decisions. In this experiment, the researchers attempted to isolate the lack of resources as a cause of poor decisions by eliminating the question of intellect. The conclusion reached was that the scarcity of poverty renders everyone less capable regardless of intellectual capacity.

As one could predict, pundits were quick to point out that the Princeton experiment was not a real-life situation and could not predict how intelligent people would perform under the weight of poverty. Then a perfect storm occurred: Mullainathan and colleagues were conducting experiments in India. They came upon sugarcane farmers who get their income in one lump sum at harvest time once a year. That meant farmers would be flush with cash at one point of the year, and if everything went well, they would have sufficient funds to make it until the next harvest. However, if unexpected expenses occurred, they could find themselves economically disadvantaged before the next harvest. The researchers administered the Raven's Matrices tests two months after the harvest and two months before the next harvest. They tested the farmers' cognitive control, their ability to control their emotions, their fluid intellect, and their ability to think logically. The farmers tested two months before the next harvest who were barely scraping by scored lower in cognitive control and registered a drop of 10 to 15 points in fluid intelligence when compared to their earlier tests. The farmers were compared to themselves, with only financial variables changed. Even the occurrence of temporary poverty produced lower cognitive performance, resulting in a reduced decision-making capacity.

Severe cognitive overload can manifest itself as disinterest or lack of engagement as students apply their cognitive capacity to cope with the rigors of everyday life.

Poverty's impact on cognitive capacity has enormous implications for education. The primary concern is that students coming from extreme poverty may arrive at school cognitively overloaded and not have the capability to engage in learning. Severe cognitive overload can manifest itself as disinterest or lack of engagement as students apply their cognitive capacity to cope with the rigors of everyday life. However, disinterest can quickly shift to impulsive or volatile behaviors when stressed or when placed in environments with too much stimulation.

Overstimulation is more likely to occur in current school settings because elementary, middle, and high schools are being built bigger. In 1920, there were 271,000 public schools in the United States, but by the late 1980s, there were only 83,000. While the number of schools decreased, the U.S. population more than doubled between 1920 and 1980 (Berry, 2004). So, today about 60 percent of American high schools have over one thousand students (Toch, 2003). This trend is especially troublesome as it relates to students coming from low-income settings because they are experiencing lower cognitive capacity, making it challenging to function in larger environments. In addition, larger educational settings are more likely to trigger impulsive behaviors. If the students living in poverty come from neighborhoods where they are exposed to violence, impulsivity can often take the form of aggression.

Concerning academics, cognitive overload produces periods of significant drops in fluid intelligence, which reduces academic performance. Fluid intelligence is the ability to reason and solve problems in novel situations, as well as synthesize new information quickly. What is often overlooked is that poor academic performance not only causes the teacher to underestimate the mental capacity of low-income pupils but also causes the students to think they are cognitively deficient. The impact for students in the early grades is a lack of motivation to learn, which results in a negative association with school. Persistent failure produces a lack of student motivation. A chemical in the brain, dopamine, is triggered when we experience success—that hormone is the source of motivation. For example, when students get good grades and adults reinforce the practice, the students begin to associate excellent academic performance with success. Once that happens, getting good grades will trigger dopamine, which will further motivate studying, increasing the likelihood that high test scores will happen again. Once a student establishes a pattern of getting good grades, she will become self-motivated to perform well academically because dopamine has helped create a new habit. The sad thing is that many of our poor students have greater potentials than their teachers see demonstrated. It is important to remember that cognitive load can cause a drop as high as 15 IQ points. Over time, the pattern of repeated failure by low-income students causes teachers to associate poor students with the inability to excel academically. Yes, there are always exceptions. However, they do not occur with enough frequency to terminate subconscious bias. Unconscious bias influences behaviors in a range of ways. Teachers who subconsciously associate students of poverty with failure are more likely to say things or do things to convey that they do not believe the students can achieve. Further complicating this scenario

Persistent failure produces a lack of student motivation.

is that behaviors caused by subconscious bias are seldom recognized and therefore go uncorrected.

Poverty Hinders Brain Development and Function

The prefrontal cortex is the front part of the frontal lobes of the brain; it is in charge of complex cognitive tasks, personality, social behavior, and decision-making. The parts of the prefrontal cortex are mentioned in this section because they have specific roles in higher-order thinking, which poverty impacts. Using functional magnetic resonance imaging (fMRI), Dagher found that the root cause of poor decision-making relates to aberrant connections between the dorsolateral prefrontal cortex and other brain regions (Hayash et al., 2013). Economic disadvantage produces an underdeveloped prefrontal cortex, making students more susceptible to making poor decisions. The underdevelopment of the prefrontal cortex is produced by a combination of stress and environmental factors. A growing body of research now shows that poverty causes the loss of grey matter, compromising the size and function of the prefrontal cortex. Poverty is also correlated with a drop in brain white matter, lowering communication between the cortex and other regions of the brain. Atypical connections and poor functioning result in an inability to make rational decisions. Simply put, grey matter determines how well a brain region functions and white matter governs the communication between regions. Compound the issue of compromised brain development with the cognitive load experienced by the poor and you have a propensity for inferior choices. Since cognitive load is not readily apparent and does not require any significant stressors, educators usually cannot comprehend or justify many of the bad decisions made by their low-income students.

Researchers determined that the interactions between the dorsolateral and ventromedial prefrontal cortex play a central role not only in self-control but also in flexible intelligence (Rudorf & Hare, 2014). Decisions that require self-control are vital because they directly affect a person's physical, psychological, and social welfare. Flexible intelligence plays a significant role in rationally solving problems. Both self-control and flexible decision-making require efficient retrieval of prior learning to have sufficient data to decide what to do and when to do it, or the ability to shift when an alternative plan is needed. Therefore, even something that seems non-related such as the ability to recall information is vital to every decision a person makes. The cortex and hippocampus both play a critical role in memory formation and retrieval.

The hippocampus is in charge of short-term memory, and without it, no long-term memories can be formed. Deficits experienced by those growing up in poverty compromise the development and functioning of both of these brain structures, reducing memory and slowing retrieval. Imagine making a quick decision without your brain having the ability to synthesize prior information before acting quickly. Acting without thinking is the very definition of impulsive behavior. It is important to understand that the automated retrieval of information happens both consciously and subconsciously. We are aware of the factors we consider when making a decision; however, we are not aware that a vast amount of information is also processed by the subconscious mind to help influence conscious decisions toward a better outcome. Struggling with memory retrieval on a conscious level is a strong indicator that the subconscious brain does not bring back information efficiently.

The reduction in flexible decision-making also indicates a lower level of resilience. A key indicator of being resilient is the ability to adapt. Adaptability is especially crucial in moments of high emotion and crisis when quick decisions occur. Efficient communication between brain regions is necessary to demonstrate adaptability. Dagher found that pressure to make a decision can challenge the efficient processes of a healthy prefrontal cortex. However, when the dorsolateral prefrontal cortex can efficiently communicate with other regions in solving a problem, it reduces stress. Whenever an issue can be resolved quickly, we experience less stress, and our prefrontal cortex maintains control over our emotions.

RECOMMENDATIONS

Facilitate Key Productive Decisions

The cognitive load of poverty creates a sense of continuously being overwhelmed, making major life decisions feel so insurmountable that it promotes avoidance as a method of coping. As a result, disadvantaged students are less likely to take advantage of opportunities that most would perceive as commonsensical. For example, consider the Free Application for Federal Student Aid (FAFSA). Any student living in poverty who aspires to go to college should feel compelled to complete this application. The FAFSA application determines not only if a student is eligible for federal and state financial aid but also establishes whether she qualifies for scholarships, grants, and work-study. Yet studies found that most students living in poverty hoping to attend college do not complete a FAFSA form because it is complicated. A three-year study found that assisting low-income students with the completion of the FAFSA was enough to increase the submission rates by eight percentage points (Bettinger et al., 2012). Not only did facilitating this one decision increase college applications, but most of these students completed at least two years at institutions of higher learning as well.

When schools promote any productive decision proven to enhance the educational experience, it impacts not only students' immediate circumstances but also their long-term academic outcomes. For example, research suggests that participation in extracurricular activities may increase students' sense of engagement in their school, thereby decreasing the likelihood of school failure and dropout (Finn, 1993; Lamborn et al., 1992). Also, participation in extracurricular activities promotes positive self-perception (Daley & Leahy, 2003). Brown found that taking part in extracurricular activities produces better grades, higher standardized test scores, and advances in educational attainment (Brown, n.d.). Schools that actively recruit students coming from poverty to participate and maintain eligibility for extracurricular activities offer a wide range of benefits for the pupils, teachers, and the school climate. The determination to facilitate one decision can have long-term ramifications for a student's future.

> Research suggests that participation in extracurricular activities may increase students' sense of engagement in their school, thereby decreasing the likelihood of school failure and dropout (Finn, 1993; Lamborn et al., 1992).

A commonly used argument for not facilitating a significant decision is that coddling promotes dependency and only delays eventual failure. However, research does not support this position. If that were true, facilitating the completion of the FAFSA form would not have resulted in most of those students completing two years of college and 60 percent of them graduating.

Teach Crucial Skills Required to Be Successful in School

When the human brain learns something new, it expends a significant amount of energy. Increased use of energy when experiencing limited cognitive capacity causes a subconscious feeling of irritation. However, once a skill is mastered, it requires less energy, and with enough practice, it can reach a level of automation, allowing the brain to expend less energy. Consequently, training in just a few skills that students frequently use can dramatically alter their educational experience.

There are three overarching skills that schools should consider that would help pupils develop and would dramatically reduce the daily cognitive load at school. The first improves academic performance. One of the unexpected impacts of increased interaction with technology is a drop in the ability to maintain focus. Focus is required to maintain attention, process information, and comprehend. Also, reduced concentration is associated with an underdeveloped cortex found in many students born and raised in low-income settings. Therefore, improving the ability to focus benefits students who regularly interact with technology as well as students coming from poverty. A study conducted with marines prior to deployment demonstrated through the use of fMRI that focus can increase in eight weeks, using the correct exercises. The marines that received focus training showed increased memory capacity and better mood stability, and they performed better under pressure than their counterparts in the control group (Jha et al., 2010). By improving focus, the brain will require less energy when engaged in learning and improve attention, comprehension, and test performance.

The second overarching skill is social ability. Since empathy has steadily declined in individuals between 1979 and 2009, teaching social skills benefits not only students coming from low SES backgrounds but also most students (Konrath et al., 2011). Additional analyses showed that the declines in empathy are more pronounced after 2000. The average person is less empathic than three-quarters of the people living in 1970 (Konrath et al., 2011). In addition, recent researchers found that texting reduces the number of face-to-face interactions, further eroding empathy skills. Helen Weng and colleagues using fMRI discovered that people can develop empathy and altruism through cognitive reappraisal in a short period. Using this systematic approach, she found that people can build up their compassion through caring thoughts and behaviors and alter brain structures. Weng also learned that promoting caring thoughts and acts of kindness increased activity in the inferior parietal cortex, a region of the brain involved in empathy and understanding others (Weng et al., 2013). Compassion training also increases activity between the dorsolateral prefrontal cortex and the nucleus accumbens (also known as the reward pathway). The activation of the nucleus accumbens signals that an action is being rewarded in the brain promoting a new habit. By practicing acts of compassion through volunteer programs, schools can help students develop empathy and positive social behaviors.

The social skills in students coming from economically disadvantaged settings are often lower because critical activities that promote prosocial

> There are three overarching skills that schools should consider that would help pupils develop and would dramatically reduce the daily cognitive load at school.

behavior are frequently lower. Decreased social interaction with parents during crucial periods of development, higher exposure to violence, and elevated stress all slow the development of social skills. Social skills within the context of K–12 education are a set of competencies that enable students to initiate and maintain positive social relationships, achieve peer acceptance, and improve the probability of being able to cope effectively within society. A common reason teachers often may not take time from their subject matter to teach social skills is that it takes time away from academic endeavors. However, that line of thinking might be shortsightedness. The development of social skills improves all aspects of educational performance. In a three-year longitudinal study, social skills training enhanced relationships between students, increased respectful interactions, facilitated the development of self-control, and produced a 12 percentile gain in math and reading over three years (Ottmar et al., 2013). In another study, researchers found that social and emotional learning improved grades and standardized test scores by 11 percentile points compared with nonparticipating students (Durlak et al., 2011). These studies found that students can acquire social skills if the steps taken are concrete and they are allowed to practice consistently.

> The development of social skills improves all aspects of educational performance.

The third overarching skill is self-control. Maintaining self-control requires the prefrontal cortex to exercise control over the primitive limbic system. The limbic system comprises the parts of the brain that deal with automated or instantaneous actions. The impact poverty has on the development of the cortex, coupled with stress associated with low socioeconomic status, creates an increased risk of poor self-regulation. The use of meditation can improve emotion and attention regulation in students with a short amount of practice. Studies show that children as early as preschool can master meditation techniques. Neuroimaging studies have shown meditation to improve activation and connectivity in brain areas related to self-regulation. When compared with the control group, students given twenty minutes of interactive training over five days showed more significant improvement in conflict scores on the Attention Network Test as well as lower anxiety, depression, and anger (Tang et al., 2007). These same studies also found mindfulness could lower mental fatigue and improve focus in the classroom. Students who engaged in mindfulness training showed an increased ability to maintain mood stability as demonstrated on the Profile of Mood States scale and a decrease in stress-related cortisol (Tang et al., 2007).

Mindfulness training can also improve the decision-making process. Dr. Richard Davidson showed that mindfulness could both strengthen the activity of the left prefrontal cortex and reduce the activity in the right prefrontal cortex (Wang et al., 2017). Increasing positive activation in the left prefrontal cortex seems to slow the decision-making process down enough to allow students to think before they act. Slowing down the decision-making process seems to keep the prefrontal cortex involved in logical assessment longer by reducing input from the amygdala, which promotes an emotional response. In times of crisis, it is the amygdala that overrides the cortex and often uses our strongest emotional memories on which to base our actions. Also, engaging in negative thinking increases activation in the right prefrontal cortex, which lowers the control of the cortex and increases the activation of the amygdala, often resulting in impulsive acts. A calm and positive outlook helps students maintain self-control and make better decisions.

It would be shortsighted thinking to believe that teaching global skills like those mentioned above detract from academics. Most of these strategies improve grades and standardized test scores. More importantly, helping students develop these skills allow the brain to self-correct, so these skills improve brain structures and functions. One could conclude that the investment in skills that can lower the cognitive load of poor students will benefit them not only in the short term but also for their life span.

Born Behind the Eight Ball

In this chapter: The stress related to poverty is so unique that it dramatically affects infant brain development during the first two years of life. The ramification of this type of stress inhibits infant-mother attachment and certain executive brain functions. The stress problems related to low SES are evident even in the most positive low-income homes and seem to intensify in cases of generational poverty. The result is a higher pattern of stress-related issues in low-income Black families due to their overrepresentation in persistent poverty.

The Early Occurrence of Stress

Financial hardship is a primary source of stress. A large longitudinal study of infants from low-income families found a higher than average level of salivary cortisol, a stress hormone, at three different monitoring intervals during the first two years of life (Blair et al., 2011). High salivary cortisol is uniquely associated with low executive brain function and IQ by the age of three (Blair et al., 2011). The low executive functions of the brain negatively affect an infant's abilities in several areas: self-awareness, inhibition, non-verbal working memory, verbal working memory, emotional self-regulation, self-motivation, and problem-solving. Infants from low-income homes exhibited higher cortisol levels when compared with infants in average income homes as early as seven months of age. The early occurrence of elevated cortisol reveals that infants begin to experience the hardships of poverty much younger than expected. Even more disturbing was the fact that high salivary cortisol levels were present even in positive low-income home environments. The conclusion reached is that the stress produced by poverty is inherent to financial status regardless of how well families cope with economic hardships. High salivary cortisol during infancy negatively impacts IQ. Numerous studies found that IQ is more dependent on the environment than heredity (Capron & Duyme, 1989; Schiff & Lewontin, 1986), and additional studies found that when families experience a period of poverty, there is a significant negative impact on IQ on the youngest siblings (Duncan et al., 1994). Thus, early exposure to poverty has a more substantial effect on IQ than if it is experienced when children are older.

Further evidence that financial hardship is the primary source of stress is apparent in the findings that cortisol levels were lower in preschool children when low-income families received additional financial support compared to low-income families that did not receive financial support (L. Fernald & Gunnar, 2009). The unfortunate reality is that the brains of infants born in poverty are already dramatically altered within the first two years of life. It is devastating to think that the hardships of poverty are severe enough that the odds of escape are undermined so early.

The Impact on the Prefrontal Cortex

The early impact of stress on the developing prefrontal cortex seems to hinder attention, working memory, inhibitory control, and cognitive flexibility (E. P. Davis et al., 2002). Socioeconomic skill differences are apparent in various aspects of language development, including expressive language skills, vocabulary, language processing efficiency, and gesture use in the first two years of life (A. Fernald et al., 2013; Halle et al., 2009; Hoff, 2003; Rowe & Goldin-Meadow, 2009). There are actual activity differences in the prefrontal cortex based on SES seen through the use of electroencephalogram (EEG) as early as six months of age (Tomalski et al., 2013). The drop in prefrontal cortex activity is associated not only with poor language in the first two years of life but also with later development (Gou et al., 2011).

The prefrontal cortex undergoes considerable growth during early childhood (Gogtay et al., 2004). Therefore, it is not surprising that economically disadvantaged infants experience significant variance in prefrontal cortex development and function by age two as compared to infants who are not financially disadvantaged (Hughes & Ensor, 2007). Evidence suggests that the abilities of the prefrontal cortex early in childhood are a predictor of the success that one attains later in life (Bailey, 2007; Brown & Landgraf, 2010; J. C. Davis et al., 2010). As a result, prefrontal cortex development is one of the strongest predictors of school readiness (Blair, 2002; Blair & Razza, 2007; Diamond, 2014; F. J. Morrison et al., 2010; Mulder et al., 2017; Normandeau & Guay, 1998). Recent research suggests that the development of the prefrontal cortex is at the root cause of the reported income-based achievement gap found in school data in the United States (Fitzpatrick & Pagani, 2012; Fitzpatrick et al., 2014; Lawson & Farah, 2017; Reardon, 2011).

It is the prefrontal cortex that allows infants to organize the rush of incoming information and formulate goal-directed behaviors. Infants are flooded with a deluge of new information because so many experiences are novel, and the rate of new information processed can be stress inducing. An infant can learn and remember only the things in their environment on which they focus. However, infants from low-income homes have a lower capacity to focus on things within their environments, reducing the amount of information processed, understood, and remembered (Brito et al., 2016). Contributing to the low levels of attention is the fact that infants in low-income homes have fewer opportunities to develop focus skills through play, social interactions, and stimulating environments (Dilworth-Bart et al., 2010). Stimulating environments are so influential that homes with more books even when not read have been found to increase literacy skills (Sikora et al., 2018).

> Infants are flooded with a deluge of new information because so many experiences are novel, and the rate of new information processed can be stress inducing.

One of the general indicators of poor executive functioning is the inability of infants to focus. It is not surprising that infants with poor focus often demonstrate a range of deficits with other executive functions, including inhibition, non-verbal and verbal working memory, emotional self-regulation, self-motivation, and problem-solving. A series of studies illustrate that a negative impact on one executive function can have a domino effect, causing other functions to be affected. For example, the inability to focus early in life increases the risk of developing attentional disorders, which often lead to impulsive and disruptive classroom behaviors (Holmes et al., 2014). The part of the prefrontal cortex that manages focus is highly involved with inhibition. Poor self-regulation is predictive of antisocial behavior, which often occurs with poor language skills because of an inability to engage in inner speech (Goswami, 2015). The area of the cortex that manages emotional regulation is highly involved in inner speech, which is one of the things we engage in to process social behavior and reduce impulsive response. Think of the number of times you have rehearsed in your mind what you will say or said something in your head that you would never utter out loud. Educators should be aware that most executive functions are linked. The inability to focus is linked with poor self-regulation; poor self-regulation is connected to poor language development. The prefrontal cortex provides a good illustration of the fact that no brain region functions in isolation.

Poor Attention

Studies have specifically implicated low SES to poor attention (Neville et al., 2013). Infants are born with an amazing repertoire of linguistic abilities that can reach full development incredibly fast. However, language develops incrementally based on a wide range of factors. One of the most critical factors is the ability to focus. The attentional system may play a significant role in the developmental trajectory in language acquisition (Diego-Balaguer et al., 2016). Babies are endowed with an attentional system that is fully operational. Nevertheless, it requires relevant stimuli in the environment to invigorate the attentional system into overdrive. When learning language, the rhythm, pitch, number of words, and the variety of terms used influence the level of focus.

> Both attentional skills and self-control are considered critical for school readiness

Both attentional skills and self-control are considered critical for school readiness (Carlson, 2005; Hughes & Ensor, 2008; Kochanska et al., 1997; Morrison et al., 2010). The result of low focus is a reduction in the ability to learn words, objects, and their functions. Very early in life, infants begin to distinguish objects and learn their names. As early as nine months of age, infants understand that objects continue to exist even when they cannot see them. This conceptual cognitive development is a critical step in motivating speech because infants start to desire objects that are not visibly present. Shortly after object recognition and recall are present, infants can plan and execute two-step tasks. The execution of two-step tasks leads to the ability to plan that allows infants to be able to sort objects according to rules or patterns by age three (Piaget, 1977). The ability to sort objects by established standards is a foundational skill for many academic tasks. Therefore, the ramification of poor attention is widespread. Poor concentration dramatically reduces language development, object identification, memory, planning, and reasoning.

Memory

Cortisol also significantly reduces working memory. The effects of poverty attack the capacity to develop memory by reducing white and cortical grey matter in the hippocampus (Luby et al., 2013). The hippocampus is the part of the brain where all memories are initially formulated. Noble was the first to validate that economic disparities impact the cognitive domains of memory as early as twenty-one months of age by approximately eight standard deviations lower than peers not living in poverty (Noble, Engelhardt et al., 2015). A study found that issues related to memory development were proportional to the levels of economic disparity (Herrmann & Guadagno, 1997; Leonard et al., 2015). The more severe the economic depravity, the lower the ability of the prefrontal cortex to develop long-term memories. The ability to hold information in working memory is predictive of how well information will transition into long-term memory. Memory ability underlies the development of an aspect of intellect referred to as fluid intelligence (Fry & Hale, 1996; Kail & Ferrer, 2007).

As mentioned in the prior chapter, fluid intelligence refers to our capacity to think logically and problem solve when we face new situations. As a result, infants with lower fluid intellect tend not to think independently as quickly because they are often frustrated by new circumstances. In addition, when fluid intelligence is hindered, it results in an inability to identify patterns and form logical relationships between things learned. A common deficit frequently observed by preschool teachers working with low-income students is their inability to connect related information. An individual has to be able to recall information to compare and denote patterns. The identification of patterns is an essential component of fluid intelligence, and some people think it is foundational to all advanced learning.

Economically disadvantaged children are behind academically as early as preschool due to poor focus and working memory. They are significantly lagging in recognition of objects, the labeling of those objects, and the language skills to communicate accurately what they want to express. The ability to combine the recognition of letters, shapes, and colors is the foundation of early learning. For example, children distinguish building blocks from one another by the different letters, colors, and objects drawn on them. The observant infant is learning much more than one thing when playing with the blocks. She is learning the elements of letters, colors, shapes, sorting, geometry, patterns, physics, and language. It is not surprising that a sixteen-year longitudinal study that tracked preschool students who were encouraged to play with blocks found that they scored higher on the Classroom Assessment Techniques (CAT) in third, fifth, and seventh grades, as well as having a higher high school grade point average (GPA) and representation in

> The observant infant is learning much more than one thing when playing with the blocks. She is learning the elements of letters, colors, shapes, sorting, geometry, patterns, physics, and language.

honors classes, when compared to the control group (Wolfgang et al., 2001). The longitudinal study demonstrates how critical early engagement is to brain development and how cognitive skills are advanced through interactive play. The problem that infants from low SES face are that the stress associated with poverty significantly reduces positive social engagement by the primary caretaker.

Cognitive Flexibility

Children who grow up in poverty often live in environments that offer less support and stability (Evans, 2004). Research shows that home and community environments that increase stress lower the development of cognitive flexibility, and the early formation of cognitive flexibility is critical for the long-term prognosis of the skill. What is cognitive flexibility? Around nine months of age, babies are already trying alternative methods to get what they desire if established practices are unsuccessful (Piaget, 1952). This cognitive flexibility continues to develop during early childhood, enabling children to distinguish behaviors based on situations and settings—for example, using indoor voice versus outside voice. By preschool, most children have become increasingly accomplished at switching their focus and adapting their behavior to the changing rules based on settings and situations. That is why many children alter their behavior when the teacher enters the room. It is the student who does not possess cognitive flexibility that preschool teachers quickly notice. This student struggles in transitioning from the playground or the lunchroom to the classroom. Shifting between tasks is often so challenging that teachers will tense up during simple classroom transitions, anticipating the student requiring assistance to refocus. Poor cognitive flexibility coupled with poor self-control can result in a student who is susceptible to escalation when transitioning between activities, settings, or any shift in established routines.

Students need to develop cognitive flexibility because it is what allows them to look at an issue from multiple perspectives and it is a critical ingredient in problem-solving. The ability to view an experience from various perspectives is a cognitive skill and a rudimentary aspect of empathy. Students lacking cognitive flexibility view most social interactions from their own perspective and self-interest. As a result, students can display narcissistic traits, a diagnostic feature found in the most severe behavioral disorders. Furthermore, a lack of cognitive flexibility hinders the development of academic skills, including working independently. When tasks become complicated, the student needs to use problem-solving to remain engaged and avoid becoming frustrated and giving up. Cognitive flexibility is also a required ingredient in the development of grit. The most significant implication for education is that cognitive flexibility is a predictor of higher-level thinking and sound decision-making, one of the primary goals of education.

Nurturance Mitigates Cortisol

Under conditions of persistently elevated cortisol, the infants' physiological stress response system transforms, producing a pattern of over-response that diminishes homeostasis (McEwen & Wingfield, 2003). Homeostasis is a level of chemical balance in which the body and mind can perform optimally. The transformation of the physiological stress response system is obvious in situations perceived as threatening, unpredictable, or emotionally distressing. Although most individuals experience heightened levels of cortisol in those circumstances, healthy systems quickly start to regulate the effects of stress working to restore homeostasis. However, the transformation to the stress system impedes the flexible regulation of the stress hormone, cortisol (McEwen, 1998, 2000). The outcome is prolonged periods of cortisol production resulting in extreme emotional and behavioral responses. An early indicator that the stress response system is faltering is when infants are unable to soothe themselves.

Homeostasis is a level of chemical balance in which the body and mind can perform optimally.

The transformation of the stress response system will later contribute to poor self-regulation and executive decision-making (Ramos & Arnsten, 2007). The foundations of self-regulation are being established as early as six months of age when the infant can focus on a task, consider the information given, and suppress their immediate response before acting (Carlson, 2005). For example, by six months of age, most infants can stop themselves from touching something when asked not to by a parent. The ability to demonstrate self-control by aged four to five is why preschool teachers expect some capacity to control attention and motor response (Carlson, 2005). Students coming from poverty are often distinguished from their peers due to early self-regulation issues. In situations that a student perceives as stressful, he will be unable to control his behaviors and will tend to make a sequence of poor decisions that disrupt the classroom and, in some cases, the entire school. When under perceived stress, the student will misinterpret benign situations as threatening and lose self-control, turning minor issues into prolonged disruptive incidents.

Parenting is the primary mechanism nature has provided to mediate the stress experienced during infancy (Brody et al., 2005; Gershoff et al., 2007). The interactions that promote the bond between mother and infant produce an oxytocin-dopamine interaction in the brain. Oxytocin, which plays a crucial role in infant-mother attachment, was originally thought to be associated only with lactation. However, neuroscience later determined that it is intricately involved in all social bonding. Many actions mothers intuitively engage in with their babies activate oxytocin: feeding, touching, gazing, melodic conversation, and tones the baby finds appeasing. Most mothers trigger oxytocin frequently during a typical day by feeding the baby, engaging in baby talk, rubbing the baby's back, singing, or reading at bedtime. Acts of caring can trigger oxytocin receptors in key brain regions, followed by a surge of dopamine reinforcement (Francis et al., 2000). It is the dopamine reinforcement that creates the drive to repeat bonding actions because dopamine release creates habits. The reason infant-mother attachment is critical is that when oxytocin is elevated, cortisol is lowered. Therefore, the activities that produce the infant-mother bond also mediate the stress in infants that can hinder healthy brain development.

> The reason infant-mother attachment is critical is that when oxytocin is elevated, cortisol is lowered.

Stress and Parenting

A shocking finding is that the protection against stress produced by infant-mother attachment is less apparent in homes of Black multigenerational poverty (Blair et al., 2011). Blair found that the average resting cortisol level was higher for Black infants and concluded that there is an increased risk associated with deep poverty. Whites of multigenerational poverty may show similar higher resting cortisol rates, but whites are not disproportionally represented in poverty. The disproportionate representation of Blacks at or below poverty levels provides a neuroscientific explanation for consistently performing at the lower ends of intelligence and academic testing in the United States (Nisbett, 2009). A disproportional number of Black children experience higher levels of cortisol during the most critical developmental period of brain development, birth to three. The issue of intergenerational brain transformation may be one of the most significant contributors to long-standing disparities in health and educational outcomes in Blacks relative to the rest of the U.S. population (Kuzawa & Sweet, 2013; Lu & Halfon, 2003). While schools continue to focus on the achievement gap between white and Black students, they have missed a salient point: The income-achievement gap has widened substantially over the last twenty-five years. The emergence of a Black middle class and their academic performance illustrated that it is not a racial gap. The problem is that so many Blacks are included in the income gap that the fact that it is not a racial gap but an economic gap goes unnoticed (Reardon, 2011).

When the brain alterations caused by deep poverty are taken in combination with inferior quality schools and reduced educational and employment opportunities, the cycle of higher cortisol levels in Blacks is not only understandable but predictable too.

Multigenerational poverty produces a higher level of cortisol and a lower capacity to parent. Blair's research revealed that every generation in poverty increased the resting cortisol level in families. Stress by itself is a predictor of poor parenting. When healthy mothers are stressed, brain oxytocin receptors and maternal behavior are compromised (Champagne & Meaney, 2006). However, most mothers experience only temporary periods of stress. Allostatic load tests prove that poverty produces an ongoing elevated level of cortisol coupled with periods of even higher anxiety. The stress of poverty in multigenerational low-income families seems to lower the level of responsiveness and emotional supportiveness provided by the primary caretaker. Elevated cortisol also reduces the occurrences of interactive and engaging verbal and nonverbal exchanges that are found to be stimulating and rewarding to the infant brain (Landry et al., 2006; Tamis-LeMonda et al., 2001).

Maternal responsiveness establishes the early foundations for the child's social communication and independent problem-solving skills (Landry et al., 2006). Researchers found higher incidents of harmful and intrusive parenting that focused on the child's behavior beyond developmental or safety needs, which diminish the progression of autonomy and self-regulation in multigenerational poverty homes (Egeland et al., 1993; Ispa et al., 2004). The researchers found that low-income mothers were less likely to allow children to engage in age-appropriate exploratory behavior of objects, express feelings, and question the rationale for a directive. These mothers were more likely to say, "don't touch that," "I don't want to hear it," and "because I said so." It should be clear that *all* parents, when stressed, are more likely to engage in harmful parenting tactics and less likely to exhibit actions associated with positive parenting. Therefore, it is a misinterpretation of the facts to associate poor parenting traits to Black mothers. The overrepresentation of Black mothers living in poverty who suffer from persistently elevated cortisol are more likely to be the root cause of parenting problems. It is the lack of awareness of how patterns and trends have come into existence that promotes the development of unhealthy biases.

It has become all too common for educators working in concentrated poverty areas to witness actions associated with poor parenting

It is the lack of awareness of how patterns and trends have come into existence that promotes the development of unhealthy biases.

and—due to the disproportional representation of Black mothers—to connect the two. Once such a bias occurs, it will negatively influence most social interactions with these parents. A study on implicit bias revealed that the observer can innately discern subtle nonverbal cues. These cues are often expressed by anyone holding a bias against a specific group (Weisbuch et al., 2009). The unconscious demonstration of subtle cues by educators toward parents contributes to emotional reactions. The most interesting aspect of the study found that seldom were any negative statements made, yet observers still felt that the interaction was negative. Why? Implicit negative biases toward a group or individual influence facial expressions, gestures, postures, and voice tone. The recipients of these subtle cues are attuned to notice and interpret them. Once cues are noticed, negative emotions are triggered, and a social interaction is most likely to take on a negative tenor. Further compounding the problem is the fact that many parents of generational poverty have themselves had negative educational experiences, which in turn have negatively biased them toward the educational system and educators in particular. These social interactions can quickly become a toxic mixture: like bleach and ammonia, they release vapors that negatively distort the interactions of educators and parents before they begin.

Persistent exposure to stress can alter how the body processes cortisol in the future. The changes to the stress response system produce poor self-control in low-income preschool students, creating a pattern of negative behaviors observed by many teachers. Exposure to disproportionate patterns of low self-control by Black male students contributes to teacher expectations. The testosterone present in Black males produces a larger amygdala (the region of the brain responsible for crisis response to danger), resulting in higher levels of aggressive behaviors. Research also suggests that males with naturally high testosterone levels are more aggressive and impulsive (Zak et al., 2009). On the other hand, Black female students demonstrate better self-control because estrogen reduces the size of the amygdala, thus lowering aggression. The problem with many biases is that they are based on *some* facts. The brain notices a pattern and rationalizes the bias's existence. However, the truth is often somewhere in the middle. Deep poverty reduces self-regulation, producing poor behavioral control. Increased monitoring due to a bias that Black male students are more likely to be aggressive, causes teachers to observe more infractions. The outcome is evident in the data, a disproportionate representation of suspensions and expulsions of Black male students as early as preschool.

RECOMMENDATIONS

Right Intervention, Right People, Right Way

There is little debate that poverty affects the structure and function of the prefrontal cortex, which has a significant negative effect on academic achievement for disadvantaged children (Mason, 2017). However, there is growing evidence that positive changes to both brain structure and function can improve with the correct training (Zelazo & Müller, 2010). Early training targeting the prefrontal cortex is shown to reduce the achievement gap between the haves and the have-nots (Blair & Raver, 2014, 2016; Ribner et al., 2017). Studies on low-income students have found significant improvements to the regions engaged in working-memory through identified intervention programs (Diamond & Lee, 2011). Interventions such as computerized cognitive training, a range of physical activities (e.g., yoga and martial arts), and certain school curricula such as Montessori-based activities and *Tools of the Mind* have produced changes in brain structure and functioning related to memory (Diamond, 2016). However, certain key elements have to be present to produce success: the goals of the activity have to be obtainable yet challenging, and the program has to be of high quality and consistently practiced.

Another key to success is the quality of instruction or coaching. For example, a computerized memory training program, such as Cogmed, produced improvement to working memory, but only when a skilled instructor is involved in mentoring students through the process (de Jong, 2014). Such a finding on the surface might seem odd; however, the added oxytocin provided through quality coaching likely enables a higher level of prefrontal cortex engagement. Diamond found that every program that demonstrates improvements in memory is accompanied by quality mentorship that engages in the children's interests, enhances social and emotional development, and provides students with a sense of belonging and social acceptance (Diamond & Lee, 2011). In many ways, the improvements in memory capacity share the same key ingredient with promoting resiliency. In resiliency research, having a positive, accepting adult relationship is essential to becoming resilient and to gaining protective factors.

Another aspect of successful memory improvement programs is teaching skills through a multisensory approach that simultaneously engages multiple cognitive domains (Miendlarzewska & Trost, 2014). This approach increases recall because it processes the information through multiple sensory pathways. The multisensory approach also allows many regions to fire together. The adage "what fires together wires together" is validated through brain scanning technologies.

Early Music Activities

Systematic music training enhances specific cognitive structures and functions in the prefrontal cortex, and the improvements correlate to nonmusical cognitive and academic skills (Sala & Gobet, 2017b). There is even evidence that home-based musical activities during the ages of two to three improve school readiness and academic attainment (Williams et al., 2015). The home-based music activities were not taught through any formal curriculum; it required parents to engage the child in auditory songs with accompanying movements and visuals. The improvements through early musical activities seem to have the most significant impact on the areas in the prefrontal cortex involved in language acquisition (Miendlarzewska & Trost, 2014). One reason music has such a positive effect is that it involves the coordination of body movement and auditory perception refining the connection between motor and acoustic areas (Trainor et al., 2009). This enhancement seems to promote language acquisition. This research finding should encourage preschool teachers because it does not require advanced music training. Teachers need only provide consistent music activities that combine acoustic music, singing, visuals, and movements when teaching academic content to help improve the development of the prefrontal cortex. For example, the teacher shows the corresponding letters of the alphabet, while students sing the ABCs song and perform distinct movements representing each letter. However, later in life, students from low socioeconomic backgrounds will require advance musical training to achieve the same results. Advance music training, in this case, means a rigorous music curriculum led by a skilled professional in which the student participates with a high degree of frequency. The curriculum should be similar to ones that have proved to improve brain structure and functioning. Teachers should remember to implement the fundamentals of successful interventions mentioned above when engaging in music activities: positive relationships, multisensory activities, and consistent practice.

Studies on preschool musical training have shown promising results with children between the ages of four and six (Bugos & DeMarie, 2017). Short-term preschool music training that focuses on creativity, bimanual gross motor skills, and vocal development enhances inhibitory

> Teachers should remember to implement the fundamentals of successful interventions mentioned above when engaging in music activities: positive relationships, multisensory activities, and consistent practice.

control after just twenty days of consistent practice (Bugos & DeMarie, 2017). Bimanual refers to actions in which the brain must simultaneously control multiple movements, such as one hand shaking a tambourine and the other hand banging it. The result of short-term preschool music training is that students are better able to follow stop-and-start directives as well as switch focus from one task to another. During the school day, students need to demonstrate start-stop skills continually. For example, place your worksheet into your math folder and line up for lunch. The student needs to be able to stop working, focus on another task, and then switch again to prepare for lunch. It is the student that the teacher has to remind several times of each task that becomes mentally exhausting during an average school day. If a teacher has to tell just one student to put his supplies away and get in line three times every school day for one school year, that would equal 540 directives.

Primary school students engaged in an intense music curriculum displayed improved verbal IQ, planning, and inhibition during follow-up assessments (Jaschke et al., 2018). Another study using fMRI with students eight to nine years of age found that years of music training increased activation in brain regions involved in conflict processing. These studies suggest that systematic extracurricular training in music when students are in advanced primary grades provides a potential strategy for improving the cognitive control networks in the brain, provided the student is engaged consistently over an extended period (Sachs et al., 2017). With both of the above-mentioned studies, a structured program meant consistent participation in which a significant portion of the time combined singing with movements. Many teachers are aware of the wealth of studies that identify learning to play an instrument early in life with profound benefits for a range of cognitive functions. The reason is that learning movement patterns that are coordinated with acoustics enhances all the regions of the prefrontal cortex involved with language and memory.

The studies mentioned above reveal a few salient points when attempting to improve the brain functions of students impacted by poverty. Early intervention seems to provide faster gains without the need for formal music training that appears to be required later in the child's development. Studies indicate that music training needs to become more rigorous as students from low-income backgrounds get older. Brain functions can improve at any age; however, the approach will have to be modified based on the student's age. As a rule, the more severe the presenting cognitive issues are and the older the child, the greater the need for consistency, intensity, quality of intervention, and the skill of the instructor.

CHAPTER
4

Speechless

*In this chapter: Poverty diminishes language devel-
opment and expressive language, altering academic
achievement, social growth, and emotional stability.
Because of these limitations, low SES has acted as a
gag on the voices of the poor. Poverty reflects a perception that causes those who are socially advantaged
to dismiss poor people as unintelligent.*

Poverty's Impact on
Language Development

Low SES negatively impacts executive functions of the brain because
the prefrontal cortex takes longer to develop. Executive function refers
to seven advanced cognitive tasks, one of which involves language
development. The extended development of the cortex affects language ability because the brain regions involved in language processing
undergo prolonged maturation and are susceptible to environmental
factors (Sowell et al., 2003). Language disparities are widely considered
the most consistent negative outcome related to low socioeconomic
status: including vocabulary, phonological awareness, syntax, and
delayed speech development during critical periods (Evans, 2006;
Farah et al., 2006; Noble et al., 2007). Language impairment and
speech impairment are usually rooted in genetic issues rather than
resulting from environmental problems. However, there is growing
evidence that low SES is becoming a source of language and speech
impairments. For example, children born to young mothers with both
low education and income are at higher risk of developing language

and speech disabilities (Gianaros et al., 2011). When you control for economic factors, most children with speech impairments who are not living in poverty do not demonstrate speech deficiencies by early adulthood as long as they receive proper remediation (Young et al., 2002). In other words, students who are not born with genetic speech impairments successfully overcome speaking problems except for economically disadvantaged pupils. Children born into poverty are more likely to continue to demonstrate speech impairment into adulthood.

Studies show that the effects of poverty negatively influence the development of language by attacking two major regions of the cortex: the temporal lobe, which is responsible for executive functions, and the frontal lobe, which plays a significant role in linguistic performance (Hackman et al., 2010; Kishiyama et al., 2009; Noble et al., 2006). The temporal lobe is essential for forming long-term memory and language comprehension, such as connecting sounds with letters, word recognition, and attaching meaning to words. Patricia Kuhl (2010) found through her research that many financially disadvantaged children do not hear or say words correctly. The lack of auditory accuracy means they will have problems recognizing words, spelling words, and associating words to their meaning. Kuhl used advanced brain-scanning technologies to measure the phonetic processing abilities of infants during their first year of life. Infants are born with the ability to process every phonetic sound associated with all dialects across the world. After establishing a baseline, the researchers can easily track the loss in the ability to process phonetic sounds not commonly heard in the infant's native language as well as the increased speed in processing of phonetic sounds familiar to the baby's native language.

Kuhl found that the ability to process sounds during the first year of life accurately predicts the level of language skills displayed between eighteen and thirty months of age. However, a more surprising finding was that phonetic skills during the infant's first year were also predictive of language abilities and pre-literacy skills at the age of five (Kuhl, 2011). The ramifications for students who do not process discrete language sounds are significant. Without proper intervention, the areas of speech, pronunciation, spelling, and reading are negatively impacted throughout their academic careers.

Students cannot learn effectively without the ability to process information and attach meaning to words and letters (Sousa, 2011). A finding from multiple studies reveals that children from low socioeconomic backgrounds have problems with recognizing shapes and associating them with their identified names and definitions. The hippocampus, which is a brain structure that plays a central role in processing spatial information with associated meaning, is reduced in size and function by the issues of poverty (Sousa, 2011). It is spatial reasoning that allows a child to be able to distinguish one letter from another. It is the function of the hippocampus that helps children recognize letters and remember their meaning. It is easy to see how the foundations of language are significantly compromised. Not only do children coming from poverty have difficulty in hearing letters and words correctly, but they have difficulty in associating those letters with the correct shapes too. The hindered development of the hippocampus only compounds the problem by slowing the student's ability to remember the information learned. The lack of recall means initial language learning will be difficult and frustrating. Students who struggle with self-regulation work harder when performing cognitive tasks, making them more taxing (Mensebach et al., 2009). The result is an aversion to cognitive tasks that are challenging. If an aversion to language learning develops during a student's initial exposure to school, it can set a precedent that all academic work is unpleasant.

Teachers see how early language deficits caused by poverty play out every day in classrooms across the country. A group of boys from a poor neighborhood struggle academically in school from the time of their initial placement. They each begin not to like school because motivation produced by the human brain is intricately linked to success. The boys are eventually drawn to one another because the amygdala (responsible for the fight-or-flight reaction) is calmed by commonality and thus causes attraction to other similar individuals. In addition, most schools group students based on their performance; therefore, the same boys spend extended time together. Children are smart enough to deduce that they are in a struggling group, and with the repeated failure and embarrassment, they quickly discover that they don't like school. They often start to engage in harmful behaviors to avoid doing academic tasks that cause their brain's irritation. Their behavior only exacerbates an already tenuous situation further. Eventually, they take on the mindset that tells them they cannot learn and that school is not for them.

The issues will only intensify at each subsequent grade level as the academic work becomes more challenging. This scenario is producing a lost generation of boys from low SES. However, girls' brains have advantages when it comes to learning and language processing. For example, language centers develop faster in female brains and therefore are not as

> Not only do children coming from poverty have difficulty in hearing letters and words correctly, but they have difficulty in associating those letters with the correct shapes too.

impacted by the environment. The language advantage might explain why research finds that girls are more likely than boys to have a positive motivation for reading (Wigfield et al., 2016). Also, girls have larger hippocampi, which improve memory. They also have a robust connection between the hippocampus and the prefrontal cortex. The more substantial the connection is between these two areas of the brain, the faster long-term memories are formed. In addition, girls have a thicker corpus callosum, which connects the left and right brain hemispheres. This means girls can transition between the left and right brain more efficiently. Although language is commonly viewed as a left- or right-brain dominant function, the efficiency of the communication between the two sides is predictive of increased language acquisition. All of these factors result in girls having some natural insulation from the devastation poverty reeks on the language centers of the brain.

> All of these factors result in girls having some natural insulation from the devastation poverty reeks on the language centers of the brain.

Cortex Development Is Susceptible to Environmental Factors

Because the brain seems to be able to rebound from many forms of trauma, many perceive it as resilient and too often overlook the impacts of poverty. However, the brain is delicate, especially to toxic environments, which affect the highly evolved brain regions performing the complex cognitive functions (Sousa, 2011). The cortex is more susceptible to environmental influences than the other areas of the brain (Gluck et al., 2008; Schacter et al., 2009; Woolfolk, 2014). As a result, the effects of poverty are most apparent in the primary region critical to language processing and learning. Since the prefrontal cortex develops over an extended time frame, it is exposed longer to the ill effects of poverty. It is similar to one elementary student getting the flu and exposing his peers. Even as some students are getting over the flu, others are contracting it. The classroom goes through an extended time when someone is always sick. Eventually, the toxicity of the environment breaks down the immune systems of even the healthiest adult and child. The length and severity of the exposure increases the overall risk. In the same manner, the toxicity associated with low-income settings reduces the number of children whose brains are not negatively transformed in some way. That is why studies warn that the longer the exposure to poverty, the more significant the academic deficits (Hair et al., 2015).

The frontal lobes, the parts of the brain affected by prolonged exposure to poverty, include functions involved with working memory, impulse regulation, visuospatial, language, and problem solving (Noble et al., 2005). Not only are the frontal lobes affected by poverty, but the temporal lobes, which deal with sound, music, and face and object recognition, are affected as well. The temporal lobes also play a role in the development of long-term memory and speech. The altered development of both the temporal lobes and the hippocampus illustrates how severely poverty diminishes memory capabilities. The hippocampus helps in the formation of short-term memory, while the temporal lobes help in creating long-term memories. The reduction of grey and white matter to both lobes results in less information held in short-term memory and a lower percentage achieving long-term retention. In the brain regions mentioned above, grey matter is reduced in direct proportion to the length and severity of poverty. Losing grey matter in these regions inhibits the processing of information, and the reduction of white matter lessens the communication between brain regions.

It is a commonly held belief that the loss of white and grey matter primarily impacts language development. However, white matter loss in the left frontoparietal network correlates with a student's ability to perform basic math functions, such as addition and multiplication (Beek et al., 2014). Basic math, such as addition and multiplication, are foundational skills upon which more advanced mathematical concepts rely.

Advanced numerical cognition is dependent on the communication between the cortex, the basal ganglia, the thalamus, and the hippocampus. It is white matter that provides the communication between the above-mentioned brain areas that creates a math network. Suffice to say, poverty significantly hampers areas not only involved in math functions but also in the ability of these areas to communicate efficiently between one another. The damage to the communication pathways between regions is correlated to how severely white matter is impacted by economic hardship. More advanced math tasks require an increased level of interaction between the areas of the brain executing the task. The result is a lower number of poor children excelling in math or taking part in advance placement courses. The ramifications are apparent, the inability to major in degrees that require the performance of advanced math as well as underrepresentation in math-related fields.

Features of Impoverished Environments

A wide range of environmental elements associated with low-income settings negatively impact language development. The environmental influences of poverty are far reaching: including but not limited to parenting quality, the in utero environment, home atmosphere, potential toxin exposure (e.g., lead), nutrition, and stress, both chronic and acute. Children from low SES consistently have higher levels of salivary cortisol, the stress hormone (Lupien et al., 2001). This early exposure to persistent stress seems to impair all the brain structures involved in managing cortisol levels, including the hippocampus, amygdala, and prefrontal cortex. The level of stress exposure is associated with the loss of grey matter in all of these brain areas, which decreases brain activity and impairs brain functions during childhood and into adulthood (Gianaros, Horenstein, Cohen et al., 2007). The inability to regulate stress interferes with the acquisition of language both by the hippocampus impeding memory formation and executive processing by the prefrontal cortex.

Research has proved that the intensity and length of exposure to impoverished environments usually determines the extent of brain impediment. Merely one of these environmental factors can have devastating effects on brain activity and development. For example, poverty decreases resources resulting in home environments that lack mental stimulation. Studies on infants found that lower mental stimulation produces lethargic brains. Electroencephalogram (EEG) is a standard method of testing the level of brain activity in infants. EEG measures the electrical activity of the human brain by placing electrodes on the scalp and translating them into oscillations occurring at different band frequencies. Gamma is the frequency associated with peak cognitive performance, beta with alertness, alpha with a relaxed not thinking state, theta with deep meditation, and delta with a state of dreamless sleep. Researchers found that infants coming from low stimulating environments exhibited excessively low oscillation levels, usually associated with deep meditation and dreamless sleep—except the low oscillation occurred during their hours awake. The infants' brains could not sufficiently focus, compromising their ability to observe and retain the environmental information (Brito et al., 2016).

Neuroscience research determined that an infant's initial social relationships influence early learning opportunities. The American Academy of Pediatrics concludes that the role of primary caregivers has a significant impact on early brain development and strongly advocates the following (American Academy of Pediatrics, 1999):

- Nurturing, supportive, secure, predictable relationships

- Individualized and responsive care and attention for each child

- A stimulating learning environment that includes exposure to proficient language models

However, the stress associated with poverty can strain relationships by increasing the incidents of familial conflict and problematic parental behavior, such as harsh and inconsistent discipline, less sensitivity to the needs of the child, and reduced verbal communication (Hackman et al., 2010). Something as simple as a mother touching her infant less can reduce oxytocin levels, resulting in increased stress for the infant (Morhenn et al., 2012). It is an oversimplification to think that the negative parenting practices of the poor are primarily a result of their being uninformed or uneducated. The fact is that many positive parenting practices have been found to be intuitive when not impeded by stress. Consider how stress can negatively impact the ability to parent appropriately. For example, imagine yourself responsible for maintaining a family of four on $25,750 annually. Even if you qualify for food stamps, that only allows for a $1.40 per person per meal. The daily stress of meeting the needs of a family on such a meager budget is continuously present. Now think of one of your most stressful days; did you snap at your children unfairly, ignore something important your daughter attempted to convey, or forget to do something you promised to do for one of your sons? Consider that parents living in poverty experience constant financial burden and encounter additional daily stressors like anyone else. Parenting is challenging on a good day. It requires emotional control and a fully engaged prefrontal cortex to make thoughtful sound decisions. In many ways, poverty robs adults of the ability to parent by producing stress that inhibits emotional control and reduces brain functioning. Poor parenting can have biological ramifications. Parents who cope poorly with stress produce children who are less capable of regulating cortisol.

Many studies have identified that parents in poverty talk less to their children. Most educators are familiar with the well-known Hart and Risley study that found less educated parents are more likely to use fewer words, less complicated syntax, and fewer references to past or future events when communicating with their children.

Many individuals overlook the fact that language, when primarily focused on the present, contributes to a loss of future expectations. Less exposure to words slows auditory accuracy, pronunciation, and vocabulary development. A study using audio recordings in economically diverse households with children four to six years of age found that the increased frequency of word usage by the parent(s) resulted in greater brain activation within the children's brains, specifically the left inferior frontal (Broca's area), which predicts verbal acquisition (Romeo et al., 2017). The study found that the number of words spoken in the home corresponded to household income: the lowest-income households

The study found that the number of words spoken in the home corresponded to household income: the lowest-income households recorded significantly lower utterances than middle- and affluent-income households.

recorded significantly lower utterances than middle- and affluent-income households.

Huttenlocher studied the role of caregiver speech and found significant differences between low SES households and middle-income households. The differences became most pronounced in the expression of directives and discipline. For example, "pick up the ball" was the type of directive heard in low SES households, while "Can you please pick up your ball and put it into your toy box" was a more common form of a directive in a middle-income household (Huttenlocher et al., 2010). The expression of complex ideas, comprising multiple aspects, including quality and diversity of lexical utterances, did not initially affect the child's speech. Lexical utterances refer to the variety of words used to express a thought. However, between fourteen and forty-six months, when language usually undergoes an increase in both a variety of words and syntactic structures, parental expressions made an exponential difference in language acquisition. Longitudinal studies on language development concluded that SES and the speech of the caregiver show a pervasive influence on language growth.

Researchers recognize that neighborhood quality accounts for over 40 percent of the variance for health vulnerabilities (Hertzman & Boyce, 2010). The Early Development Instrument (EDI) is a widely used measure of children's readiness to learn and reflects levels of physical health, well-being, social competence, emotional maturity, language development, cognitive development, and general knowledge. The EDI found a consistent correlation between poor physical health and slowed cognitive development, especially in language acquisition (Kerkshaw et al., 2005). A lack of preventative health care coupled with poor diet and exercise habits are common among those living at or below the poverty line. An often-heard adage is what is good for the body is good for the brain. What neuroscience has now found to be true is what is bad for the body is devastating to the brain. Poverty in America is bad for the body; it makes preventative health care a luxury and a healthy diet unattainable; sleep is hampered and motivation and time available for exercise is limited.

Further complicating health for individuals in poor neighborhoods is the finding that health disparities are partially attributable to how poverty influences self-identity. The researchers found that if an individual feels unrespected or undervalued because of social status, it increases the risk of health complications (Hertzman & Boyce, 2010). Poor self-perception based on social status negatively influences amygdala development, which inhibits emotional control and the ability to regain composure. Poor self-image related to poverty alters brain structures critical in developing empathy. Empathy plays a significant role in language comprehension. It is the chemical experience produced by empathy that gives emotional words a deeper level of meaning (Niedenthal et al., 2009). The chemical experience felt is instantaneously associated with past relevant experiences providing context and a deeper level of comprehension. The brain can subconsciously provide relevant context at an emotional level that plays an essential role in language comprehension.

Language Bias

One of the often-overlooked outcomes of poverty is that those who are economically advantaged and well educated are subconsciously biased to dismiss or discount the voice of the poor. Our auditory process identifies emotional tones at 150 to 200 milliseconds. At the speed of 150 to 200 milliseconds, only the subconscious brain has registered the thought process. Sound, or voice, tones activate the amygdala to assess positive or negative emotions in vocalizations (Fecteau et al., 2007).

If the amygdala determines a positive or negative sentiment in the tone of voice, it will release a chemical reaction, producing a physical response. That is why we often change our facial expressions in response to positive or negative voice tones. The brain is predisposed to give dominance to low tonalities because it conveys emotional control. Individuals who feel that others perceive them as second-class citizens based on their social status are prone to elevate their voice tone because the amygdala increases tonality during the loss of self-regulation. Everyone should be able to understand how the loss of emotional control relates to voice tone. We have all experienced heated emotional exchanges in which we hear ourselves shouting but are unable to lower our voices. The constant stress of poverty seems to produce tonalities that subconsciously signal poor self-regulation. When we identify a tonality that reflects a high level of emotion, the amygdala subconsciously dismisses the information as coming from someone who lacks self-control. Consider the number of times you engaged in intellectual discourse, and the other person is becoming emotional and begins yelling. Did you give his opinions the same thoughtful consideration or discount them as irrational rantings?

At around 300 milliseconds, our brains engage in identity matching when processing voice tone. Once again, at this speed, we are not

> We have all experienced heated emotional exchanges in which we hear ourselves shouting but are unable to lower our voices.

conscious of all the implications we have made relating to the voice tone. However, inferences are made that bias our options concerning the speaker nonetheless. We usually fail to notice that we encode a vast amount of information about the speaker based on tone alone: who, gender, age, health, race, emotional state, education, and so on (Spreckelmeyer et al., 2009).

It is after conducting emotional assessment and identity matching that the brain processes words. Bias research has determined that we make a wide range of decisions based on who is talking rather than on what words are said. Kraus found that Americans could accurately determine social class from small snippets of speech (Kraus et al., 2018). In the experiments, individuals predicted educational attainment and income bracket with over 90 percent accuracy from only a small snippet of speech. The research concluded that individuals are biased against the poor before they are able to process the actual content of their words. The poor in America have too many strikes against them, reducing the probability that the general population will listen to them. The level of stress or anger associated with their tone, the difference in race, and the assessment of lower educational attainment causes the brain of the listener to be negatively biased before words are ever processed. The feeling that society is ignoring what the poor are saying intensifies emotions, further marginalizing their message. Teachers are not exempt from subconscious bias. Many times students from poverty can make brilliant observations that are discounted because of how it is said and who is saying it.

Poverty's impact on the environment produces persistent exposure to stress. Enduring financial hardships create a sense of insecurity regarding the future. The demoralizing feelings of marginalization or social exclusion impact the brain and are evidenced through non-verbal expressions. It is now well known that a person's perception of his ranking in a social hierarchy affects emotional and physiological processes (McEwen & Gianaros, 2010). In 2008, the American Association for the Advancement of Science presented findings on the impact of stress due to poverty. Krugman summarized the results by saying, "The effect is to impair language development and memory—and hence the ability to escape poverty—for the rest of the child's life. So now we have another, even more compelling reason to be ashamed about America's record of failing to fight poverty" (Krugman, 2008, para. 1–2).

RECOMMENDATIONS

Don't Stop the Music

The previous chapter illustrated how music instruction could improve general intelligence and self-control. These recommendations explain how music can improve brain regions related to language processing and acquisition. Music and language share brain features that allow it to improve language processing. However, many of the early studies on music were correlational, inferring causation, which resulted in schools taking note but not altering programming. Advancements in neuroimaging have given birth to a range of studies that now conclude that music training improves not only language processing but improves many of the structures in the brain involved in language acquisition as well. By providing music training, schools can address capacity issues related to underdeveloped brain structures due to poverty through the promotion of a rigorous music program.

Several studies have demonstrated that music training improves performance in the cognitive domain of language (Chan et al., 1998). These studies focused on determining student performance pre- and post-music training and looked for increased activation in certain language regions of the brain as well as improved academic performance. Research shows that music training helps students coming from poverty who struggle with symbol identification and meaning by improving spatio-temporal reasoning and visuospatial abilities (Hetland, 2000; Rauscher et al., 1995; Hassler et al., 1985; Brochard et al., 2004; Gromko & Poorman, 1998). In relation to language acquisition, spatio-temporal reasoning relates to understanding a sequence of words to draw meaning. Visuospatial abilities refer to the ability to recognize letters and words and associate them to their sounds and definitions. In the studies, students were better able to recognize letters and later words and associate them with their corresponding meaning. Also, verbal memory has shown significant improvement with music training by the increased stimulation to the hippocampus (Chan et al., 1998; Ho et al., 2003). Since music training improves general intelligence, it also helps with language comprehension and expression (Schellenberg, 2004, 2006).

Through advanced brain imaging techniques, researchers discovered that music training can modify the brain structures related to language

> Advancements in neuroimaging have given birth to a range of studies that now conclude that music training improves not only language processing but improves many of the structures in the brain involved in language acquisition as well.

processing. The improvement to brain structures through music provides education with an alternative method to address many language deficits associated with poverty. School performance data indicate that academic strategies alone are not sufficient to overcome many of the language processing issues related to low SES. Research shows a significantly larger anterior half of the corpus callosum in musicians that have engaged in intensive training (Schlaug et al., 1995a). A larger corpus callosum increases the speed of communication between the brain's hemispheres, improving complex left-to-right processing. Several additional studies have also shown structural differences with students who took part in music training versus students who did not in the planum temporal, which involves verbal memory and identification of absolute pitch (Keenan et al., 2001; Luders et al., 2004; Schlaug et al., 1995b; Zatorre et al., 1998).

Music training also increases the anterior-medial part of the Heschl's gyrus, which helps restore the auditory processing ability that is often not developed in students from poverty because they do not hear certain discreet language sounds (Schneider et al., 2002). Music training restoring auditory processing explains why Kuhl found that many of the students from low socioeconomic status picked up discreet sounds related to their native language. In contrast, low socioeconomic students who did not take part in music training could not discern the discreet sounds. Also, music training helps with the auditory processing of language by increasing the size of the inferior lateral temporal lobe, which was identified earlier as playing a significant role in auditory language processing (Gaser & Schlaug, 2003; Luders et al., 2004). Perhaps the most significant benefit of music is its impact on the inferior frontal gyrus, which helps promote executive functions such as attention and language comprehension. Low SES correlates with how the left inferior frontal gyrus is activated during language tasks in young children, indicating decreased language function in the left hemisphere (Noble, Norman et al., 2005). The improvements to the inferior frontal gyrus are not limited to language but will also improve decision-making, emotional control, and overall learning.

Schools might consider investing in developing a comprehensive music program as too daunting a task in the face of other existing fiscal demands. However, music training, especially in schools with a concentration of students coming from poverty, might be one of the most effective and well-researched strategies for improving not only the immediate performance of students but also the long-term capacity of their brains by improving underdeveloped structures. Strategies such as music training should be considered mandatory for students coming from deprived environments that have altered brain development. The research supports that the earlier the training begins, the more immediate and long-term the benefits.

Improve Initial Learning and Emotional Control

The neuroscientist Brody conducted an independent review of a training program designed to help poor Black at-risk children. The researcher conducted pre- and posttests related to the seven-week training program that promoted four specific skills to help children achieve better life outcomes. Brody found that the program increased the capacity of the hippocampus and amygdala, improving memory and emotional control. This outcome was fairly astounding but paled in comparison to his finding that at age twenty-five, all the young participants continued to show the increased function and size of the hippocampus and amygdala (Brody et al., 2004). These findings are relevant to educators because all learning begins in the hippocampus and requires a level of emotional control. The human brain can retain no information without it being held in the short-term memory of the hippocampus. Poor emotional control is an indicator of poor focus, which often prevents students from being on task and responding appropriately to directives.

The training course focused on teaching two skills to the parents and two skills to the children. Schools can adapt the training course and implement the elements by training teachers to exhibit the two adult skills and teach the other two skills to the students. To reinforce the gains of this training program, schools could also offer similar training to parents to use with their children in the home.

The following is a brief description of the four skills:

Skill 1. The Adult Expresses Nurturing Skills

The definition of nurturing related to skill development is to support and encourage while someone is learning and becoming proficient. Nurturance was found in studies of children born in poverty to promote resilience. Therefore, by a teacher associating the development of a skill as an attempt to nurture students, using the above-mentioned definition, skill building can promote grit. It is important to remember that the brain is better able to internalize an abstract concept when associated with something concrete. Embodied cognition teaches us that the human brain's mental processes can increase when performing a concrete physical action. Skill 4 is for students to learn strategies for dealing with stress. By encouraging students while they are becoming proficient, the teacher provides nurturance, enhancing the benefit of the intervention. Teachers can associate practicing stress coping strategies as an act of providing nurturance. Nurturance has been found to increase hippocampal development and will, therefore, promote academic achievement in all subject areas (Rao et al., 2010)

Skill 2. The Adult Applies Effective Discipline Strategies With the Students

Most schools have already adopted nonpunitive methods of dealing with negative student behaviors. One reason for the discontinuation of harsh discipline tactics is that it makes the brain susceptible to emotional disorders (MacMillan et al., 1999). However, many teachers don't realize negative emotions, such as elevated voice tones used while administering discipline, negates nurturance and reduces empathy. Teachers should make every attempt to separate the student from the behavior. It is also vital that schools consistently remind students that the responses to negative actions are to teach appropriate practices to make the student more successful. Reducing negative emotions and emphasizing that discipline measures are in place to help the student will increase the benefits of the nonpunitive discipline model and increase empathy by both teacher and pupil.

> Teachers should make every attempt to separate the student from the behavior.

Skill 3. Offer the Student a Healthy Future Orientation

The restoring of hope for the future is not only a protective factor found in resiliency research but also helps the brain better regulate stress and regain homeostasis (Duggal et al., 2016). There are two critical elements to restoring hope and expectation for the future (see the lesson in Appendix B on restoring hope and expectation for the future). One is for the student to learn and believe that they can be successful. Schools are encouraged to have students learn about different professions and have people who relate to the students because of shared backgrounds come in and speak to them. The second step is for students to take active steps to work on things that will make their future dreams a reality. One method is to establish how the school curriculum applies to real-world goals and experiences. Students are more likely to take part in learning activities that relate to them personally and to their goals.

Success for students coming from severe social and economic conditions often requires a shift in mindset that they can do it. Students must repeatedly hear that hard work changes the brain and will make them more successful in school (Dweck, 2006). Although many now debate the research conducted on *growth-mindset*, what is not in dispute is the power that a positive attitude has on the human brain. Several studies attempted to duplicate Dweck's findings with none producing similar outcomes (Bahník & Vranka, 2017; Sisk et al., 2018; Wilkinson, 2019). The challenge is to boost morale and prevent making the curriculum intimidating while not lowering academic expectations.

To make the curriculum both attainable and challenging, teachers should first understand the nature of the problem students coming from poverty face related to brain function. Since classrooms have students from varied backgrounds and abilities, teachers should adopt multiple instructional approaches and strategies to meet the learning needs and improve the educational outcomes of all students (Burden & Byrd, 2010; Sousa, 2011; Woolfolk, 2014). The ability of learners, especially those with learning difficulties to retain information, requires modifications in delivery and review of the data (Sylvester, 2003). A brain-based approach to teaching and retention provides strategies for stimulating multiple senses simultaneously because what fires together does wire together. Also, persistent periods of review are required because information heard repeatedly increases its importance to the brain, making that information more likely to enter long-term memory. The brain selects only a small percentage of what it has learned to fortify during REM sleep. The brain is prone to give priority to messages frequently heard.

> Skill 4. Teach the Student Skills for Dealing With Stress and Peer Pressure

Students who learn and practice techniques for dealing with stress improve self-regulation and promote the development of the prefrontal cortex (Shapiro et al., 2015).

The prefrontal cortex plays a significant role in advanced language learning. A preferred method for helping students develop techniques for dealing with stress is called *mental shift*. Mental shift is a strategy designed to help manage negative emotions by shifting the focus away from the problem to restore chemical balance. Since the human brain cannot focus on two things simultaneously, the individual learns to refocus the brain by doing specific cognitive tasks to slow negative emotions and prevent it from spiraling out of control. This approach shares many of the same benefits with the *body-calming method*, but it is a concrete task that is easier to teach. Most teachers are familiar with the body-calming method that teaches students to use a breathing technique to calm the body and mind. Individuals who struggle to focus seem to be better able to engage in concrete tasks.

As with any approach, mental shift also has some drawbacks. Students struggling to manage negative emotions initially need help in remembering to apply these strategies when required. Practicing coping strategies regularly when the person is calm increases the ability to use them effectively when aroused. The students have to complete the tasks at a high rate of speed for the appropriate amount of time to enable the brain to shift from emotional to cognitive processing. Convincing students that the process will help them is critical, or they will not use it.

An example of mental shift is the *mental grounding* strategy. Mental grounding is a process that has students rapidly list as many items as quickly as possible under a designated category within an allotted time frame. Recalling items rapidly within a given category in rapid succession forces the brain to shift from the emotional region to the executive functioning region. Attempting to list items under a few different categories allows the brain time to make the transition. Practicing mental grounding means that someone who is becoming agitated can have an effective method to shift from focusing on a negative emotion to engaging in a concrete task. Since the practice of listing items is concrete rather than abstract, the individual can rate how well he or she attends to the action. Students can chart their improvement and gain confidence that they are proficient in the activity; this assurance will increase the ability to use the technique in times of arousal.

> Recalling items rapidly within a given category in rapid succession forces the brain to shift from the emotional region to the executive functioning region.

The following are a few examples of mental grounding:

- Identify as many colors as you can that you see in the room.
- List as many square shapes as you can find in the room.
- Name as many cities as you can.
- Name as many TV shows as you can.
- Name as many music artists as you can.

Enrich the Home Environment

Many programs have found that providing parents with books and encouraging them to read to their infant and child positively influences language acquisition (Son & Morrison, 2010; Storch & Whitehurst. 2001). It is well known that early exposure to stimulating environments has the most significant impact on language development. Studies show that even a small number of reading materials in the home is still better for improving language development than sparse literary environments (Sarsour et al., 2011). Schools can impact the home literary environment by identifying any student enrolled with a sibling at the ages of preschool or younger and offering those parents' books and reading aloud training. Early intervention is desirable; a study by Noble found that kindergarten children from low SES families already test a full standard deviation below middle-class children on specific cognitive measures (Noble, Tottenham, & Casey, 2005). The SES disparities are not subtle; Hurt found that by age 6 the average IQ score of low-income children is 81. Only 20 percent scored in the normal range, which is 90 or above (Hurt et al., 1998). Successful programs designed to improve the home literary environment have found that merely having a mother and child attend story time conducted by a proficient reader is effective modeling on how to perform it in the home. Also, schools should provide the parents with copies of the same books read at any of the scheduled story time events. The studies showed that parents are more apt to read a book that they have heard read to them than books just provided to them.

You've Lost That Loving Feeling

In this chapter: The emphasis on self, which is common to an individualist culture, coupled with access to information, negatively impacts the self-esteem of people living in poverty and is contributing to a drop in empathy.

Cultural Bias and Cognitive Function

Cultural neuroscientists define an individualist culture, such as that of the United States, as any culture that stresses the needs of the individual over the needs of the group. Collectivist cultures like China emphasize the needs and goals of the group over those of the individual. Recent advancements in cultural neuroscience have found that the complex interaction of environmental, cultural, and genetic factors alter brain structures and functioning. When cultural climates influence the overall focus to be either on the individual or the group, these influences affect individuals' perceptions and reasoning. For example, East Asians are more likely to engage in holistic awareness, improving the ability to see the entire landscape, and rely heavily on dialectical reasoning. In contrast, Westerners are more likely to attend to central objects rather than the contextual background and rely heavily on analytic reasoning (Ji et al., 2001). Simply put, Westerners will focus on the primary object when viewing a picture, while East Asians will focus on the context surrounding the central object. In the same manner, people from high and low SES backgrounds often perceive the world differently (Stephens et al., 2012).

One of the central aspects of the human brain is the awareness of one's self and others. The perception of self illustrates one of the significant differences in brain function between individualist and collectivist cultures. People who live in individualist cultures think of self as autonomous from others, whereas those in collectivist cultures think of self as connected to others. People living in the United States are more likely to show an increased neurological response within the ventral and dorsal anterior medial prefrontal cortex when asked to think of themselves. The ventral and dorsal anterior medial prefrontal cortex is the same area of the brain that activates when someone makes an "I am" statement like, "I am strong." However, people living in a collectivist culture when asked to think about themselves demonstrate increased activity in the posterior dorsal medial prefrontal cortex, which activates when adopting the perspective of another person (D'Argembeau et al., 2007). This emphasis on self in an individualist culture means that the brain is prone to having a strong chemical reaction to a negative or positive self-image.

The New Poverty

A distinguishing feature between poverty thirty years ago and today is that being economically disadvantaged is more likely to produce a negative self-image, which has a devastating impact on brain structure and functioning. A commonly heard mantra of many people of previous generations who grew up poor is, "I did not know we were poor." The reason many families did not think they were poor is that the people around them were also disadvantaged. Many of them could even maintain a positive self-image and aspirations of a better life for themselves and their family. Linda Chavez, the president of the Center for Equal Opportunity, in an editorial published in the *New York Times* (2005), painted a typical picture of many individuals growing up in poverty years ago:

> Growing up in the mid-1950s and early '60s, I had no sense that we were poor or struggling, even though my father had to stop working as a house painter during Denver's long, cold winters. We shared a bathroom on the first floor of the apartment house with two other families. It was my job to post the sign-up list for bathing hours each week so that no family monopolized the bathroom. Inevitably, the hot water ran out if you didn't take your bath early in the evening. Today, because this is America and you are not destined to remain in the class into which you were born, I live in a house with four bathrooms, and there is always enough hot water. (Chavez, 2005, para. 3)

The question is, what has changed between the poverty of yesteryear and poverty today? In a word, *technology*. In the past, many people who grew up poor experienced a level of isolation. They remained in their communities for school, work, and play. A familiar adage and one you may have heard recited during professional development in schools is that families in poverty, on average, travel within a three-mile radius (Murakami & Young, 1997). Today, regardless of income, most students have a cell phone and are aware of how the rich and famous live, what they drive, how they dress, and where they go to have fun. Television shows targeted at the young tour the homes of their favorite singers, actors, and athletes. The cameras walk you through their six-car garage, by the pool, into a twenty-room house, showing walk-in closets more massive than most apartments, and record excesses like a $15,000 dog collar belonging to their little Pomeranian. Constant visual reminders drive home the differences between the haves and the have-nots that can assault one's self-image. In an individualist culture, self-image is every-thing. Some living in poverty set their sights on obtaining the trappings of wealth by any means necessary. Even with the shortcuts of crime, few acquire the materials of wealth, leaving them further demoralized. Educators not familiar with the burden of poverty might wonder why more poor students don't focus on education to escape their current circumstances. The research is clear: The higher your stress or emotional instability, the lower the ability to delay gratification. Cognitive load reduces the ability to devise and maintain long-range plans.

Individuals who perceive themselves as having a lower socioeconomic status than others can experience a decrease in the volume of the cin-gulate cortex (Stanley et al., 2012). The cingulate cortex is part of the limbic system, which is often referred to as the primitive brain because it evolved first. The limbic system has an integral role in emotion formation and processing, learning, and memory. Youths with psy-chopathic traits have also shown a reduction to the cingulate cortex, which dampens empathy response (Marsh et al., 2013). In the simplest of terms, empathy is the ability to internalize the emotional state of another by experiencing similar feelings yourself. Through advanced brain-scanning instruments, studies have identified that in pain-related experiences, the cingulate cortex plays a vital role. For example, one experiment found that when you are being pricked by a pin as well as when you witness someone else being pricked, the cingulate cortex becomes active (Morrison et al., 2004). It has long been established that adolescents with disruptive behavior disorders also exhibit a muted response to pain in self and others (Hoffman, 1982). I am not saying that youths growing up in poverty will develop psychopathic traits, but living in poverty has been shown to increase the risk for impaired empathy and developing behavioral disorders.

Many adolescents suffering from disruptive behavior disorders are victims of trauma, which is linked to changes in the cingulate cortex. Children exposed to urban poverty face a disproportionate risk of exposure to trauma when compared to the general population (Collins et al., 2010). Factors associated with urban poverty such as unsafe neighborhoods, daily disturbances, and racial discrimination increase the risk of trauma. How disturbing is the fact that being poor in America can be associated with trauma? Schools may soon face a time where poverty is identified as a traumatic event leading to behavioral disorders. Teachers should know the implications this change to the cingulate cortex can have on empathy, social behavior, and emotional control.

Many youths with behavioral disorders suffer from both reduced cingulate cortex and an amygdala lacking the capacity to interpret emotional non-verbal expressions (Jones et al., 2009; Marsh et al., 2008; Viding et al., 2012; White et al., 2012). The stress of poverty can also impede the ability of the amygdala to accurately read and respond to non-verbal cues (McEwen & Gianaros, 2010).

Teachers working with students coming from concentrated low-income neighborhoods have witnessed disruptive behaviors, which the lethal combination of a reduced cingulate cortex and impaired amygdala can produce. For example, Michael glances at Jacob. Jacob immediately becomes agitated and says to Michael, "What are you looking at?" Michael, confused, says, "Nothing." Since the situation seems inconsequential, the teacher ignores it, only to find that in the time she glanced away, Jacob was standing up yelling at Michael, and before she can reach them, he has struck Michael in the face. Michael takes an ugly fall out of his chair, catching the edge of the desk with his forehead and is bleeding profusely. All the other students are immediately distraught and seem worried about Michael. Jacob does not display any remorse but rather looks even more agitated by Michael's sounds of pain. The fact is that the combination of a reduced cingulate cortex coupled with a reduction in the amygdala response can increase violence in reaction to fearful, sad, or pained facial expressions (Blair, 2005; Marsh et al., 2005; Marsh & Ambady, 2007).

A thinner cingulate cortex is shown to compromise two parts of the cingulate: the dorsal region, which is involved in cognitive processes, and the ventral area, which is engaged in emotional regulation. The cingulate cortex's role in connecting the amygdala to the prefrontal cortex

---

Teachers should know the implications this change to the cingulate cortex can have on empathy, social behavior, and emotional control.

cannot be understated. The strength of the connection determines how capable we are at interpreting and displaying emotions as well as responding rationally. When the anterior cingulate cortex is compromised, emotional regulation diminishes—in some cases to the point of psychosis. The cingulate cortex is involved with emotion formation, learning, and memory.

The dorsolateral prefrontal cortex is located in the frontal lobes toward the top and side of the cingulate. There is a wealth of research concerning the dorsolateral prefrontal cortex role in memory. It has been well established that the hippocampus is where learning begins and is vital to short-term memory. Since so many studies use the term *working memory* and *short-term memory* interchangeably, most people are unaware that there is a difference. Short-term memory is a limited aspect of the formulation of recent memories performed by the hippocampus. Working memory, on the other hand, in which the dorsolateral prefrontal cortex plays a vital role, refers to the process by which we temporarily store a new recollection to perform a task. For example, someone hears a phone number, recalls the information long enough to make the call, but does not retain the knowledge long term. Recent studies on the hippocampus and the prefrontal cortex have advanced our understanding of the distinct roles these brain regions play in the encoding and retrieval process. The studies have led to an alternative model of how the hippocampus forms and replays memories and how the prefrontal cortex connects new recollections to meaningful contexts to improve retrieval. Both the hippocampus and prefrontal cortex play a vital role in memory consolidation.

Poverty's Impact on Empathy

The ventromedial prefrontal cortex, the backside of the cingulate, processes feelings of empathy, shame, compassion, and guilt. A reduction of the ventromedial prefrontal cortex compromises an individual's ability to function on a social-emotional level. It is important not to gloss over the implications of lowered feelings of empathy, shame, and guilt.

Empathy is almost as crucial as procreation in ensuring the continuation of the human race. Neuroscience describes empathy as an automated motor reaction that occurs in the mind of anyone observing the emotions of another. That is why we cry when friends cry, laugh when others laugh, and turn our faces and wince when witnessing a gruesome accident. Empathy allows us to share the chemical and emotional experiences of another and produces compassion. Those who lack empathy, like sociopaths and psychopaths, are callous to the pain their actions cause others because they lack understanding. It is the lack of empathy that allows a sociopath to con the life savings of an elderly woman and feel no remorse. It is the lack of compassion that enables psychopaths to torture others because their ability to feel is so dampened that they resort to extreme measures to experience any pleasure. Consider the crimes of the real Dr. Hannibal Lecter, Albert Fish, who killed fifteen children and mutilated many others. His lack of empathy enabled him to torture his young victims. No one whose brain produces empathy could witness that level of pain and horror even once, much less repeat the process a hundred times. In times of crisis, it is empathy that moves individuals to sacrifice time and resources and sometimes risk their very lives to help those in pain. Dr. Sean Mackey of the Stanford Pain Management Center concluded after decades of studying pain that without the automated empathy response, humans would have wiped one another off the face of the Earth long ago.

When considering the impact of poverty on empathy, it is important not to think of it like a light switch that can only go on or off. Poverty's impact on empathy is more like a light dimmer that can gradually intensify or lessen. Students from poverty can manifest a wide range of empathy issues. On the lower levels, lacking empathy might be viewed as being oblivious to the feeling of others. In more severe cases, the lack of empathy might be expressed by a complete lack of remorse, which would allow a student to not only trip and injure a peer but even take pleasure in their pain.

One of the elements of concentrated poverty is the association with lower empathy due to exposure to violence.

One of the elements of concentrated poverty is the association with lower empathy due to exposure to violence. Consider an experiment conducted by Bushman and Anderson, which showed that temporary exposure to violent media could briefly dampen the empathy response. The researchers staged a scene outside a local cinema, where a young female actress with a cast on her ankle pretended to fall with her crutches and struggled to get up. The experiment observed 162 people exiting the cinema. While all the patrons helped the woman, those who had just seen a violent film took 26 percent longer to come to her aid than those who had seen a nonviolent movie (Bushman & Anderson, 2009). Bushman and Anderson explained that even brief exposure to violence created a more callous response than patrons who did not see a movie containing acts of violence. Now consider students in poverty exposed constantly to violence in their neighborhood and suffering from a perceived lower social status. Some researchers believe that many personality profiles growing up around violence deliberately shut down the empathy response to better survive the surrounding brutality.

One of the challenges for education is that teachers think they understand violent neighborhoods because they have seen them portrayed on television and have heard about violent incidents involving their students. However, awareness alone does not produce real comprehension. The reality is people born into violent communities are indoctrinated before they can form opinions on their own and view violence as a way of life, even for those who attempt to avoid acts of aggression. One factor that makes overcrowded prisons so volatile is the mere fact of confining so many desperate people into one confined space. In many ways, high-rise housing projects provide a similar setting. Because even the poor know that you have to be a special kind of broke to live in government-subsidized units. Children learn that violence is not optional. Mothers who love their children send them back out to fight the child they ran from because they know that running from violence will make life even more unbearable.

One of the worst things about concentrated poverty is the learned paranoia. Some people will fight only if provoked; however, some will shoot over seemingly nothing. The problem is you cannot discern who is who. There is a constant feeling of paranoia because you never feel safe. The locks on your doors are meaningless because you and all your friends' apartments have been broken into many times. The ride to school is an hour of torment because, for sixty minutes, you are on constant alert because an incident can happen without warning. The only adult on the school bus has to focus on keeping 30,000 pounds of metal from careening out of control. You never let your guard down because once a drug addict robbed you at gunpoint for the $4.25 in your pocket. The one person on Earth who loves you also has an unpredictable temper and can become physically abusive without apparent cause or provocation. Even sleep provides no rest because at any moment, one of mom's intoxicated boyfriends might lose control, and you awake to violent screams and are afraid to leave your room. Once you internalize the distorted value that violence is not optional, the world changes. You learn to numb your feelings to survive. A smile is no longer pleasant and a kind word no longer nurturing because you are always on high alert, waiting for things to get worse. Teachers don't understand; how can they unless they grew up in a combat zone? Teachers might be aware of the violence related to poverty, but few truly comprehend it.

Teachers might be aware of the violence related to poverty, but few truly comprehend it.

The issues related to empathy further intensify when one considers that the impact to the ventromedial prefrontal cortex not only reduces empathy but also increases the risk of mental health issues. Adolescents who perceive themselves as having a lower social status and who experience a thinning of their anterior cingulate cortex can demonstrate aggressive responses when they perceive that they are being looked down upon by others (Gianaros, Horenstein, Cohen et al., 2007). Teachers who know students from economically disadvantaged neighborhoods have become very familiar with the *dissing* response. The dissing response is an aggressive reaction to a perceived slight that is often misinterpreted or disproportionate. The risk of demonstrating a disproportionate response when feeling slighted is often compounded in cases of generational poverty. In an individualist culture that stresses self-reliance and social status, it is almost impossible not to feel belittled. Feelings of being seen as a second-class citizen intensify every time students are reminded of how much more material wealth and opportunities other people have. The sad truth is that lowered empathy is becoming a symptom of poverty. The outcome is more impoverished youths suffering emotional disorders associated with poor impulse control and aggression.

RECOMMENDATIONS

The field of behavioral psychology has debated whether empathy is trainable. However, recent studies in the field of neuroscience have determined that it is (Srivastava & Das, 2016). In one study, researchers found that individuals can develop identified skills through practice that enhances empathy, improving social interactions even across cultures (Case & Brauner, 2010).

The practice of expressing what someone says in your own words primes the brain to see things from another person's perspective.

Active Listening and Comprehension

The ability to listen and accurately reflect not only the content but also the emotion of speech are critical components in enhancing empathy (Hojat et al., 2009). Hojat found that exercises where students actively listen and then repeat back what is said in their own words increase empathy. The practice of expressing what someone says in your own words primes the brain to see things from another person's perspective. Mimicking voice inflection also helps in identifying the emotional intent of the speech. The exercise increases the likelihood that the brain will engage in the practice more frequently, increasing the occurrence of empathy. A crucial element to empathize accurately with what is said is the ability to interpret voice tone correctly. One experiment found that the simple phrase, "I never said she stole my money," can have seven different meanings based on inflection alone (Dichter et al., 2018). Students who can accurately interpret voice tone are less likely to misinterpret what others say.

It is imperative to help students better understand how the brain processes speech in order to enhance the accurate interpretation of spoken words. When hearing words, the first thing the brain does is to identify emotional tones (Fecteau et al., 2007). As we have evolved, the things that are most important to survival are what the brain performs faster, as evidenced by the speed of emotional identification, which is within 150 to 200 milliseconds. There are 1,000 milliseconds in a second, meaning this action takes place so fast it happens at a subconscious level (Fecteau et al., 2007). Immediately after emotional identifiers, the brain engages in what we call identity match, "asking" questions such as who said it and their age, gender, and race. An identity match occurs at about 300 milliseconds. The last thing the brain analyzes is the meaning of words (Spreckelmeyer et al., 2009). Students should learn that the adage "it is not what you say but how you say it" is correct for how the human brain processes speech. The brain's focus on tone further explains why students and teachers often react to the emotion in verbal exchanges far more than to what is said. Teachers should be cognizant of voice tone, especially when interacting with students from low SES.

In addition, the brain focuses on facial expressions, body posture, and hand gestures when processing language and producing empathy. The mind is automatically alerted to focus on non-verbal expressions to help us feel what another might be experiencing. The mirror neuron system, which simulates the movements of others in our brains, activates motor neurons as if we were doing the movements ourselves (Rizzolatti & Craighero, 2004). Then our limbic system produces chemical signals that code responses for us to experience the emotions related to the non-verbal cues seen (Carr et al., 2003). Immediately afterward, the insula acts as an interface between the mirror neuron system and the limbic system to translate what is seen for emotional significance based on prior experience (Leslie et al., 2004). This process is crucial to comprehending emotional behavior as evidenced by children with autism who show no mirror neuron activity, which helps explain why their ability to understand emotional expressions is impaired (University of California–Los Angeles, 2007).

As with spoken words, the human brain processes emotional facial expressions well before the conscious brain can register them, at 50 to 200 milliseconds (Smith & Smith, 2018). The automated tracking of facial expressions is so hardwired that our brains react to them even from our peripheral vision. The reaction of the brain to facial expressions affects our chemical disposition. For example, one experiment discovered that we detect and react to non-verbal emotional cues even when they occur up to 30 degrees in our peripheral vision (Smith & Smith, 2018). The subconscious processing of faces means that others unconsciously influence our moods. The school climate is important because the non-verbal expressions of students continually influence behaviors and learning. The pervasive attitude of students within a school can positively or negatively alter the dispositions of students and teachers without conscious awareness. In schools where teachers focus on projecting positive attitudes and being supportive of students, the teachers' facial expressions improve the moods of everyone in the building.

> In schools where teachers focus on projecting positive attitudes and being supportive of students, the teachers' facial expressions improve the moods of everyone in the building.

Gesturing plays an essential role in language processing. Gestures reduce the load on working memory and cognitive load (Marstaller & Burianová, 2013; Pouw et al., 2014). The brain engages in a few distinct processes when we observe a gesture. In milliseconds, the subconscious brain recalls additional times and circumstances we have seen the gesture. If you and the person gesturing are close friends, the mind recalls past situations when your pal used the same gesture, providing a deeper level of context thereby improving understanding. Also, motor neurons activate in our brains as if we are performing the observed gesture. This mimicking in our minds allows us to experience a similar chemical experience as the person making the gesture. As a result, the ability to process gestures accurately enhances comprehension of what is being communicated. Gestures help us better remember what others say and reduces cognitive load, allowing the brain to focus longer.

It would be helpful for students to learn that the more they improve their level of empathy, the better they will interpret non-verbal communication. Hand gestures also receive pre-attention occurring within 200 to 700 milliseconds. Positive and negative gestures get the earliest subconscious attention as quickly as 200 milliseconds (Flaisch et al., 2011). The rapid reaction system means the brain is hypersensitive to any non-verbal signal that conveys a positive or negative message. However, it is unfortunate that negative messages receive greater vigilance and have a more significant impact on our brains. Researchers found that our brains are biased to give priority to anything that is perceived to be negative (Cacioppo & Berntson, 1994). The take-home message is that we always notice and respond to emotional non-verbal expression. Most of the attention and reaction occur subconsciously and chemically. Improved awareness increases the ability of the brain to observe these cues with increased frequency, enhancing comprehension and empathy.

Empathy increases when students learn to reciprocate with the correct emotional response to produce the best outcome during a conversation (Kelm et al., 2014). The ability to respond appropriately to emotional cues takes a significant leap forward for most students between the ages of thirteen to fourteen (Kolb et al., 1992). Students continue to refine their abilities further to meet the emotional needs of others through their teens, reaching a peak response between the ages of twenty and thirty-nine. Many students raised in callous environments do not develop the ability to respond to emotional cues, resulting in an inability to defuse volatile interactions appropriately. The ability to practice identifying and responding to the emotional cues of others is a vital skill to develop. Research has found that the skill to react appropriately can be acquired through the consistent practice afforded through role-playing. Having students role-play everyday emotional situations that occur at school and practice how to best respond can increase empathy over time. The assumption that students growing up in stressful environments should know how to react is clear evidence of a lack of comprehension of the profound impact poverty can produce.

Practice Practice Practice

When it comes to improving empathy, there is no replacement for practice to promote long-term behavioral change (Case & Brauner, 2010). The brain rewards repeated practice with dopamine. The moment dopamine activates in response to repeated behavior, a new habit begins to form. If, as an adult, you make your bed every morning, the practice generates dopamine. In most cases, as a child, you were told by your parents to make your bed, and you likely had some initial resistance. However, over time it became easier, signaling the occurrence of dopamine reinforcement. Now, as an adult, even after recognizing that it is not the best use of your time, you still consistently engage in the practice. You have considered that you are the only person who sees your bed made, only to return in the evening to unmake it. It is estimated that it takes 5 minutes to make your bed daily, multiplied by 365 days a year over an average life expectancy of 78 years, for a total of over 9 months or nearly 1 percent of our lifetimes (Patterson & Stewart-Patterson, 2001). The value of the practice is not the aesthetics but rather the chemical reinforcement you receive from making your bed daily. Contrary to popular opinion, there is no magic number to how many times something has to be repeated for it to become a habit. Brains with a lower level of chemical balance usually take longer to develop a new habit and, in some cases, significantly longer. The challenge is that teachers will often judge that a behavior has received sufficient practice when most students are complying independently. Students who need the most time to change have a different experience as the practice times reduce or stop altogether before they achieve the internal motivation needed to maintain the behavior. Therefore, teachers should continue to practice opportunities even after most students are complying to allow all students enough time to develop the behavior as a new habit. It is also worth noting another added benefit to engaging in a consistent practice: the repeated action strengthens the prefrontal cortex, improving discipline and focus.

See No Evil, Hear No Evil, and Speak No Evil

In this chapter: Neuroscience has established that culture can alter brain function and can even produce brain mutations. In the same manner, poverty can modify certain hardwired brain functions that produce social bias. Much of a child's intuitive understanding of the social world is a product of how humans have evolved to notice facial, hand, posture, and voice tone cues. Under normal circumstances, our focus on these cues creates instantaneous biases concerning others. The purpose is to help us identify individuals who are safe and avoid people who are threatening. However, under the stress of poverty, our abilities to read and appropriately respond to these hardwired cues can be compromised and negatively influence social behavior.

How Social Bias Occurs

Individuals are continuously processing the emotional cues produced by the faces, hands, postures, and voice tones of others; most of this processing happens at a subconscious level. A part of processing emotional cues includes the interpretation of these signals, which produce bias on a subconscious level. The result is that we are often unaware of our preconceptions. Unfortunately, most people go through life oblivious of their biases and are ignorant about how these biases have altered their social behavior. Individuals who develop negative biases are usually unaware that a problem exists, so they do nothing to correct it. Although we are born programmed to notice emotional cues, the ability is not fully developed at birth and is highly influenced by our environment, the quality of social interaction, and how the brain develops. Poverty negatively influences the elements responsible for accurate social assessment. Individuals who do not assess and respond appropriately to emotional cues struggle to forge relationships and build healthy social networks. Our ability to create a healthy social network is predictive of academic and vocational success, long-term relationships, and physical and emotional health. At the root of all social behavior is our ability to notice and accurately interpret the non-verbal cues that we are programmed to see.

The Monitoring of Faces

We know that all non-verbal emotional cues produced by our facial expressions, gestures, postures, and tone of voice are hardwired because of our pre-attentive system. The pre-attentive system is the brain's subconscious focus on specific cues that improve or diminish our chemical dispositions. The unconscious focus on particular physical behaviors biases our perceptions and attitudes toward others. For example, humans are predisposed to notice and respond at a subconscious level to facial expressions at a speed of 50 to 200 milliseconds. At 50 to 200 milliseconds, the conscious brain does not register that the process has transpired. Our eyes automatically track facial expressions, and our brains react chemically. The chemical reaction to facial expressions produces feelings that influence our thoughts and responses at a subconscious to a conscious level. Consider an experiment that had individuals make a facial expression at someone in their peripheral vision. Participants detected and reacted to the non-verbal facial expressions made even at 15 or 30 degrees to the right or left of their vision (Smith & Rossit, 2018). The instruments registered that the eye noticed the moment the expression was made, and the brain produced a chemical reaction. The brain produced positive chemical secretions when registering a positive facial expression and an adverse chemical reaction to facial expressions interpreted as negative. Even though the participants were unaware of what they saw, their eyes tracked when emotional expressions occurred, and their brains responded accordingly.

The brain responds chemically to emotional facial expressions even when registered only subconsciously. The positive expressions of others usually trigger positive chemical responses, while negative emotions will trigger adverse chemical reactions. The chemical responses to facial expressions bias our perceptions of others. Consider the meta-analysis studies conducted by Nalini Ambady and Robert Rosenthal when they found that observers make a wide range of assumptions concerning individuals they see within thirty seconds. It was the subconscious assessment of facial expressions, hand gestures, and tone of voice that biased the observer to experience a positive or negative gut response concerning the person they saw.

Ponder the impact of poverty on the hardwired process of noticing and responding to facial expressions. Poverty is known to rob individuals of their hope for the future. It is common for the faces of the homeless, addicted, and depressed to appear void of hope. Concentrated poverty is an area where a high proportion of residents are poor. For researchers, more than 40 percent of the households have to fall below the poverty line. It is also associated with violence and aggression, producing the angry scowls that become a common daily expression. Imagine the chemical impact of always observing these facial emotions daily. It is not surprising that teachers report seeing more and more students in high-poverty schools displaying expressions of sadness, anger, or disinterest even in the elementary school grades. As the issues of poverty intensify with generational poverty, the faces of poverty influence not only what the brains of children notice but also portray. The mind quickly becomes programmed to notice first what is most familiar.

The amygdala is attracted to itself. The state of high alertness of the amygdala when seeing faces and things that are different creates a subconscious negative feeling to the unfamiliar. However, the amygdala is comforted by the familiar, creating an attraction to things and people to which we are accustomed. Students coming from poverty often seek out other students with the facial expressions associated with poverty and lose comprehension and tolerance for variances. A frequent question from students who experience intense poverty is to ask teachers why they are always smiling. The human brain produces smiling and laughter at a very early age because it stabilizes the brain from the overwhelming experience of having to process so much new information. Infants are overwhelmed with a barrage of novel information and are calmed by the nurturing expressions of mom and the reflective smiling and laughter responses when modeled. Imagine environments so decimated that smiling and laughter are perceived to be expressions of weakness. We are attracted to people who are happy because it improves our mood and increases our sense of safety. Children from poverty are often averse to smiling and laughter. In more extreme cases of exposure to violence and abuse, they are attracted to individuals expressing anger because it

> It is not surprising that teachers report seeing more and more students in high-poverty schools displaying expressions of sadness, anger, or disinterest even in the elementary school grades.

has become a familiar expression that offers some level of comfort based on it reflecting what is expected.

In dangerous communities, the reading of facial expressions is so closely tied to survival that the amygdala can undergo a strange mutation. When scanning facial expressions is linked to survival, students can become hypersensitive to any looks they perceive as unfavorable. The vigilance for negative expressions results from growing up in environments in which one false look can lead to explosive life and death confrontations. The stress of dangerous environments often causes the amygdala to be in a state of constant alertness. The vigilance creates a hypersensitive limbic system prone to misperceive benign expressions as aggressive. These students can explode in class at any moment because of a perceived slight. Schools in low-income communities often report incidents that began by one student asking, "What are you looking at?" The problem is that the perceived slights are usually not interpreted as threatening by the teacher or other students. The outcome is that most students become fearful and attempt to avoid social interactions with the volatile students coming from poverty. The fear evidenced by the other students only promotes a state of paranoia, increasing incidents of misreading the facial expressions of peers. As a result, schools become a setting where students from poverty are more likely to inaccurately read non-verbal facial expressions of peers, resulting in a higher risk of emotional outbursts and confrontations.

The intense environments of poverty that expose children to violence can even change individuals at a cellular level. Adolescent males coming from low socioeconomic backgrounds are more likely to develop chemical tags near the SLC6A4 gene, which dispenses serotonin to the amygdala (Swartz et al., 2017). Chemical tags attach themselves to genes, altering genes in ways that affect the brain and behavior. When our brain dispenses serotonin to the amygdala, it helps calm us down so we can regain composure. But the tags alter the SLC6A4 genes flow of serotonin, which slows the calming of the amygdala. The outcome is an enlarged amygdala, quick to agitation, and slow to regain equilibrium. A more disturbing fact is that once an adolescent develops this mutation, he can pass it on to his child (Grabe et al., 2005). This passing on of a genetic trait caused by experience is called biological embedding (Hertzman & Boyce, 2010). The erroneous conclusion often made is that poor genetics is at the root of anger management problems. This justification absolves society from facing the sinister effects poverty is having on generations of families. We are ignoring the fact that the

---

In dangerous communities, the reading of facial expressions is so closely tied to survival that the amygdala can undergo a strange mutation.

experience of poverty is producing biological embedding, altering a child's development from birth.

Although noticing and interpreting facial expressions is a hardwired feature, we are not born with it fully developed. As early as age one, we possess the ability to label facial emotions accurately (Gross & Ballif, 1991). Most children experience a significant improvement in accurately reading facial expressions between the ages of nine and ten. By ages thirteen and fourteen, there is a considerable increase in the ability to read facial expressions accurately. More importantly, at ages thirteen and fourteen, the ability to respond appropriately to the facial expressions begins to evolve (Kolb et al., 1992). We experience a discrimination and response peak related to facial expressions in early adulthood during the ages from twenty to thirty-nine. Between the ages of fifty and sixty-four, we experience a mellowing in our emotional response to the facial expressions of others (Carstensen et al., 2000; Charles et al., 2001; Magai et al., 2006; Phillips et al., 2006). During this same period, individuals experience a decrease in the magnitude of emotional memory. In other words, emotional memories no longer produce the same levels of chemical reaction, and that is why so many people can bury the hatchet during this stage of their lives. However, around age sixty-five and older, some older individuals lose the ability to detect a threat in the facial features of others (Mather & Knight, 2006). It is this drop in threat detection that makes the older population a target for financial scams. Poverty slows or alters the ability to assess facial expressions and appropriately respond at each of these stages. Consider the negative impact on the quality of life produced by the inability to read and respond to the facial cues of others. How many of us would remain in a relationship with someone who was not only incapable of accurately identifying our facial expressions but also inept at responding to them?

Researchers found that the brain processes facial features of individuals outside our race primarily by category at the expense of seeing individual features (Bernstein et al., 2007; Ostrom et al., 1993; Sangrigoli et al., 2005). The less we notice detailed features, the more likely our level of empathy is diminished. Research has demonstrated that there are differences in own-race versus other-race face processing at the neurological level. In other words, the brain processes the faces of distinct races differently (Walker et al., 2008). It seems that our ability to process faces of other races correlates to our level of experience with different races while the facial identification process is developing. Individuals with more other-race exposure show a similar process in identifying the faces of other races as with someone of their own race. The face processing shortcut was likely developed to help individuals quickly identify others belonging to their clan. However, this shortcut can result in a lower level of empathy for individuals of distinct races.

The Monitoring of Hands and Gestures

We subconsciously monitor hand movements because it is an intricate part of unspoken communication. What is not commonly known is that we subconsciously monitor hand movement when discerning if someone is telling the truth. The monitoring of hand movements to determine honesty is where the concept of tells evolved: because subtle body movements convey true intentions that people are attempting to disguise. Individuals, when being dishonest, often place their hands over their mouths, touch their nose, tug on the ears, or do other movements with their hands. We understand this on an intuitive level and experience a gut instinct. Hand movements work similarly to facial expressions. We subconsciously notice hand movements made at speeds between 50 and 200 milliseconds. It is important to note that negative gestures are observed faster than positive ones. In addition, negative gestures trigger a higher level of chemical response in the brain. However, the chemical impact of a negative gesture is diminished when followed by a positive one and vice versa. Environments where people engage in a lot of negative gestures or a lot of positive gestures influence our moods for the better or for the worse. Consider a middle-class neighborhood in which everyone waves when passing each other. Contrast that with a community where people flip off individuals passing by, engage in gang signs, or use threatening gestures. These gestures, because of their negative messages, challenge the recipient's homeostasis by producing chemicals that impede the brain's stability and performance.

Many scholars believe that speech and gesture both constitute human language as part of one system (McNeill, 1985). Whenever speech is limited, gestures are able to take over much of the communication burden. Research illustrates that gesture and speech in children emerge simultaneously with parallel developmental trajectories and patterns (Goldin-Meadow, 2003). People all over the world make many of the same expressive gestures without ever being taught. What child has not shrugged her shoulders to show that she does not know the answer to her parent's question? Researchers have found an evolutionary link between gestures and language. The National Academy of Sciences' researchers found that blind individuals produce many of the same emotional gestures as people who have sight, demonstrating that it is

People all over the world make many of the same expressive gestures without ever being taught.

a product of the limbic system since it could not have been learned by observing others (Corballis, 2003; Harnad et al., 1976; Hewes et al., 1973; Rizzolatti & Arbib, 1998).

Studies have shown that mothers who gesture frequently while they speak improve their child's language acquisition (Goodwyn et al., 2000). Gestures will continue to play a role in communication throughout our lives. Studies using fMRI have shown that gestures during conversation reduce the burden on working memory and cognitive load (Marstaller & Burianová, 2013; Pouw et al., 2014). Cognitive load, in this case, reveals how hard the brain has to work to achieve comprehension. Because of the association with survival, individuals coming from poverty focus on gestures with higher intensity than others; thus, educators' use of gestures becomes paramount in improving comprehension. Susan Goldin-Meadow validated the concept by incorporating simple gestures when teaching math concepts and proved that it increased comprehension and test scores of struggling students (Goldin-Meadow et al., 2009). For example, the teacher would have all students use two fingers on one hand to point to one side of an equation and use only one finger to point to the blank on the other side of the equation. The students that gestured solved more math problems correctly than children told not to move their hands at all. The study suggests that body movement is a part of how people learn; it helps the process of linking old ideas to create new ones. The math study also highlights how movement helps learning in cognitive tasks and should be incorporated when teaching concepts.

Research has shown that when we have a good rapport with others, gestures convey a deeper meaning. The increased understanding is because the amygdala brings back subconscious emotional memories concerning the gestures and provide context. When you are very familiar with a person, your brain subconsciously remembers when the individual used the same gesture in the past. Having the level of context that rapport provides produces a far deeper insight than observing a similar gesture made by someone you hardly know. Also, having a rapport with someone produces a higher level of empathy. Greater empathy means the brain is more likely to mimic the movements in our own mind, sharing the chemical experience of the speaker (Chu et al., 2014). For example, Mary is comforting Susan, who is experiencing problems in her marriage. As Mary talks to Susan, she notices how tightly clenched Susan's fists are. Then Mary sees that she too has clenched her fists so tightly that they hurt. Mary not only senses the tension and stress Susan is going through; she feels it as well. Studies found that close friends subconsciously mimic each other's postures and gestures, sharing a level of brain chemistry. As a result, gesturing between friends conveys a more accurate meaning of the message.

Gestures promote communication and increase empathy. When an individual uses gestures and mannerisms familiar to us, our brains are biased toward the positive impression of that person. When gestures and mannerisms are foreign to us, it biases our opinions toward the negative. It is here where we encounter a catch-22. Unfamiliar gestures and mannerisms produce a subconscious negative impression of others. Once a subconscious negative impression transpires, it will influence us to respond with subtle negative gestures the other person will notice on a subconscious level. Therefore, a negative first impression is usually validated by an equally disapproving response. When the brain is on high alert for any negative signal, it will typically notice undesirable cues and is prone to miss positive ones.

Hand gestures as a form of communication are considered more primitive than speech. The ability to speak is one of the things that separates us from our less evolved cousins. There are two primary theories on how language developed. In one theory, Steven Pinker and Paul Bloom theorize that over time, gesture combinations gave birth to language (Pinker & Bloom, 1990). In the other theory, Chomsky and Gould hypothesize that gestures and language evolved simultaneously (Chomsky, 1959). Regardless of how language came into existence, most believe that gestures have always been a primary form of communication. As a result, hand movements continue to accompany language today. When we are under stress, there is a tendency to use hand gestures more. Groups living in high-risk situations tend to use hand gestures more frequently. Many people in America are familiar with the use of gang signs by youth gangs across the country. Associating hand signs with only inner-city gangs is incorrect. Groups in high-risk environments in Sarajevo, the Middle East, and Africa have been observed communicating with unique hand gestures. One theory is that hand gestures are part of our innate communication method that we revert to when placed in deprived and dangerous environments. The point is that when our prefrontal cortex maintains control, hand gestures are a subconscious accompaniment to language. However, when emotional control is jeopardized, the use of hand gestures to communicate becomes magnified. Think of the many times you have observed someone who is emotionally out of control, flaying their arms around and hand gesturing furiously.

Hand gestures as a form of communication are considered more primitive than speech.

The physical risk that individuals experience living in concentrated poverty—that is, communities with over 40 percent of homes below poverty line—reduces social bonding. Many studies found that language development slows because of poverty. The common reasons identified are the limited exposure to languages and overall stress. Poverty persistently erodes working memory, making acquiring words difficult (Evans & Schamberg, 2009). There is also the often-overlooked fact that being on constant guard with whoever you meet limits rapport building. The ability to develop a good rapport with an extensive social network improves language comprehension on a deeper level. Over time, a comprehensive range of gestures and their meanings are accurately recognized and understood. Advanced understanding of gestures occurs only through repetition and practice. It is not surprising that the subtleties of language elude the poor. In addition, when we read, it is empathy that helps our brains to trigger motor neurons to mimic expressions associated with emotional words and provide a higher level of comprehension. It is the repetition of accurately recognizing and responding to a wide range of gestures that helps the brain become efficient at interpreting gestures. Poverty is robbing individuals of the ability to engage in in-depth interpersonal conversations with an extensive social network. It is not surprising that expressive language scores are lower for students from low-income homes.

The Monitoring of Body Postures and Movements

The brain processes body postures and movements in much the same manner as it monitors hand movements. Positive and negative body postures and movements are registered by the eyes and processed in the subconscious mind within 190 milliseconds (Thierry et al., 2006). Once again, this is showing that we monitor body postures and movements at an unconscious level. As with all negative non-verbal expressions, undesirable body postures and movements register significant activities in the brain as opposed to neutral ones (Olofsson et al., 2008; Schupp et al., 2006). Emotional movements and postures that elicit fear register the most significant activation in the brain (Olofsson et al., 2008; Schupp et al., 2006).

Movements that alert us to a threat produce enhanced activation in the amygdala, the region of the brain most associated with flight or fight (Adolphs, 2013; de Gelder et al., 2004; Hadjikhani & de Gelder, 2003; LeDoux, 2014; Van de Riet et al., 2009). The impact living in poverty has on the ability to interpret body posture accurately is in direct correlation to the increased exposure to threatening postures and movements. Repeated exposure to threatening actions produces a brain in which the prefrontal cortex, the logical part of the mind, loses the ability to exercise control over the amygdala (Keysers et al., 2010; Rizzolatti et al., 2014). The result is a state of hyperarousal to any postures or movements. Many times during the school day, the pose or movement of teachers and students can convey a range of negative emotions. Most of the adverse postures or movements are not interpreted as threatening by students not coming from poverty. However, for students in a state of hyperarousal, these negative postures can cause an overreaction that result in aggressive reactions.

The Monitoring of Voice Tone

In the same manner we are biased by facial expressions and hand gestures, voice tones influence us. The brain assesses the emotional tone in our voice in 150 to 200 milliseconds. Functional magnetic resonance imaging shows that the amygdala reacts to positive and negative vocalizations compared to neutral ones first (Fecteau et al., 2007). After we identify emotion, at around 300 milliseconds, the brain engages in *identity match*. Identity match is the process the brain performs when people are speaking that assesses who is talking, the gender, age, health, race, and a range of other identifiers, automatically (Friderici et al., 2020). We take for granted the many things we assess from voice tone alone. How many times have you said something like, "you sound tired" or "you don't sound well." After we evaluate emotions and identifiers, we engage in word recognition (Spreckelmeyer et al., 2009). It is difficult to comprehend that when people speak, the brain takes part in so many decisions that it minimize the processing of words. Years of extensive science has proved the old adage: it is not what you say but how you say it.

Teachers should understand that the conditions of poverty increase a student's sensitivity to the emotional tones contained in language and de-emphasizes the words themselves. As a result, in schools with a concentration of students from poverty, it is not uncommon for incidents to stem from how something is said and not what is said. Our subconscious biases influence our voice tone at a very subtle level. However, individuals living in at-risk situations have a higher sensitivity to negative tonalities and are prone to react strongly to perceived harsh voice tones. The reaction is logical when one considers that harsh voice tones in high-risk environments are often associated with life-threatening events.

Teachers should understand that the conditions of poverty increase a student's sensitivity to the emotional tones contained in language and de-emphasizes the words themselves.

Familiar tonalities and diction bias us toward a positive impression. Consider how differently people react when listening to unfamiliar accents. People all over the world react emotionally when they call for tech support for their laptops and have to deal with someone with a foreign accent. These same biases occur in schools every day. Students are biased against teachers who speak using unfamiliar tones, accents, inflections, and dialects. Teachers are biased against students who talk using distinct tones, accents, inflections, and dialects. If there are differences in pronunciation and tonality, the brain is negatively biased before we can even process the words. The negative influence of different tones or intonations is further influenced when we associate them with students of a distinct race or socioeconomic status. Remember, we engage in identity match, automatically guessing as to the gender, age, health, race, and a range of other factors before we begin to process the meaning of the words heard.

The brain gives dominance in every conversation to individuals who speak at low frequencies. However, when the amygdala is alerted, voice tones are automatically elevated. When people are in stressful environments, they often generate higher voice tones. Individuals who experience long-term exposure in stressful environments can develop the habit of maintaining a higher voice frequency, which can produce a subconscious tendency to dismiss what they are saying by the hearer. The result is that teachers are more likely to dismiss the importance of what students who speak in high frequencies are saying. Since the amygdala is attracted to commonalities, individuals who speak in high frequencies are attracted to one another. People with shared behaviors often group together, making it easier for the brain to not think of them as individuals but as part of a distinct group. Once the brain perceives a person as part of a distinct group rather than an individual, both the desire to connect and empathize are lessened.

The brain developed this shortcut to quickly identify individuals who are not a member of your in-group to alert you to strangers as a survival mechanism. However, distinguishing between members within your clan is necessary to be productive within the group. The outcome is that once others perceive students as part of an out-group category, they will notice fewer details about them, which will reduce empathy toward them. Over time, familiarity and safety help us to overcome the out-of-group shortcut to enable us to see people we have to deal with as individuals. However, if we view an out-of-group person as a threat, the ability to view him as an individual remains compromised. As a result, teachers will see out-group students who exhibit poor self-regulation less as individuals (or less personally), and express less empathy. The reverse applies; students from poverty who perceive out-group students and teachers as threats will show a lower empathy response. The difference is that when low SES students from violent communities see an out-group student as a threat, they are at higher risk of behaving aggressively. Also, aggressive actions in these instances can have a high level of callousness because of the lower empathy response.

As we learn to read and appropriately respond to social cues, we develop social skills that enable us to overcome differences and cultivate rapport.

Humans are born to be able to read each other's non-verbal cues. Initially, it is to ensure survival. The ability to interpret non-verbal emotional cues evolved to provide insight and empathy. Over time, the ability to interpret non-verbal cues led to responsive social behavior. As we learn to read and appropriately respond to social cues, we develop social skills that enable us to overcome differences and cultivate rapport. The depraved existence produced by concentrated poverty alters the ability to read and accurately respond to non-verbal cues. Neuroscience has proven that a healthy and diverse social network not only enhances the quality of life but is also necessary for maintaining biopsychosocial health.

RECOMMENDATIONS

The hardwired functions of the brain that bias social perceptions perform better in positive environments. Establishing a positive school climate is the foundation for stabilizing and improving the automated brain functions that monitor and interpret facial expressions, gestures, postures, and voice tone.

Model Good Self-Regulation

Teachers need to model self-regulation, especially when responding to issues in the classroom. Children start to understand self-regulation by studying parent responses to occurrences. Poverty produces less self-control due to overwhelming problems and stress. For many of the children living in poverty, consistent modeling of self-regulation is not found in the home and must be observed in other adult role models. For many students, adults who consistently display good self-regulation can be found at school. Modeling is a natural form of instruction to the human brain. If teachers can consistently model self-control when dealing with students, the practices will become predictable. When the brain expects certain behaviors because it is consistently observed, mirror neurons will play past experiences like a film when expecting the action. Nature designed this aspect of mirror neurons to influence human behavior. Mirror neurons record consistent activities displayed at reliable times or circumstances. Then mirror neurons play predictable events like a film in our subconscious mind when the incident is anticipated. It is the consistency of the adults in the school modeling good self-regulation that can begin to combat the intensity of poor self-control expressed by many students from low SES environments. Over time, students will start to anticipate good self-control by adults when dealing with specific behavioral incidents. The film playing in the subconscious minds of students will eventually influence their own behavior.

Nurturance and Empathy

Some of the adverse impact poverty has on the brain is diminished if the primary caretaker can show nurturance and empathy toward the child during times of distress (Rao et al., 2010). Many students living in poverty come to school in distress, and the demonstration of nurturance and empathy can help them recognize and cope with their negative emotions. When parents are dismissive or disapprove of expressing emotions, it can cause maladaptive self-regulation (Lunkenheimer et al., 2007). Studies have found that a punitive response to the expression of negative emotions results in increased anger management problems. Teaching students how to improve self-control with concrete strategies is a more constructive response.

It would be wonderful if we could teach all students with poor self-regulation how to meditate, control their breathing, and lower their heart rates. However, the likelihood that a student can go from a lack of self-regulation to controlling body functions is rare. Initially, it is best to teach students active measures that promote emotional control. For example, mental shift teaches students that when you focus attention on something else, the mind cannot remain focused on the issue that is causing you emotional distress. A simple technique is to have students focus the brain on tasks like making lists. Have the students list consecutively as many things as they can under a selected topic such as sports teams, music artists, cities, or television shows within a specified time frame. Repeat the exercise with different topics based on the age and capacity of the student. Another exercise is to challenge the student to hold a physical pose for an identified length of time that requires balance and concentration. The concept of mental shift is

> It is the consistency of the adults in the school modeling good self-regulation that can begin to combat the intensity of poor self-control expressed by many students from low SES environments.

founded on the fact that the human brain cannot focus on two things at the same time.

Another approach is to teach students they have the power to change their perspective on any situation at any given time. This skill can be practiced by beginning a story then having the student take an adverse event and describe how something good can come from it. Cognitive reappraisal is not only an accepted psychotherapy practice but is also based on the neuroscientific principle that our perspective influences our brain chemistry. A positive outlook insulates the brain from the impact of unfavorable circumstances. An example of this approach is discussed in more detail within Appendix B.

The problem teachers face with demonstrating nurturance and empathy is that their bias toward students from poverty creates a tendency to focus on directives or confrontation of negative behaviors with little compassion. The Yale Child Study Center found that early education staff observed students from poverty more closely than others, especially if they were minorities, based on the expectation of negative behaviors (Todd et al., 2016). The researchers at Yale concluded that teachers are biased to expect negative behaviors from minority male students. Neuroscience found that when there is an expectation of negative behaviors, the eyes track those students closely at a subconscious level. The increased tracking results in the student being noticed more frequently and feeling targeted. The feeling of being picked on only intensifies the student's lack of emotional regulation, which increases behavioral problems. Because many forms of bias are subconscious, teachers are unaware of the need to alter their behaviors. The Yale study found that the anticipation of negative actions only intensifies as students become older. Teachers who demonstrate nurturance and empathy when dealing with behavioral issues promote greater self-control in the students and an increased willingness to engage in self-regulation activities. Nurturance does not mean turning a blind eye to negative behaviors. It means being compassionate when confronting those behaviors and avoiding negative emotions influencing the response.

Improve Emotional Identification Skills and Appropriate Response

Students who struggle socially often do not read emotional cues accurately, nor know how to respond best to defuse volatile situations. Teaching students how to interpret emotional non-verbal cues and

> Neuroscience found that when there is an expectation of negative behaviors, the eyes track those students closely at a subconscious level. The increased tracking results in the student being noticed more frequently and feeling targeted.

appropriately respond is a valuable preventative strategy. These three steps improve the identification of and response to non-verbal cues:

1. When an individual cannot correctly read non-verbal cues, the insula, the part of the brain that plays a role in accurate interpretation, becomes less active. This inactivity hinders the student's ability to predict behaviors, making many actions unanticipated and therefore perceived as threatening. Conduct lessons that illustrate non-verbal emotional cues and appropriate responses. The consistent exposure to different non-verbal emotional signals and how best to respond retrains the brain on what to notice. It is essential to focus not only on negative cues but on positive ones as well. Students prone to seeing negative cues will generally not notice the existence of positive ones in their environment. When students learn to read cues more accurately, their tendency to misperceive diminishes.

2. Teachers should take great care to model consistent identification of emotional cues and suitable responses. For example, if a student seems down, the teacher might say, "You look sad today. Is there anything I can do to help?" The constant identification of student emotions helps not only the student become more self-aware, but also it increases the empathy response in the teacher. When individuals consciously focus on the non-verbal cues of others, it increases the empathy response in their brains. Increased empathy over time will also help students improve their self-regulation.

3. Have students practice appropriate responses to emotional cues. Practicing how to respond correctly can begin as early as primary school. For example, the teacher says, "Sam seems down today. If you are in his work group, you might want to check in on him and ask him if he is ok." These types of prompts help students become more adept at recognizing and responding to emotional cues. Also, the prompts have the added benefit of helping students feel that their emotions are recognized. This practice teaches students how to react to identified emotions appropriately. When feelings are acknowledged, it validates self-worth and improves self-regulation.

Poverty Is a Story of Risk

In this chapter: Poverty and resiliency are so closely correlated that poverty usually predicts poor resiliency, and poor resiliency often predicts poverty. Socioeconomic status is not an organism that can interact directly with people's brains and bodies. It is the predictable risk factors that usually occur with economic hardship that produce the outcomes commonly associated with poverty. Resiliency studies identified the specific risk factors associated with failed life outcomes. Unfortunately, the majority of the risk factors found in resiliency studies are associated with poverty.

Resiliency Theory

Resiliency theory came into existence from a rich body of longitudinal research that identified specific risk factors associated with reduced life outcomes. For example, in 1955 Emmy Werner tracked every infant born on the island of Kauai for forty years and found those who acquired a high number of identified risk factors consistently had poor life outcomes (Werner, 2001; Werner, 2005). Examples of poor life outcomes include school failure, criminal involvement, mental illness, substance abuse, incarceration, vocational instability, inferior health, and failed relationships. A closer examination of the risk factors identified in resiliency studies begins to clarify the relationship between poverty and resiliency. Out of 31 risk factors identified in resiliency research, poverty increases the risk of having 25 of them. The following is a comprehensive list of risk factors identified in all the validated resiliency studies (Sanchez, 2003).

Early Developmental Risk Factors

- Premature birth or complications
- Substance use by mother during pregnancy
- Difficult temperament
- Poor infant attachment to mother
- Long-term absence of caregiver in infancy
- Shy/anxious temperament
- Siblings born within two years of a child
- Developmental delays

Childhood Disorders

- Pattern of aggression
- Juvenile delinquency
- Substance use
- Psychiatric disorder
- Chronic medical condition
- Neurological disorder
- Low IQ < 70

Family Stress Factors

- Low socioeconomic status
- Separation/divorce/single parent
- Five or more children in the home
- Frequent family moves

Parental Disorders

- Parental substance use
- Parental emotional disorder
- Parental criminality

Experiential Risk Factors

- Removal from home by a public agency
- Witness to extreme conflict or violence

- Neglect
- Physical abuse
- Sexual abuse
- Conflicted relationship with either parent

Social Drift Factors

- School failure
- Negative peer group
- Teen pregnancy

The Story of Risk

The following paragraphs illustrate how poverty often produces the risk factors listed above in the life of those growing up economically disadvantaged. The reality is impoverishment is the story of risk. However, it is essential to remember that resiliency studies found that 25 percent of individuals who have numerous risk factors are resilient and have success in life despite the presence of risk.

Poverty Increases Risk at Infancy

Before life begins for an infant, poverty can already leave an indelible mark. Poverty is so debilitating that Hallum Hurt said it "is a more powerful influence on the outcome of inner-city children than gestational exposure to cocaine" (FitzGerald, 2013, para. 27; see also Farah et al., 2006). Allostatic load tests, which measure the wear and tear on the body, have established that poverty produces continuous stress, which accumulates over time. In many ways, chronic stress causes premature aging. The impact of prenatal stress is also well documented. Prenatal stress can have long-term ramifications on cognitive, behavioral, and physiological functions. For example, impaired cognitive performance at age five and a half was present in children whose mothers experienced significant stress during pregnancy (Laplante et al., 2008). The study compared the Full-Scale IQs, Verbal IQs, and language abilities of children exposed to persistent prenatal stress to children not subjected to constant tension. The researchers concluded that prenatal exposure to severe stress is associated with lower cognitive and language abilities of the child in early development. Also, prenatal stress is an increased risk for psychiatric disorders (King et al., 2009). The prenatal stress experienced by the mother can impair the infant's ability to regulate the stress hormone cortisol (Gunnar et al., 1995). What is not

> Prenatal exposure to severe stress is associated with lower cognitive and language abilities of the child in early development.

commonly understood is that high levels of cortisol experienced by the mother can impair the amygdala before birth—creating a brain that is easily agitated and less capable of calming down. The stress related to poverty is so unique that pediatricians have referred to it as toxic stress (Shonkoff & Garner, 2012).

Mothers from all economic situations are at risk of postpartum depression; however, mothers living at or below the poverty line are at a higher risk. Economically disadvantaged individuals suffer from depression or chronic stress more than those in middle- and upper-income groups (Almeida et al., 2005). Fifty-five percent of all infants born into poverty are raised by mothers with some form of depression (Evans & Kim, 2007; Falconnier & Elkin, 2008; Leventhal & Brooks-Gunn, 2000. The combination of depression and stress dramatically increases the risk of substance use (Vericker et al., 2010). Postpartum depression and substance use are two of the highest contributing factors in reducing parental responsiveness, warmth, and supervision (Bailey et al., 2009). The poverty-related issues mothers face jeopardize what many believe to be the most salient event in an infant's young life: infant-mother attachment. Infant-mother attachment helps newborns feel and learn to believe that they are safe and loved. The attachment process stabilizes infants chemically. Moments of infant-mother bonding bathe the infant in oxytocin, a hormone critical to early brain development. The bond between mother and child cultivates social-emotional intelligence and empathy. It is common for newborns who do not bond with their primary caregivers to struggle socially for a long time and be at higher risk of developing emotional disorders rooted in anxiety.

Postpartum anxiety is as common as postpartum depression, and financial hardships increase the occurrence of postpartum anxiety. Postpartum anxiety produces negative intrusive thoughts of harming self or the baby, which can become all consuming. The worry can lead to a mother's inability to eat, sleep, or function. New mothers are at risk for both anxiety and depression due to elevated hormones such as estrogen and progesterone during pregnancy, which plummet after giving birth. The drop makes new moms vulnerable to mood swings (Schiller et al., 2015). When a new mother is dealing with the stressors of poverty, postpartum anxiety jeopardizes her ability to respond to the infant's emotions to restore a feeling of calm. Increased periods of arousal experienced by the infant can lead to an inability to self-regulate later in childhood, heightening the risk of poor self-regulation throughout childhood and adolescence. Poor self-regulation places a student at a high risk of poor academic focus and behavioral control.

Postpartum anxiety is as common as postpartum depression, and financial hardships increase the occurrence of postpartum anxiety.

Schools serving a concentration of low-income students frequently report higher incidents related to poor self-regulation, even as early as preschool. School discipline data show that incidents of poor self-regulation during primary school usually result in increased problems in the upper grades.

A mother's inability to provide the basic necessities for her child can cause her to feel she has neglected and abandoned her responsibility as a mother (Schweder, 2009). There is a direct link to mothers with symptoms of depression and the inability to provide for their children. A study found that mothers experiencing food and monetary insecurities often manifest signs of depression (Casey et al., 2004). The pressure to provide can be so intense that even a small decrease in financial support is associated with an increased risk of depression (Casey et al., 2004). People who do not comprehend the stressors of poverty conjure up images of low-income mothers willfully being neglectful. However, that is not the complete story. Studies reveal that the fear of not being able to provide for the bare necessities, such as food, increases the occurrence of depression (Casey et al., 2004). Mothers displaying symptoms of depression are at risk of being neglectful. The outside world sees only the neglect, failing to see that the root cause is often depression. Regardless of the cause of the neglect, the damage to the infant is the same. Neuroscience research has established that neglect is more damaging to a developing brain than physical abuse (Center on the Developing Child, 2013).

Poverty Increases Risk During Childhood and Adolescence

Based on the stressors, common circumstances, and general environment that economic hardship creates for parents, infants born into poverty are already at a higher risk of accruing multiple risk factors, including substance use by mother during pregnancy, poor infant attachment to mother, long-term absence of caregiver, anxious temperament, and siblings born within two years. During childhood and early adolescence, impoverished environments unfairly continue their assault of mounting risk factors. Resiliency research determined that each risk acquired increased the probability of obtaining even more risk factors. Although exposure to violence transcends age and SES, individuals living in poverty face increased risk of exposure and the likelihood of suffering trauma related to violence. Children coming from poverty are more than twice as likely as their higher socioeconomic peers to experience three or more adverse experiences during childhood (Murphey et al., 2013).

Adverse childhood experiences (ACEs) increase the risk of emotional disorders, chronic health conditions, academic failure, low life potential, and premature death (Centers for Disease Control and Prevention, 2016).

Safe and nurturing relationships and predictable environments make up the first line of defense against physical, emotional, and cognitive issues. A curious and alarming thing is that the lack of economic investment in preventing early child maltreatment results in a financial toll on our welfare, medical, mental health, legal, and education systems (Fang et al., 2012). Neuroscientists found that as little as a $10,000 annual increase to families living below the poverty line can substantially counteract many of the developmental brain issues consistently found in children living in destitution. The monetary increase resulted in a 600 percent rise in high school graduation for low-income students (Duncan et al., 1998).

> The lack of economic investment in preventing early child maltreatment results in a financial toll on our welfare, medical, mental health, legal, and education systems.

Poverty increases exposure to violence during childhood and adolescence, which can have long-term consequences. Merely being subjected to violent neighborhoods has been found to negatively impact elementary students' mathematical and reading abilities (Milam et al., 2010). Individuals exposed to community violence only during their adolescence are at higher risk of poor high school grades and lower vocational attainment (Borofsky et al., 2013). The researchers found that it was the concrete outcomes of exposure to community violence that reduced school engagement. Exposure to community violence causes sleep disturbances, alcohol and drug use, avoidant behavioral responses, fearfulness, self-blame, and decreased self-efficacy, which reduce the ability or desire to perform in school. Even when a child only observes violence and family conflict, there is an increased risk of depression by the time the student enrolls in high school (Eisman et al., 2015). Neuroscience research has established the link between success and motivation. Individuals cannot maintain motivation in any endeavor when they are persistently unsuccessful. Students in schools with higher incidents of bullying consistently get lower grades than in educational settings that prevent harassment (Strøm et al., 2013). Experiencing violence during adolescence can change life's trajectory, decreasing the odds of ever getting married, lowering educational attainment, and reducing income earning potential throughout adulthood (Covey et al., 2013).

> Individuals cannot maintain motivation in any endeavor when they are persistently unsuccessful.

Delinquency is another product of socioeconomic disparity and violent communities (Birckhead, 2012; *OJJDP Statistical Briefing Book*, 2017). Although adolescents from affluent homes also engage in delinquent behaviors, it is an anomaly rather than the norm. The majority of juvenile offenders come from the ranks of the poor. Youth living in poverty attempt to survive in low socioeconomic communities that lack high-quality education, job opportunities, financial support, and mental health and medical services. The lack of resources focuses the brain on the unfairness of the system. Studies show that when the mind focuses on inequalities, aggressive outbursts toward people or institutions deemed responsible can occur (Fehr, 2018). The brain begins to reinforce risk-taking behaviors. The outcome of juvenile delinquency is usually incarceration. The prisons are overcrowded with disenfranchised adults who were products of childhood poverty with limited opportunities for success.

Poverty or even a brief period of economic struggle during early childhood increases the likelihood of substance use from adolescence to adulthood (Buu et al., 2009; Ensminger et al., 2002; Najman et al., 2010). Two characteristics identified by researchers related to substance use during adolescence and young adulthood are poor self-control and poor parenting. Several studies associate poor self-control with substance use (Moffitt et al., 2011). Neuroscience has established that poverty reduces the functioning of the prefrontal cortex, which is responsible for self-regulation. Reduced cortex performance increases risk-taking behaviors, which is limited to just drug use (see Brown, S. A., Tapert et al., 2000; Giancola & Tarter, 1999; Pharo et al., 2011; Wilens et al., 2010). Another contributing factor to poor self-control is poor parenting (Blair & Raver, 2012; Karssen et al., 2008; Wills & Dishion, 2004). Indicators of poor parenting are a lack of nurturance, home structures, rules, awareness of child activities, and punitive discipline in response to household conflict. The stressors related to poverty are a gateway to substance use.

Poverty Increases Risk in Adulthood

Before they reach adulthood, children living in poverty are at higher risk of acquiring additional risk factors such as a pattern of aggression, juvenile delinquency, substance use, psychiatric disorders, school failure, negative peer group, and teen pregnancy. Individuals who grow up in poverty become parents of children born into low socioeconomic circumstances. The longer an individual is exposed to poverty and stress, the greater the impact on cognition, emotions, self-regulation, and learning (Lipina & Colombo, 2009). Each consecutive generation born into poverty is exposed to incrementally higher severity obstacles. Several physical and mental disorders carry genetic markers that make the next generation susceptible to many of the negative issues their

Each consecutive generation born into poverty is exposed to incrementally higher severity obstacles.

parents faced. In addition, neuroscience has validated the theory that people suffering from emotional disorders are often attracted to other individuals exhibiting similar disorders (Nordsletten et al., 2016). A large nationwide study found that individuals with a psychiatric diagnosis were two to three times more likely to marry or partner with another person suffering from a mental health disorder than people without a psychiatric diagnosis. The reason for this phenomenon is stunning: The amygdala is attracted to itself. One might ask, what about opposites attracting? The reality is that attraction to variance is more likely to occur with individuals who are emotionally healthy because they possess a better capacity to deal with differences. The sad fact is, generational poverty chips away at physical and emotional health. Over the course of generations, those most impacted by poverty are more likely to produce children who are less capable of escaping its sinister grasp.

Consider the fact that substance-using adolescents often become substance-using parents. Parents who are using substances are less likely to know the whereabouts of their children (Griffin et al., 2000). Nurturance and acceptance are less likely to occur with parents who abuse substances (Rohner & Britner, 2002; Wills & Cleary, 1996). A parent who struggles with substance use is more likely to be absent, display poor self-control, and use manipulation as a parenting technique (Barnes et al., 2006; Taylor et al., 1997; Barber & Harmon, 2002; Bean et al., 2003; Garber et al., 1997; Peterson et al., 1983; Trzesniewski et al., 2006; Wild et al., 2004). The cycle is clear; each of the factors mentioned above increases the risk of a child growing up to abuse substances, develop poor self-esteem, and suffer from emotional disorders.

Poverty studies found that parental emotional disorders are not only widespread but also as much as 11 percent of parents from low SES suffer from severe or multiple disorders (Evans & Kim, 2007; Falconnier & Elkin, 2008; Leventhal & Brooks-Gunn, 2000; Vericker et al., 2010). The presence of parental emotional disorders increases the probability of domestic violence, substance use, health complications, and additional mental health issues (Vericker et al., 2010). Children born into poverty are at higher risk of having brain structures that place them at risk of mental and emotional disorders. Increased risk does not mean that every child born with brain structures associated with specific disorders will suffer from the condition. Consider the story of neuroscientist James Fallon who performed a brain scan on himself and discovered he shared all the features commonly found in psychopaths. The scan revealed that he had all five major gene variants linked to psychopathy (Fallon, 2006). Fallon then found out that he was adopted, and in his biological family line were eight individuals accused of murder. The point is, all individuals who are psychopaths share the same abnormalities in brain function, but not all individuals with those same abnormalities are psychopaths. An individual's environment and experiences regardless of brain abnormalities matter.

An often-overlooked risk factor associated with parents living in poverty is criminality. Juvenile delinquents are more likely to become adult criminals. An outcome of living in concentrated poverty is exposure to high levels of criminal behavior that lowers the brain's standards to determine right and wrong. The ventromedial prefrontal cortex (VMPC) is the part of the brain involved in moral processing. However, certain emotions like stress and anger reduce the engagement of the VMPC, producing a gut type decision approach when making a moral choice. The reduction of the VMPC means that the part of the brain that should be engaged when contemplating an ethical decision is overridden by the area of the brain responsible for taking emotional action. Deplorable living conditions associated with poverty in the United States account for the world's highest rate of incarceration. America has 730 prisoners for every 100,000 citizens. The high rate of imprisonment equates to more than 2.2 million prisoners. Over 60 percent of those in prison are African American and Latino, coming from poor communities (The Sentencing Project, 2010). Two-thirds of the people incarcerated in America reported an annual income under $12,000 at the time of arrest (Alexander, 2012). Incarceration contributes to the cycle of poverty; being convicted creates employment barriers, reduces earning capacity, and creates a constant fear of termination. A convict is the first to be terminated when something goes missing, when the economy slows, or when there are temporary layoffs. Consider the cases of inmates who, upon release, owe thousands in traffic violations because the fines accrued while incarcerated. Such irrational injustices consistently happen to the poor and create a defeatist attitude toward ever becoming productive members of society.

The story of poverty is the story of acquired risk factors. Being disadvantaged in America is to possess so many risk factors that becoming resilient is almost an impossibility. Being poor is being robbed of resiliency that allows an individual to escape the grasp of poverty by having the fortitude to climb out.

> An individual's environment and experiences regardless of brain abnormalities matter.

The Other Half of the Story

Risk is only half the story. Resiliency researchers have found individuals with numerous risk factors who are still successful. These are indicators of success, as defined by resiliency research:

- graduating from high school

- avoiding criminal involvement

- stable mental health

- vocational stability

- good physical health

- maintaining positive long-term relationships

The researchers reviewed the lives of individuals at risk and found common experiences and skills, labeled protective factors, that mitigated the risk in their lives. The key is to have enough protective factors to offset the number of risk factors experienced or present. These individuals are referred to as "the resilient population" because they overcome a wealth of risk factors to experience success. Resiliency research answered the age-old question: How can twin brothers be exposed to similar negative experiences and have dramatically different life outcomes. The answer is simple. One obtains more protective factors than the other.

Each protective factor improves brain function, which helps an individual's overall well-being.

What makes protective factors so impactful? Each protective factor improves brain function, which helps an individual's overall well-being. For example, having a long-term relationship with at least one adult is a protective factor. What makes relationships so vital is their impact on the brain. Positive nurturing relationships produce oxytocin, a hormone that plays a role in social bonding. When in the presence of an individual with whom there is a positive relationship, oxytocin levels elevate in the brain. Oxytocin is a natural regulator of stress. When oxytocin elevates in the brain, the hormone cortisol lowers. Cultivating positive relationships is one way we regulate cortisol levels, which will improve brain functioning and emotional stability. We have already discussed how living in poverty increases stress. A positive relationship with an adult provides some regulation to the chemical imbalance caused by poverty. Resiliency research found that most of the individuals who overcame risk in their lives developed such a relationship. Many of the participants in the resiliency studies identified a relationship with a teacher as the significant adult mentor in their lives.

Once a relationship is established, certain actions within a relationship continue to trigger oxytocin levels. For example, actions that denote trust produce an immediate increase in oxytocin following the act (Zak et al., 2005). Also, higher oxytocin levels are evident when someone is giving or receiving empathy. On the other hand, exposure to violence and depravity mute empathetic responses. Resiliency research found that having a positive relationship with at least one parent promotes the development of empathy. Students who did not have a positive relationship with a parent but had the opportunity to cultivate and maintain a relationship with an adult outside of the family were better able to maintain or restore the ability to respond empathetically. Improved empathy increases positive social behavior, enabling the student to continue to cultivate a broader social support network.

A positive relationship in adolescence provides long-term benefits throughout a student's life span. A longitudinal study by Schwartz and colleagues found that a student's relationship with an adult immediately reduces the risk of dropping out of school. Beyond the immediate impact, the ramification of having a positive adult relationship statistically improves educational attainment, longer employment, higher earning, and fewer arrests throughout adulthood (Schwartz et al., 2013). Resiliency studies determined, out of all the protective factors identified, that having a positive long-term relationship with an adult was consistently present in everyone who overcame risk. Furthermore, the studies showed that relationships are a catalyst for obtaining additional protective factors. Therefore, this single universal protective factor can change a person's life trajectory.

It is important to note that all resiliency studies identified only naturally resilient individuals. However, one mental health agency proved they could promote protective factors in children and adolescents with severe biopsychosocial issues (Sanchez, 2003). The mental health program focused on identifying individuals who built or who could build relationships with vulnerable clients and through that relationship target protective factors to develop. The program evaluated how existing and gained protective factors influenced life outcome indicators four times a year. As the clients acquired protective factors, their life outcomes (mental health issues at school, in the community, with family, and with vocational placement) improved. Schools whose staffs become skillful at promoting protective factors will see an improvement in the academic and behavioral performance of students regardless of presenting issues. Resiliency research provides schools with a proven strength-based approach for improving student outcomes. For schools

Schools whose staffs become skillful at promoting protective factors will see an improvement in the academic and behavioral performance of students regardless of presenting issues.

serving students living in poverty, promoting protective factors might be the difference between success and failure. The following is a comprehensive list of protective factors gathered from all resiliency research (Sanchez, 2003).

Early Developmental Protective Factors

- Easy temperament
- Infant-mother attachment
- Autonomy and independence as a toddler
- Firstborn

Family Protective Factors

- Lives at home
- Consistently employed parent
- Parent has a high school education or better
- Adult or older sibling available to help the family with child care
- Regular involvement in church
- Rules, routines, chores, and curfews in the home
- Discipline with discussion and fair punishment
- Child feels cared for by at least one parent
- A positive relationship with at least one parent
- A parent consistently monitors the child's whereabouts

Child Protective Factors

- Problem-solving skills at school age
- Ability to function as a good student
- Good reader
- Perceived competencies
- Involved in extracurricular activities
- IQ > 100

Child Social Skills

- Gets along with other children
- Gets along with most adults
- Interpersonally engaging, "likable"
- Sense of humor
- Empathy

Extra-Familial Social Support

- Adult mentor for the child outside the immediate family
- Support from an adult at school
- Support for the family from church
- Support from inner faith
- Support for the child from friends
- Lives in a community where other adults provide supervision and support

Adolescent Protective Outlook/Attitude

- Feels confident that life events are under his control
- Has positive and realistic expectations for the future
- Actively plans for the future
- Female is independent minded

RECOMMENDATIONS

Schools should consider implementing strategies based on neuroscience research to promote protective factors. A neuroscientific approach will not only help schools determine which protective factors to prioritize but also how to instill them effectively. Early resiliency research treated all protective factors as equal. However, neuroscience research found that certain protective factors improve brain functions so that the individual can gain additional protectives. The protective factors prioritized by neuroscience promote the chemical balance in the brain needed to facilitate a student's ability to gain additional protective factors. Without physiological homeostasis, an individual will lack the discipline and self-control required to obtain and maintain protective factors.

Restoring Homeostasis

Neuroscience research determined that routines and rituals play a vital role in regaining and maintaining physiological homeostasis (Heintzelman et al., 2013). Studies have found that the consistency and qualities of rituals in an individual's life are predictors of not only the person's homeostasis but also how quickly the person rebounds from adverse events and trauma. The protective factor of *rules, routines, chores,* and *curfews in the home* plays a significant role in promoting

> Studies have found that the consistency and qualities of rituals in an individual's life are predictors of not only the person's homeostasis but also how quickly the person rebounds from adverse events and trauma.

homeostasis. Within the home, the most vital rituals relating to maintaining homeostasis are wake-up, main meal, and bedtime. These critical events are the anchor points of each day. Anchor points, in this case, refers to regular daily activities that anchor our lives, providing predictability and improving physiological homeostasis.

Viewing these three rituals through the lens of neuroscience can help clarify their importance. When we wake up in the morning, our bodies secrete a high level of cortisol hormone to jump-start our immune system. An individual's temperament determines if the increase in cortisol will have a negative social and emotional impact. For example, individuals with easy temperaments usually show little social and emotional change resulting from the increase of morning cortisol. However, individuals with anxious or difficult temperaments can show irritability and even anger because of the increased cortisol levels the brain produces in the morning. The inability to regulate morning cortisol can lead to poor social behavior resulting in conflicts with others during the early part of the day. Individuals who have established morning rituals seem to regain homeostasis quicker because predictable routines trigger dopamine, which lowers cortisol. The inability to gain homeostasis early in the day helps explain why some students seem consistently irritated in the morning and prone to behavioral incidents in the first hour of school.

The main meal of the day can also improve physiological homeostasis. Food provides a level of nurturance when predictability and positive social interactions accompany the meal. When the main meal of the day has some established rituals, it triggers the release of the oxytocin hormone. Oxytocin helps regulate stress and increases social bonding, bringing the family closer together. Therefore, the main meal of the day can be therapeutic by helping us connect and control daily stressors.

Individuals who have consistent bedtime rituals transition into deep sleep quicker, improving their cognitive and physical function when they wake up. When we enter deep sleep, often characterized by rapid eye movements, commonly referred to as REM, our brain engages in three critical functions. The brain reinforces new information learned that the individual perceives as valuable. Without the nightly reinforcement process, our ability to recall information decreases. Our brains also connect information while we sleep, helping us figure out complex problems. Many of us have experienced going to bed thinking about a problem and waking up with a solution. The phrase, "sleep on it," likely evolved from real experiences as our brains make vital connections while we sleep. Also, our brains undergo a level of recalibration each night when we are in REM sleep to help us perform more efficiently when we are awake. Anyone who has experienced multiple sleepless nights has found that their brain becomes inefficient. One of the brain calibrations performed is the production of proteins that improve synapse function. In many ways, sleep primes the brain to transmit chemicals efficiently—in other words, to function (Brüning et al., 2019; Noya et al., 2019). Another reason sleep has restorative powers is because when asleep, cerebrospinal fluid (CSF) flushes toxic waste out to cleanse the brain. Neuroscientist Laura Lewis has recorded this process and notes that many memory and psychiatric problems are experienced by individuals who do not get a sufficient flush of CSF.

For many students who come from homes and communities lacking in structure, the only ritualized environment in their lives is school. When schools offer safe and predictive environments, they can promote the students' physiological homeostasis. However, schools can undermine students' homeostasis when they are unsafe and unpredictable. Overstimulation causes the brain to work at high levels to process large amounts of information. The dramatic increase in stimuli during major school transitions explains why many schools experience an increase in impulsive behaviors during those times. Schools that teach students what to do during transitions and have pupils practice how to transition provide predictability and structure to these unstructured times. The anchor points in a school day are admission, lunch period, and dismissal.

A ritual to the human brain is an established pattern, predictable in its occurrence. When the brain has learned a pattern and can predict when it will occur, mirror neurons rehearse the routine in the brain before the event takes place. One of the functions of mirror neurons is to shape social behavior. If a family has dinner every night at 6 p.m. and follows a consistent dinner routine, shortly before 6:00 p.m., mirror neurons will play the dinner time routine, improving the likelihood that the child's behavior will conform. The repeated playing of the practice is not only subconsciously teaching the practice but also influencing the individual's behavior. How established routines influence the brain explains why it is so essential to teach desired behaviors. The brain can play a predictable practice to help train students to complete required actions. However, the brain cannot play practices that are not consistently seen. When schools seek to teach desired practices, they are attempting to create new habits.

Neuroscience has identified the critical elements required when establishing a new habit. Schools should consider incorporating these elements when teaching students how to perform the three major

> For many students who come from homes and communities lacking in structure, the only ritualized environment in their lives is school.

transitions in the school day. The chemicals in the brain that promote habits reinforce actions, not concepts. Therefore, schools should teach students the specific behaviors that are expected. For example, when transitioning between classes, students should walk on the right side of the hallway. For the practice to become a habit, it must be something that the individual values. The amygdala, the part of our brain responsible for our survival, universally values anything that promotes safety or success. If schools can explain to students that the desired action is in place for their safety, the amygdala will learn to value it over time. When the amygdala values a practice, it remains active in the subconscious even when the prefrontal cortex is compromised. The outcome is that the student will remember what to do, even when emotionally overwhelmed. A message associating the practice with being safe has to be repeated with regularity to promote acceptance. The brain is prone to accepting repeated messages.

The brain is more likely to develop a new habit when there is a cue alerting it to the fact that the action is about to take place. For example, a chime that plays two minutes before the hallway transition bell will help motivate the practices that have been taught. A cue that signals something is about to happen primes the brain to anticipate the action. Habits develop faster if the brain is aware when the behavior is expected to be performed. The school staff's role is to let students know when they are performing the behavior correctly. Reinforcing the correct behavior will also help focus teachers and other school personnel on encouraging desired practices rather than focusing on negative behaviors. When all these steps are in place, a habit is more likely to be developed because the brain will secrete dopamine reinforcing the behavior and motivating the practice. Keep in mind that students with poor self-regulation require maintaining the practice of the new actions for an extended period to produce the chemical reinforcement.

Promoting Social Behavior and Empathy

As discussed earlier, resiliency studies found that establishing a long-term relationship with a positive adult was a consistent factor in the lives of children and adolescents who overcame risk factors associated with poor life outcomes. We know that a primary benefit of the long-term relationship is its ability to elevate oxytocin levels, which promotes the social bond between two people. Oxytocin also promotes prosocial behaviors in humans and helps recalibrate the mechanisms in the brain that produce empathy. Therefore, teachers who can develop a long-term bond with a student can also help improve the student's social behavior toward others and help restore her ability to be empathetic.

The impact of a teacher-student relationship can have short-term as well as long-term ramifications in a student's life. Remember, Schwartz found that a mentoring relationship with an adult immediately improved academic performance and behaviors and reduced the risk of dropping out of school. Also, the benefits of that relationship are seen later in life through higher educational achievement, longer employment, greater earnings, and fewer arrests (Schwartz, Rhodes, Spencer & Grossman, 2013).

Neuroscience research also provides an effective strategy for successfully developing a relationship with an at-risk student. The strategy is based on the human brain comprehending abstract concepts by relating them to concrete things. Take, for example, the concept of time. A study showed that when students try to understand the concept of past and future, participants sway about two millimeters backward when thinking of the past and two millimeters forward when thinking about the future (Miles et al., 2010). Researchers concluded that these imperceptible movements were our bodies' attempt to help us understand the abstract concept of past and future by making it as concrete as possible.

The human brain also subconsciously engages in helping us understand the abstract concept of relationships through concrete actions. The brain anchors the concept of love with actions associated with caring. Teachers can show students they care by establishing an action that they do for students that is a demonstration of caring. If the teacher defines an action as an act of caring and reminds students why she engages in the behavior, the perception of being cared for occurs quickly. Why engage in these steps to develop relationships with students coming from poverty? Because poverty alters social behavior by reducing the amygdala's ability to relate to people who are not similar to you. Therefore, poverty places barriers to natural relationship building. As a result, teachers should take a more prescriptive approach that helps students who struggle socially to build rapport.

> If the teacher defines an action as an act of caring and reminds students why she engages in the behavior, the perception of being cared for occurs quickly.

Competencies That Count

Resiliency research determined that having a perceived competence did not require a student to obtain a superior level of mastery. Instead, the person had to engage in actions consistently to develop the skill over an extended period. Two competencies that we can assume that students coming from poverty require are the ability to focus and the ability to memorize.

Students living in poverty usually struggle to focus due to low grey matter in the prefrontal cortex. Increased grey matter in a region of the brain enables optimal performance. The conditions caused by poverty reduce grey matter in many key brain regions. The loss of density to the prefrontal cortex reduces executive functions, one of which is the ability to focus. The human brain can learn nothing without first focusing on the information. Researchers found that focus can be improved in a brief period. For example, one study had participants engaged in focus training for only twelve minutes a day over eight weeks. Participants showed not only improved focus but also improved memory, better emotional stability, and better job performance when compared with the group that did not engage in focus exercises (Jha et al., 2010).

Memory in students with low socioeconomic status is usually weak due to the damage to the hippocampus associated with the stress of poverty. Teaching students standard mnemonic strategies and having set times when they can practice the techniques help students develop an approach for improving their memory. These are the three most common mnemonic techniques:

- Expression Mnemonics
  - *Every Good Boy Does Fine* can help you remember the lines of the treble clef in music (EGBDF).

- Music Mnemonics
  - Learn the alphabet through the ABC song

- Rhyming Mnemonics
  - *30 days hath September, April, June, and November*

When working with older students, teachers should consider introducing a strategy called memory palace. Memory palace is the technique used by almost every contestant competing in memory competitions. Contrary to popular belief, memory competitors are not memory savants or even individuals with excellent memories. Most memory contestants began training their minds because they suffered from lousy recall. Although the memory feats sound astounding, they have been performed by individuals who practiced the simple strategy of memory palace. In one category of memory competitions, contestants are given five minutes to memorize binary digits and allowed fifteen minutes to recall as many numbers in the sequence shown within an allotted time. The current record is 1,080 binary digits recited in the correct order. The memory feat may sound incredible, but this example validates that individuals with meager memories can achieve amazing things with just three months of training.

When using memory palace, the student visualizes a location, like a room in their house, and places information in specific locations. Then, when retrieving the information, the student visualizes the room in their mind and retrieves the information. If students can begin improving their memories early in life, it will dramatically improve academic performance. When the brain can recall the desired information quickly, it allows more energy to be devoted to advanced concepts and conclusions.

Students engaging in any practice consistently for an extended period alter their brains for better or worse, depending on the nature of the action. Since protective factors improve brain function, then each competency gained enhances the brain's overall performance. Consider the changes in the brain found in studies of students who learned to play an instrument. Many of the students never achieved mastery of the instrument; however, the studies still showed that consistent practice improved focus, memory, spatial reasoning, and language development (Hetland, 2000; Ho et al., 2003; Roden et al., 2014; Rueda et al., 2005).

Principles of Good Instruction for Students from Low SES

In this chapter: This chapter seeks to highlight the validated principles of good instruction that have success with students from low SES across the globe. Neuroscience research supports these evidence-based principles. When teachers have confidence that instructional strategies will work, it increases perseverance and certainty, which positively affects outcomes.

Interventions Matter

The British Cohort Study of 1970 proved one thing: what you do after a child is born is what matters. The study tracked all British children born from the 5th to the 11th of April 1970, equaling a sample size of 17,287 individuals. Researchers measured cognitive performance percentiles by the British Ability Scales II, which is a battery of twelve tests of cognitive ability and educational achievement (Elliott et al., 1996). The battery of tests can be administered to children as young as two-and-a-half years old. They tracked the children's academic performance for ten years. The study attempted to exclude children with any other obvious issues that contribute to poor academic performance. Those born with the lowest cognitive performance percentile and low SES demonstrated consistently poor academic performance during the ten-year period. However, those born with the same low cognitive performance percentile and high SES showed steady improvement academically during the same period. Even more surprising, children born to the highest cognitive performance percentile had very different academic outcomes based on SES. Students born in the highest cognitive percentile and economically disadvantaged demonstrated a consistent drop in academic performance during the ten-year study, while their counterparts in the highest cognitive percentile and high SES showed consistently high academic performance over the ten years. The conclusion was that SES matters more than cognitive capacity. How else can you explain children with low cognitive capacity consistently improving if they had better resources and instruction, while students with superior cognitive ability steadily dropped in performance because of a lack of resources and quality of instruction? One take-home message for teachers is, what they do matters regardless of students' circumstances.

Studies that focus on low- and middle-income children show that the quality of instruction can be one of the most significant life events that help students overcome the deficits associated with the sparsity of resources. Good instruction shows an estimated 0.36 to 0.54 standard deviations in student test performance (Buhl-Wiggers et al., 2017). That standard deviation is equivalent to more than two years of academic progress (Evans & Yuan, 2017).

In addition to academic progress, the impact of quality instruction is associated with lower teen pregnancy, increased college attendance, and improved earnings across a life span (Chetty et al., 2014). The study found that when teachers improve a students' performance by one grade level, it raises not only the probability of college attendance but also the quality of the colleges that students attend. Quality instruction that raised a child's academic performance by one grade level also improved earning trajectories in a student's life cycle by approximately $39,000 on average. Also, the same academic improvement significantly reduces the probability of having a child while a teenager, increases the quality of housing, and raises participation rates in 401(k) retirement savings plans.

Despite the amount of time and resources dedicated to improving instruction, there still seems to be little consensus on what to do to improve outcomes in schools serving poor students.

One of the most baffling things related to education is that no one questions the impact it can have on improving the lives of students from low SES. However, not all educators can say with the same level of confidence which instructional strategies they should employ to have success with students from poverty. Despite the amount of time and resources dedicated to improving instruction, there still seems to be little consensus on what to do to improve outcomes in schools serving poor students. A study that had teachers and principals identify which teaching strategies are the most effective found that less than 50 percent of experienced teachers and principals correctly selected the most effective instructional approaches (Strong et al., 2011). The result is that more than 50 percent of educators might not use effective strategies. An unfortunate consequence is that even when teachers are using effective practices, if they are not confident that the method will work, they are at risk of prematurely abandoning the approach when students do not demonstrate expected progress. For many struggling students, effective instructional strategies still require consistency over an extended time. Therefore, the most successful teachers will have both an awareness of what strategies are effective and a belief that the approaches will eventually work that allows them to stay the course and ultimately see improvement.

The remainder of the chapter identifies the primary principles found in effective instruction based on outcomes regardless of the culture, school resources, and the socioeconomic circumstances of the students (Molina et al., 2018).

The Importance of Respect

The environment has a significant impact on brain development because the prefrontal cortex takes an extended time to mature. The prefrontal cortex develops from birth through late adolescence. The extended period of development means that experience and environment shape the most vital part of our brains. For similar reasons, school and classroom environments can have an immediate and long-term impact on the prefrontal cortex because students are exposed to educational settings for extended periods during their early development. Instruction takes place not only in a physical classroom but also within the climate and culture created by both teachers and students. Children coming from low SES are readily affected cognitively and emotionally by the classroom environment. One reason for this sensitivity to the classroom climate is that poverty often compromises the ability to manage stimuli and regain homeostasis. Homeostasis refers to maintaining a stable equilibrium at a physiological level required for optimal performance. Many of the circumstances associated with poverty negatively impact physiology, producing a loss of homeostasis. The outcome is students who are less able to cope in unpredictable and rejecting environments.

Classroom culture refers to a jointly shared set of beliefs, attitudes, and behaviors established by the teacher and students (Fullan, 2007).

Developing a positive classroom culture requires a caring community of learners (Solomon et al., 2000). A process that teachers can use to establish a positive climate will be to get students to focus on things they share in common early in the school year. Identified commonalities will lower the arousal of the amygdala, which is on alert in new social settings as an automated response. The amygdala is always on high alert in new social situations to assess the environment. The alertness of the amygdala in novel settings explains why adults attending a conference walk into a large room filled with strangers and search for a familiar face to feel the calming effects of familiarity. In addition to helping students learn what they share in common with each other, have them engage in group activities that they can accomplish only through physical teamwork. The required cooperation will help students learn that they can be supportive peers. The embodied cognition experience of these activities will help students learn the abstract concept of cooperation through exercises that require working together to achieve success. Remember, the brain attempts to help us learn abstract concepts through concrete experiences. Calming the amygdala by focusing on commonalities and teamwork prevents the amygdala from focusing on differences, which can induce conflict. Each school year, teachers should develop a supportive learning environment by engaging in activities that calm the amygdala, thereby allowing the prefrontal cortex to perform to its potential.

Many of the negative behaviors that occur in the classroom are directly related to a lack of consideration for the mental condition of children coming from impoverished environments. One of the foundational principles of good instruction is creating a supportive learning environment by treating all students respectfully (Gasser et al., 2018; Jennings & Greenberg, 2009). Students who feel that they are looked down upon based on their social status are susceptible to the *dissing effect*. These students are hypersensitive to any behavior that can be interpreted as an act of disrespect, often producing a temporary loss of emotional control in response. It is important to note that students who lack self-regulation are prone to misinterpreting benign actions as acts of disrespect. It is experiencing the outcomes of the dissing effect in dangerous neighborhoods that causes so many students to be in a state of constant survival mode because any action interpreted as disrespectful can quickly escalate into a life-and-death situation. The dissing effect explains why a teenager in a movie theater shot another adolescent for accidentally stepping on his new $200 sneakers. The teen who was stepped on lacked self-control because of his exposure to volatile responses toward any action perceived as disrespectful at home and in the community.

It is important to note that students who lack self-regulation are prone to misinterpreting benign actions as acts of disrespect.

In many ways, the disproportionate response is modeled so frequently that it becomes an obligation in order not to lose the respect of others in the community. Remember, the perception that people think less of you because of your social status diminishes the ability of the cingulate cortex to produce empathy and regulate emotions to regain equilibrium. It is the lack of empathy that contributes to misreading intent and inflicting pain on others.

Teachers are instructed to be respectful toward students; however, the concept is seldom successfully operationalized. The human brain first determines intent by interpreting non-verbal emotional expressions that convey our feelings toward others. As discussed earlier, emotions are conveyed through facial expressions, hand gestures, body postures, and voice tone. Teachers need to be consciously mindful to guard against implicit biases that influence subtle expressions produced by the subconscious mind. The most common biases the teachers face are racial, cultural, and gender biases that result from patterns in our society. The Harvard Implicit Bias Studies found biases related to these three areas are still prevalent in America. In addition, teachers can easily develop implicit biases toward any consistently low-performing subgroup within their school. This implicit bias often occurs because so many schools have underperforming subpopulations. The pattern is so consistent that it is almost impossible for a teacher to see a student belonging to the subgroup and not subconsciously associate them with academic failure. Educators can also develop biases based on where students live. Teachers are too keenly aware of conversations concerning students who come from specific neighborhoods that consistently produce some of the most challenging students. Therefore, teachers who wish to be respectful have to be aware of common biases and guard against them to avoid showing (certain) non-verbal expressions when dealing with students from low SES.

Positive Language and Attitude

Another aspect of respect is apparent in our use of language (Reeves et al., 2004). Positive language denotes greater respect than negative communication, especially when dealing with students from poverty. Low SES students are conditioned to hearing negative messages and directives in their homes and communities. In poor economic settings, individuals who convey negative messages are frequently allowed to do so because of their level of authority or ability to intimidate. For example, there are many recorded accounts of mobsters incarcerated for perpetrating extreme acts of violence on someone for some action that most in society would perceive as trivial, but which they interpreted as disrespectful. When teachers use negative language or give a directive using a harsh tone, students coming from poverty can perceive it as a threatening statement without the mitigating element of intimidation. Individuals who use such harsh tones in low-income environments are often willing to *back it up* physically. It should not be surprising that language interpreted as a challenge by someone unable to back it up is perceived as dissing, triggering aggressive responses. The sensitivity to people thinking less of you because of your social status creates a need to not allow anyone to disrespect you.

The perils of focusing on negative behaviors and the use of directives further explain why classrooms that focus on the actions they want students to demonstrate have better outcomes when serving students from low SES. One reason is that classrooms that focus students on desired behaviors don't assume that students know what is expected of them (Koestner et al., 1990). Teaching desired practices also helps students to know what they have to do to be successful rather than focusing on what they are not to do. When the focus is on desired practices, it provides teachers with an effective strategy for redirecting misbehavior. Rather than the negative approach of telling a student to stop a behavior, the teacher can remind the student of what they should be doing to be successful. It is important to remember that success produces motivation in the human brain.

> Rather than the negative approach of telling a student to stop a behavior, the teacher can remind the student of what they should be doing to be successful.

When teachers use positive language to get students to engage in academic work, it promotes on-task behavior and autonomy (Koestner et al., 1990; Bandura, 1977; Deci & Ryan, 1985). Consider the importance of positive and encouraging language from a neuroscientific perspective. Teachers who have positive demeanors are likely to demonstrate hopeful non-verbal cues as well as use encouraging language. Positive teachers are better able to build rapport with students from low SES, provided that they are not naive or easily manipulated. Rapport activates the default mode network (DMN), which is a system in the brain that is engaged to improve focus and learning (Jack et al., 2009). Even more important, the default mode network opens the student to consider new ideas and attempt new behaviors (Jack et al., 2009). Students coming from poverty require the DMN activation because the ability to focus and be open to new ideas is both compromised when living in poverty. Studies have shown that teachers who focus on desired behaviors from students promote socio-emotional skills and self-regulation (Reinke et al., 2013; Rimm-Kaufman et al., 2009; Rimm-Kaufman et al., 2015). Improved self-regulation increases students' academic success by enhancing the activation and the development of the prefrontal cortex (Bradshaw et al., 2010; O'Brennan et al., 2014).

Promoting On-Task Behavior

On-task behavior means all students are actively engaged in specific assignments that have a pattern of immediate feedback, repetition, and self-correction and eventually leads to autonomous actions. Students being on task is a predictor of learning (Christenson et al., 2012). The key here is that the teacher designs each activity to be brief actions in which all students understand expectations and believe that they can accomplish what is being asked of them. For example, the teacher engages in the *think-aloud* method, providing a step-by-step logical explanation on how to perform the task by modeling the process. She asks if anyone does not understand. If there is no need for clarification, she has a student come to the board and perform the same problem, while engaging in the same think-aloud explanation of how they should solve the problem. Then, the teacher gives all the students one similar problem to complete. When they have completed the problem, the teacher selects another student to show how he solved the last problem, while engaging in thinking aloud. The teacher repeats the practice until students seem confident with the process and then allows them to work independently on a few additional problems. Literature has found that on-task behavior requires a high level of organizational skills from the teacher and promotes enhanced behavioral management skills because of the level of teacher engagement and checking for understanding (Bruns et al., 2016). On the other hand, off-task behavior can become cancerous. A few students not on-task leads to more students off-task, which interferes with learning and results in disruptive behaviors (Hanushek et al., 2003; Feld & Zolitz, 2017).

What Is the Concrete Goal of the Lesson—What Will the Student Be Able to Do Successfully?

The human brain does not function well in a vacuum. However, when the brain knows what to expect, especially when it is made as concrete as possible, it primes the brain to focus on that outcome (Valenstein et al., 1987). For the brain, there is an enormous distinction between, "today we will learn to divide" and "by the end of this lesson, everyone will be able to divide large numbers by the number two." Sometimes, teachers lose the value of creative activities by merely failing to tell students how it relates to the lesson goal. The brain naturally learns by making connections. When the brain makes clear connections, it is more likely to retain the information. Research shows that teachers who establish specific learning goals for each lesson are themselves more focused on the objective (Brophy, 1999; Clearinghouse, 2009; Shield & Dole, 2013). Teachers who clearly communicate lesson objectives help the students' brains focus on the goal (Ribera et al., 2012). Better focus improves academic performance and retention (Dunlosky et al., 2013; Hattie, 2009; Seidel & Shavelson, 2007).

> The brain naturally learns by making connections. When the brain makes clear connections, it is more likely to retain the information.

A Clear Explanation of the Content

Teachers who explain concepts in a manner that students can easily comprehend are more likely to achieve academic outcomes (Reeve, 2009). There are three simple methods for improving comprehension:

1. Relate information to what the students already know

   The brain learns with the least amount of energy when it can attach new information to what it has already learned. When the brain can make a quick connection, it reduces cognitive load, releasing the mind's capacity to achieve other more advanced insights. It also increases recall because it is connecting the new information to prior knowledge.

2. Make the information concrete

   Embodied cognition demonstrates that the brain attempts to make abstract concepts concrete to improve comprehension. For example, having the body lean two millimeters back when we think about the past is the brain's attempt to help us understand the abstract concept of the past. A visual representation of a complicated concept reduces cognitive load and increases comprehension over verbal explanation alone because it is concrete (Klingner et al., 2011; Boakes, 2009). Since the brain naturally understands abstract concepts by associating them with concrete actions or things, it is only logical that this approach will facilitate learning and comprehension.

3. Attack the senses

   Memory is not like replaying a digital video. It is placing segments of what happened into a discrete string of events. For instance, students might remember that they went to lunch at a specific time last week but may not recall that they passed the custodian mopping up soda, a class walking on the other side of the hall, or that they had pizza. The mind designates a mental basket for *walking* and another for *lunch;* once accessed, many of the finer details become available. Research shows that what makes details memorable is how much they stand out compared to the regular routine or how significantly they influence the senses. Teachers should choreograph what stands out and what stimulates the senses to help the brain determine what to remember.

All of our senses are processed in the hippocampus where short-term memories develop. Stimulating multiple senses simultaneously increases retention—what fires together wires together. Teachers should attempt to stimulate distinct senses to improve recall because each sense travels through separate pathways. The more pathways aroused during the presentation of information, the better the memories are formulated. For example, when students recite information and visually view something, they use distinct brain regions that improve recall (Kirchhoff & Buckner, 2006). Coupling a simple movement with a verbal explanation increases comprehension and recall (Goldin-Meadow et al., 2009). Effective instruction seeks creative ways to stimulate multiple senses whenever possible.

Relate Information to the Students' Daily Lives

As discussed earlier, when lessons are relevant to students' lives, they increase focus, importance, and recall (Bransford & Johnson, 1972; Tharp & Gallimore, 1988; National Research Council, 2001). Relating lessons to students' lives is especially important for school children from low SES because in deprived neighborhoods there is a tendency to view academics as unrelated to their unique existence. In impoverished communities, people often lose hope of escaping poverty, which can diminish the value of getting an education. It is helpful to students who struggle to make connections to be told what the relevance of the lesson has to their lives. The precise significance of a lesson combats messages that school is irrelevant as well as improves the application of the information. The application of information is the ultimate goal of education. Applied learning is evidence that the information is comprehended and valued.

It is helpful to students who struggle to make connections to be told what the relevance of the lesson has to their lives.

Promoting Independent Thinking

We often assume logical thinking is a product of intellect rather than a learned process. However, many of the top law schools in the

United States have taught a logical thinking process to students to help them work through legal problems posed in the bar exam. If students at top universities are taught how to think independently, then children in public schools can be exposed to logical thinking methods to be better able to determine a correct answer. The most common technique for helping students learn how to become independent thinkers is for teachers to engage in think-aloud when modeling a step-by-step approach for solving a problem or reaching a logical conclusion. Think-aloud should be used when doing both math problems and reading comprehension (Davey, 1983; Schon, 1987; Tishman et al., 1993). Research has validated that exposure to hearing how a problem is solved promotes the cognitive ability to problem solve (Bandura, 1986; Brainerd, 1978; Rosenthal & Zimmerman, 1978). A synthesis of over 800 meta-analysis studies found that analytical thinking done out loud in a step-by-step process promotes independent thinking (Hattie, 2009). For many students from low SES, this will be their initial exposure to a logical step-by-step process to solving a problem. Once students begin to engage in a step-by-step problem-solving model, the cognitive load lowers when solving issues improving self-regulation (Rosenshine, 2012). Remember, students who struggle academically find cognitive tasks taxing and reach cognitive load quickly. Once students become accustomed to a step-by-step problem-solving process, then they can easily transition to a similar method for solving social conflicts in the classroom.

Check for Comprehension

Students who expect to do poorly on a quiz or test learn to dislike taking exams. For some students, the fear of test failure can produce anxiety, which will inhibit performance because anxiety lowers the activation of the prefrontal cortex. One of the essential characteristics of effective teaching is to check frequently for comprehension in non-threatening ways. The process of repeatedly checking for comprehension reshapes test time into an exercise where students want to show what they have learned because they are confident in their understanding of the subject matter (Lemov, 2015). Teachers should reframe test taking as an opportunity to demonstrate progress and an acknowledgment for working hard. This message should be consistently said, so students think of the phrase before taking any test. An individual's perspective influences the chemical response of the brain. Therefore, what an individual thinks influences how well the brain performs a task as well as its chemical disposition.

A straightforward method to check for comprehension is to ask questions to check for understanding (Good & Grouws, 1977; Rosenshine, 2012). The trouble with this technique is that some teachers use questions that are not thoughtfully prepared or do not assess for comprehension. Teachers should develop questions ahead of time and gauge the effectiveness of the inquiries by asking themselves two questions: is the question clear, or can it be misunderstood, and does it assess what I am attempting to evaluate? This practice will also improve the quality of tests created by the teacher. It is astounding how many teachers invest hours in preparing high-quality lessons only to follow up with tests that are hastily created. A trivial question on material that was not central to the lesson confuses students and takes the focus off of the core objectives. Another strategy similar to asking a question is to require students to show their work, which is a natural progression from the think-aloud method (Evertson et al., 1980).

An additional approach for verifying understanding is monitoring students during independent and group work. Classroom observation in a low socioeconomic neighborhood school often focuses on monitoring if students are on-task (Knapp et al., 1995). When teachers monitor to check if students are working, it shifts the focus from the importance of the work to behavioral monitoring. Also, teachers monitoring on-task behavior have a tendency to see students diligently working on something and assume that they understand the assignment. Students will avoid frustration caused by misunderstanding the assignment if teacher monitoring focuses on the quality of work and not on the appearance of on-task behavior. When teachers pass by and address only off-task students, they are setting a precedent that behavior is more important than achievement. The goal of monitoring is to help students whose comprehension seems inaccurate and encourage students who are doing the work correctly (Rosenshine, 2012). In a positive classroom, teachers focus equally on students meeting expectations and on students struggling with comprehension. The first rule of psychology is that you get more of what you reinforce.

When checking for understanding, teachers need to be prepared to provide alternative strategies or explanations for the same content (Lemov, 2015). The key is mastery of content. Individuals who genuinely know their content can simplify it easily. Lack of knowledge limits the number of ways the brain can explain an idea (Borman & Overman, 2004; Connor et al., 2010; Decker et al., 2007; Reyes et al., 2012; Roorda et al., 2011; Vygotsky, 1978). Think of the last time you attended a

> Teachers should develop questions ahead of time and gauge the effectiveness of the inquiries by asking themselves two questions: is the question clear, or can it be misunderstood, and does it assess what I am attempting to evaluate?

conference and then had to present on a session you'd just heard to your peers. If the content was new, you could repeat the information you'd heard but felt incapable of answering questions. However, on subjects for which you have a wealth of knowledge, you can explain an idea in various ways to improve the comprehension of others. Until teachers have mastery, they can prepare several differentiated instructional strategies to explain the major concepts of any lessons (Corno, 2008; Lavy, 2010). Preparing for the lack of student comprehension reduces the probability that students will leave without a clear understanding of the lesson.

Immediate Positive Feedback

Before considering the feedback provided by the instructor, it is essential to note that the informal responses provided by students also contribute to classroom climate and culture. In classrooms where students are supportive of other students' comments, participation is higher, and students are more willing to take a risk. However, in classes where students are critical and make fun of remarks perceived to be unintelligent, participation diminishes, hampering an important part of the learning process. Teachers should establish that all contributions to the learning process are welcomed and treated with respect. An embodied cognition activity at the elementary school level can help internalize such a concept by having students do two claps after each student comment related to the learning process. The teacher can reinforce the concept by continually repeating that every contribution is an opportunity to learn. This approach emphasizes participation rather than whether student comments are right or wrong.

Effective teacher feedback is predictive of academic growth in students (Hattie & Yates, 2014). Teachers who provide consistent and process-oriented feedback improve students' self-regulation and achievement (Good et al., 1975; Good & Grouws, 1977; Hamre & Pianta, 2005; Nicol & Macfarlene-Dick, 2006; Taylor et al., 2003; Wharton-McDonald et al., 1998). Helpful feedback is positive because it focuses on ways to solve a problem or on what the student can do next (Hattie & Timperley, 2007; Shute, 2008). In contrast, ineffective feedback is result oriented, primarily concerned if answers are right or wrong (Kramarski & Zeichner, 2001). What makes results-oriented feedback ineffective for students from low SES backgrounds? They have often experienced repeated school failure. An established pattern of failure often produces students who are not resilient enough to cope with getting an answer wrong and perceive that the other students are being critical of them. The motivation to continue to work hard comes from achieving success. However, success is not just getting things right in a supportive classroom. Students can feel successful by participating in the learning process and feeling accepted for contributing. Teachers should also be aware that publicly identifying that a student's answer is incorrect can even be perceived as disrespectful and trigger negative emotions. Effective feedback has been found to decrease off-task and disruptive classroom behaviors, while increasing academic engagement (Johnson et al., 1996; Lane et al., 2003; Lo et al., 2002; McNamara et al., 1986; Sharpe et al., 1995; Rosenberg, 1986). It is equally important that teachers recognize when students participate. Once again, this reinforces the message that every student response is a learning opportunity for the entire class. Teachers who acknowledge participation increase motivation of the students not only to contribute but also to have the prefrontal cortex active because they are not anxious about sharing (Brophy & Good, 1985; Levin & Long, 1981; Wilen & Clegg, 1986).

> Students can feel successful by participating in the learning process and feeling accepted for contributing.

Promote the Development of Key Academic Skills

One can assume that most students coming from low SES will have some academic skill deficits based on poverty's impact on brain development. Teachers should accept the robust findings related to poverty and brain development and proactively seek to combat the impact. Since specific skills and how they can be cultivated have been elaborated on earlier in this book, no detailed explanation is provided in this chapter. The following is a reminder of the academic skills that schools should promote to improve outcomes with students coming from poverty. Assume poor focus and engage in periodic focus exercises with the entire class. Presume that memory issues will be present and teach specific memory strategies and have times when students practice and demonstrate these skills. It would be remiss to exclude social-emotional skills because a significant part of academic learning is developing social ability. Positive interactions with peers contribute to students' academic, psychosocial, behavioral, and emotional well-being (Kindermann, 2007; Skinner & Pitzer, 2012). Mindfulness exercises improve self-regulation, which is the foundation for positive social interactions. Also, skills on how to greet and find commonality with peers will serve students throughout their lives. Finally, schools should teach and practice problem-solving methods, so students learn that emotional situations do not require a response of equal or higher levels of expressive intensity.

The Only Academic Protective Factor

In this chapter: Reading is the only academic protective factor identified in resiliency research. One reason might be that the ability to read is not only reflective of a healthy brain but also a student's ability to maintain grade-level reading milestones signifies normative brain development. The process the brain uses to read changes as we age. Perhaps reading is the most crucial academic skill primary school students should master because if reading lags, the brain begins to produce alternative pathways to compensate for the brain regions not performing efficiently. Once the brain develops alternative pathways, it becomes difficult to correct as children age. However, if a struggling reader can attain and maintain reading on grade level, it improves the structure and functioning of many regions of the brain, providing a wide range of unrelated benefits.

Advancements in neuroimaging studies on language have identified more parts of the brain involved in language development than was previously thought. Due to the specificity of these studies, specific brain terminology is often used rather than a general term. The naming of specific parts of the brain does make reading this chapter a bit more challenging. For readers that are not concerned with the parts of the brain and are more focused on just the meaning, feel free to substitute *la la la* when brain terminology is used.

The Brain

- The brain is composed of the cerebrum, cerebellum, and brainstem.

- The cerebrum is the largest part of the brain and is composed of right and left hemispheres.

- Each hemisphere has four lobes: frontal, temporal, parietal, and occipital.

The Lobes' Role in Language

- Frontal lobe
  - Speech: speaking and writing (Broca's area)

- Parietal lobe
  - Interprets words
  - Interprets signals from vision, hearing, motor, and memory
  - Spatial and visual perception

- Occipital lobe
  - Interprets vision (color, light, movement)

- Temporal lobe
  - Comprehends language (Wernicke's area)
  - Memory
  - Hearing
  - Sequencing and organization

Language

- In general, the left hemisphere of the brain is responsible for language and speech (one-third of left-handed people have language and speech function in the right hemisphere).

- The right hemisphere plays a large part in interpreting visual information and spatial processing.

The Three Main Areas of the Brain Responsible for Language

- Broca's area lies in the left frontal lobe and is associated with speech production and articulation.

- Wernicke's area lies in the left temporal lobe and is primarily involved in language comprehension.

- The angular gyrus is located close to the parietal lobe and occipital lobe and allows us to associate multiple types of language-related information, whether auditory, visual, or sensory.

Structures That Connect Language Areas

- The arcuate fasciculus is the fiber pathways connecting the Broca's area and the Wernicke's area.

- The dorsal and ventral pathways connect the language regions in the prefrontal cortex and the temporal cortex.

Two Key Regions Involved in Reading

Neuroimaging studies on reading conducted while individuals decoded letters and words consistently found a reduction or even an absence of activation in the left parietal and occipital lobes (Shaywitz & Shaywitz, 2005). The lower the activity in these regions, the more severe the reading issues. The conclusion is that these two regions play a significant role in the reading process. The occipital lobe is involved in making word recognition automated. Competent readers perform word recognition instantaneously, which promotes fluency. The moment a word is seen, the visual processing triggers a mental lexicon that not only brings back the definition but also considers context to refine the meaning (Pugh et al., 2000; Shaywitz et al., 2002). In other words, when we see a word, our brains are able to not only quickly associate it to a definition but also in milliseconds recall past usages of the word in a range of contexts. This simple process provides an accurate connotation of words within a passage. The automation of word recognition is critical for fluency in reading and comprehension. Imagine how tedious reading would be if the reader had to stop and remember the meaning of every word encountered. Experienced readers take this ability for granted until they are learning new information that requires them to learn new terminologies. For example, this chapter identifies many parts of the brain, and readers unfamiliar with the terms might find the need to return to the place where the words are defined.

> Imagine how tedious reading would be if the reader had to stop and remember the meaning of every word encountered.

Compensation

Underactivation of the regions mentioned above are associated with reading difficulty and poor word recognition. Poor word recognition is also a result of issues with phonological processing. Whenever there is an area of the brain with underactivation, there is usually overactivation in other regions. The term for this is compensation. For example, when a blind individual does something that should involve sight, there is underactivation in regions of the brain involved in vision and overactivation in the areas governing the other senses. This same process of compensation is present with the poor reader: the reduction in the parietal and occipital lobes are accompanied by increased activation in the left prefrontal area (Pugh et al., 2000; Shaywitz et al., 2002).

Compensation related to reading can be detrimental because it alters the natural reading progression that has evolved since the inception of reading. Established pathways are usually the most efficient in accomplishing a task. Consider someone who suffers a stroke and loses specific physical movements. If the regions of the brain responsible for those actions cannot be repaired, the brain will seek alternative pathways to restore the physical motion. However, even if restored, it is unlikely that the process will be as efficient as the procedure that has evolved over millions of years of brain evolution.

Each of the brain regions required for reading seems to be critical in the development of competent reading skills. Once a compensation is performed consistently, the brain becomes more likely to follow that pathway in the future, making the process of retraining difficult. The issue of compensation is compounded as students age. The natural process of reading transforms in the brain as we age. As a result, when you scan the brain of a young child reading, it will look different than the brain of an adult performing the same task. The earliest major transition seems to occur between the third and fifth grades. For example, the adept reader begins to increase activation in both the left and the right parietal lobes as reading skills improve. However, during sentence comprehension, poor readers start to demonstrate reduced activation not only in the left but also in the right parietal lobes. The issue is further compounded by compensation because the process signals the transition from focusing on word identification to reading comprehension. Having an alternative reading process does not mean that the student cannot achieve reading proficiency as they age. However, for the alternative process to become proficient, it will require a lot of practice, which is unlikely because students who struggle with reading generally avoid the activity. What this finding tells us is that public education should seek to address issues of reading through intense interventions as early as possible because the complexities of restoring the natural reading pathways increase as students age.

The Importance of Phonological Skills

Poor phonological processing seems to be present in poor readers, even if other factors such as general intelligence and socioeconomic disadvantage are not present (Vellutino et al., 2004). The phonological process is foundational to reading, and that is why many early reading interventions focus on it. A meta-analysis review found that phonics instruction seems to be more effective with low- and middle-income readers (Ehri et al., 2001; Jeynes & Littell, 2000). Also, phonics instruction seems beneficial when provided early to readers. It appears that students from low-income backgrounds do not do as well with a whole language approach because of the high occurrence of auditory issues with discreet language sounds. The whole language approach teaches students to read words as complete pieces of language. Researchers believe that the only reason the whole language approach has had success with more affluent students is that they experience a high level of exposure to language and reading at an early age. The rich exposure to language produces early phonetic skills, allowing the whole language approach to be successful. Reading research has found that students exposed to higher quality and quantity of language make the transition from word recognition to word meaning earlier.

It appears that students from low-income backgrounds do not do as well with a whole language approach because of the high occurrence of auditory issues with discreet language sounds.

Phonological processing corresponds with activation in the parietotemporal region. The phonological issues associated with low SES are likely caused not only by poverty's impact on the structure of the parietal lobe but also by auditory issues that reduce the ability to identify subtle tone distinctions impacting correct pronunciation. Remember, one of the roles of the parietal lobe is to connect letters and words to their corresponding sounds. It is important to recall that reading is not performed by a single area of the brain but involves a vast cortical network. In other words, reading can be hampered in distinct ways by many brain regions found to be negatively impacted by low SES. Poverty assaults the cortex so severely that it is likely to affect reading at some level for most low SES students. Multigenerational poverty will likely become associated with reading disabilities in the future. The anticipated reading issues should cause schools to consider students from multigenerational poverty as candidates for early screening.

As students age, environmental factors such as linguistic exposure and the quality of academic instruction seem to predict when the right hemisphere regions become less active during reading. It is common knowledge that the left hemisphere of the brain is responsible for language and speech; however, early in the reading process, children show higher activation in the right hemisphere. Two areas of the brain that play a central role in language development, the Broca's area and Wernicke's area, are both in the left hemisphere. The Broca's area is involved in speech production, language comprehension, as well as sensory and motor learning. The Wernicke's area plays a role in understanding words and their meaning. The right hemisphere's role related to language has to do with interpreting visual information and spatial reasoning. Simply put, in the early stages of learning to read, children depend more on visual understanding. The transition between areas performing reading is important because it indicates a shift from word identification to reading comprehension. If students are slow to make this critical transition, reading comprehension will become compromised. The adept reader experiences a gradual increase in activation in the left angular gyrus (Pugh et al. 2000; Shaywitz et al., 1998; Temple et al., 2003). The speed of this transition is dependent not only on age but also on the quality of verbal exposure and literary interaction. All teachers should understand that during the third to fifth grades, the speed and efficiency of the brain's transition in reading comprehension is dependent on the quantity and quality of the spoken and printed word students encounter. For struggling readers, the third to the fifth grade is a time when they will experience a widening disparity between themselves and their peers. During these grades, reading will no longer focus on word recognition and pronunciation but rather on comprehension of concepts, themes, and meanings. Most struggling readers recognize how little they comprehend in comparison to their peers, causing a dislike of reading because it will likely be associated with failure.

> Most struggling readers recognize how little they comprehend in comparison to their peers, causing a dislike of reading because it will likely be associated with failure.

The underactivation in the parietal lobe among underperforming readers is correlated with a range of reading issues. Underactivation reduces phonological working memory functions on many levels (Just et al., 2004). It slows the ability to associate what students see in print with the sound of the words. It also reduces the ability to remember words read, while completing a sentence. Sentences are arrangements of words that produce meaning. If students struggle to remember the order of words, it hampers their ability to understand the meaning of the sentence. It is not surprising that underactivation in this area is associated with dyslexia.

Another aspect of reading requires imagination. When children read, the regions that elicit visual imagery activate (Just et al. 2004). The parietal lobe supports the process of visualization. It would be easy to dismiss the visualization process as a minor reading function. However, students who are the most enthusiastic about reading usually show a higher visualization activity in the brain than those less engaged. It is the imagination that brings reading to life and captivates the young reader, making them excited to return to a book to see what happens next. Imagine the reading experience of the poor readers; not only is comprehension low, but reading does not stimulate their imagination either, making the printed word a one-dimensional experience.

Once the left and the right parietal lobes are incorporated in reading, verbal working memory during reading comprehension increases (Newman et al., 2003; Xu et al., 2005). The incorporation of the parietal lobe improves the level of analysis, allowing students to compare and contrast prior readings and improves the ability to detect patterns. Patterns here are not limited to story patterns but also sentence structure and sequence. The left and the right parietal lobes seem to perform in concert even though each side may perform certain functions. For example, the Wernicke area is involved in language comprehension and plays a central role in analytical thinking during reading to promote a better understanding. The adjacent structure of the left angular gyrus is active in mapping the order of words (Booth et al., 2003, 2004; Shaywitz et al., 2002). However, even if only the Wernicke area shows low activation, the performance of the left angular gyrus is also impacted. The interconnection involved in the reading network often results in poor performance in other areas when just one part of the system is impaired.

The Importance of Grades 3–5

Research suggests that the disparity between the proficient and underperforming readers is consistently increasing between the third to fifth grades. As age-related abilities continue to develop, the latter stages of the transformation to the reading process is occurring in the brain. These developmental increases reflect the gradual regional specialization in the brain. As reading skills improve, a process of neural fine-tuning is transpiring. The result is specific language functions becoming progressively localized to the cortical areas that are most proficient in performing their assigned cognitive task (e.g., Brown et al., 2005; Booth et al., 2001; Gaillard et al., 2000, 2003; Holland et al., 2001; Johnson 2001; Johnson et al., 2002; Turkeltaub et al., 2002). Because of this transformation, learning to read is like a race against the clock. Low-income students begin the race to read yards behind the average student because so many cortical structures are being affected by poverty. Low SES students are behind before they begin to learn to read because phonological abilities are already diminished. As the race starts, low verbal memory and the inability to notice word order and sentence structure cause the impoverished student to question his ability to compete. By the middle of the race, low comprehension causes increasing despair as adept readers hit their stride and increase their lead. The inability to visualize the written word causes the struggling reader to fatigue and give up rather than finish so far behind.

RECOMMENDATIONS

Summer Reading

It is highly unlikely that most elementary schools would forgo a significant portion of their curriculum to adopt an intensive reading emphasis. However, there is evidence that a greater focus on reading might be required. The 2015 National Assessment of Education Progress report found that 64 percent of fourth-grade and 66 percent of eighth-grade students were at or below reading proficiency (Wigfield et al., 2016). The same report stated that 31 percent of fourth-grade and 24 percent of eighth-grade students barely met basic reading skills. The issues related to reading in America become even more dire for minorities of color and the socioeconomically disadvantaged. By high school, Black and Hispanic students are three years behind white and Asian students in literacy skills (Reardon et al., 2012). As mentioned earlier, the fact that so many minorities of color are poor disguises the fact that the poverty issue is the country's most significant educational problem. Students from low-income families enter high school performing at literacy skill levels five years behind high-income students. Therefore, some alternative methods to support reading proficiency seem necessary. There is proof that intensive summer reading programs might be sufficient to help improve cortex structure and functioning. For example, a six-week intensive summer reading program advanced both reading and cortical thickness across the occipital and temporal lobes in low SES students aged six to nine (Romeo et al., 2017). The higher the reading advancement attained, the more significant the improvement in cortical structure and functioning.

> Students from low-income families enter high school performing at literacy skill levels five years behind high-income students.

The intense reading intervention used a version of the Lindamood-Bell® Seeing Stars®: Symbol Imagery for Fluency, Orthography, SightWords, and Spelling reading program (Bell 2007). Trained Lindamood-Bell teaching staff members provided the instruction. The participants worked in small groups of three to five students. The program had many of the consistent elements of successful interventions with low-income students, such as multisensory remediation. The program also focused on phonological processing, reading accuracy, fluency, and comprehension. The course was four hours per day for five days a week. If schools use any validated reading intervention program for struggling readers and apply the principles of effective instruction for low SES students, similar results can be expected. However, it must be said that in all studies with positive instructional results, the programs employed highly trained and highly skilled teachers.

Improve Working Memory

Working memory enables a student to temporarily store and manipulate different forms of information to carry out a cognitive task. For example, hearing a phone number and holding it in working memory long enough to dial the extension. Working memory usually has a limited capacity in both the amount of information we can retain and the length of time it is accessible. In most cases, working memory

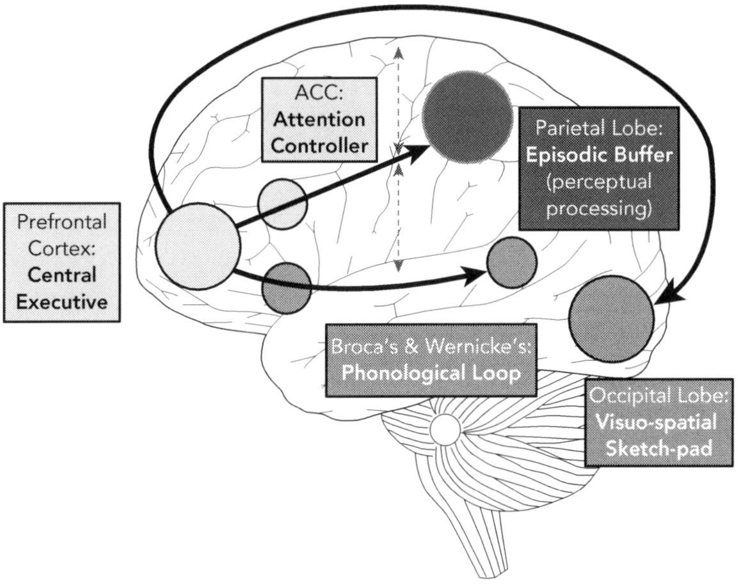

FIGURE 9.1 The many brain regions involved in memory during reading

allows us to use new information with prior existing skills or knowledge to perform everyday tasks. Low SES correlates to individuals having lower working memory. Poor readers exhibit underactivation in working memory functions related to many phonological skills.

Improve students' phonological memory skills by having them repeat sounds mimicking the frequency (how high or low), the amplitude, and duration (how long or short). Teachers can practice these exercises during stories, games, and music activities. Gradually build in the number of sounds a student has to repeat in sequence. Think of this exercise as an acoustic version of the electronic Simon game many of us grew up playing. The goal of Simon was to hear a series of tones with corresponding lights and repeat the sequence. In this activity, the students hear a series of sounds and mimic them back to the teacher, attempting to match frequency, amplitude, and duration. The same exercise is repeated using individual words and short phrases.

You can also build students' visuospatial memory by having them see simple pictures and sketch them. Remember that underactivation in parietotemporal is associated with poor auditory and visual memory. Teachers can further help students improve visuospatial memory by having them add to the number of things they sketch from memory or by increasing the time between seeing the image and having to draw it. Certain types of pictures should focus on accuracy. For example, when showing shapes, accuracy is vital because students from low SES environments often struggle to remember shapes and objects. Teachers can devise activities in which students have to replicate physical movements and continue to add to the sequence of those movements. These exercises help to promote phonological memory by improving all of its many facets.

Develop Imagination

Low activation in the parietal and temporal lobes diminishes visualization skills, which are essential for motivating reading. Imagination involves at least twelve regions of the brain, including the parietal and temporal lobes. The most crucial ability related to imagination is the ability to bring back memories efficiently. As children continue to use their imaginations, the neurons involved wire together, which improves the child's proficiency in recalling images. When neurons engage in repeated activity, myelination occurs. Myelination is the formation of a myelin sheath around nerve cells, which allows them

Teachers can further help students improve visuospatial memory by having them add to the number of things they sketch from memory or by increasing the time between seeing the image and having to draw it.

FIGURE 9.2 The many brain regions involved in imagination

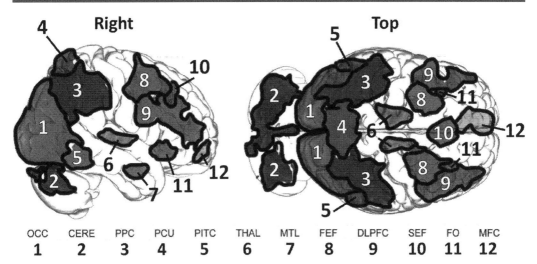

OCC	CERE	PPC	PCU	PITC	THAL	MTL	FEF	DLPFC	SEF	FO	MFC
1	2	3	4	5	6	7	8	9	10	11	12

to transmit information faster and perform complex brain processes. Consider a child reading a storybook repeatedly; each time the child imagines any aspect of the book, those images return faster, freeing the brain to engage in advance thoughts. Childhood imagination increases myelination and improves the overall speed and efficiency of the brain. There are many reasons economically disadvantaged children struggle with imagination. One reason is reduced myelination, which requires the persistent retrieval of information. Remember, memory is substantially impacted by stress. Imagination is strongly related to inner speech, which is a feature of self-regulation (Caillois, 1965). Self-regulation requires a well-developed prefrontal cortex, which often suffers a loss in grey and white matter because of issues related to poverty. Also, the limited exposure to the various experiences middle-income and affluent children have restricts imagination for low-income students. It is hard to imagine what you have never seen or experienced.

It is hard to imagine what you have never seen or experienced.

Four Ways to Improve Imagination

Think in Pictures

After reading to students, teachers can have them describe or draw what they heard in the passage. Another strategy is to have students turn math problems into visual images. Similarly, have students imagine something and then write about what they have envisioned.

Create New Inventions

Present students with an object that performs a function. Inform the students about the purpose of the object and its pros and cons. Then, have each student think of ways they could improve the existing object or invent something that could perform the task better.

Finish the Story

Have students hear a passage from the beginning of a story and guess how it will end. Alternatively, read the end of a book and have students think of how the story began.

Brainstorm, Brainstorm, Brainstorm

Identify classroom activities that are always preceded by students' brainstorming. Brainstorming is an excellent process for teaching students about any topic. For example, have students brainstorm ways you can become happier if you are sad. The ideas will help students who might lack self-regulation, and they are more likely to internalize the information because it is coming from their peers. Remember, the amygdala is attracted to itself, so children are naturally drawn to similarities with other students. The act of brainstorming promotes imagination because students are uninhibited by issues of right or wrong. Teachers should stress that there are no bad ideas during the brainstorming process.

Promoting Resiliency

In this chapter: This chapter details how schools can successfully promote protective factors so that students can become more resilient. The ability to develop protective factors is a strength-based approach to combating the adverse effects of poverty. For schools with a high concentration of students from low SES, building protective factors is a proactive approach for addressing expected academic, behavioral, and mental health issues students will face.

Why Promote Protective Factors?

A rich body of resiliency research proved that gaining protective factors helps at-risk students succeed. As established earlier, the largest at-risk group in America is the economically disadvantaged because poverty increases the occurrence of risk factors. The exciting news is that the same things that help at-risk students succeed also further strengthen healthy students to be better prepared to face the ebbs and flows of life. No school should be concerned about implementing programming that promotes protective factors because it benefits all students. Remember, the British Cohort Study validated that interventions matter. Resiliency research identified the protective factors that have the potential to strengthen the biopsychosocial health of students. Most protective factors improve brain function, helping all students to increase their capacity. It was resiliency research that began the shift from a deficit-based model to a strength-based approach. Before resiliency studies, the focus of working with at-risk populations was the identification of risk factors. Academic and mental health issues are identified by assessing risk. It was not until resiliency research proved that building protective factors helps students overcome cognitive, social, and emotional issues that caused the paradigm shift to the strength-based approach. Resiliency research was the first field of investigation to look at not only why individuals fail but, more importantly, how individuals can overcome the risk in their lives.

Resiliency research was the first field of investigation to look at not only why individuals fail but, more importantly, how individuals can overcome the risk in their lives.

The presence of risk factors leads to a variety of poor life outcomes. For example, numerous research studies have associated the risk factor of poverty to negative life outcomes such as inferior physical health (Jason & Jarvis, 1987; Pollitt, 1994), poor school performance (Dubow & Ippolito, 1994; Guo, 1998), and increased likelihood of social, emotional, and behavioral problems (Duncan, Brooks-Gunn, & Klebanov, 1994). These researchers concluded that among high-risk students with biopsychosocial issues, psychiatric symptom severity might be a less significant predictor of behavioral outcomes than the presence of risk and protective factors. By studying resilient children and their families, researchers identified essential features that confer protection against risk factors found in their lives. Protective factors protect no matter what the child's presenting problems. Therefore, protective factors provide a specific blueprint of proactive measures to ensure that students vulnerable to school failure can become more successful.

How can a protective factor improve brain function? One example is having a long-term positive relationship with an adult. Neuroscience revealed that a positive relationship promotes beneficial levels of oxytocin. Higher levels of oxytocin promote normal physical development, emotional stability, and healthy brain function. Oxytocin counteracts the harmful effects of the stress hormone cortisol. Studies have found that elevated cortisol slows physical development in abused children. High cortisol also lowers the ability of the prefrontal cortex to mitigate against the emotional brain overriding rational thought and producing impulsive damaging behaviors.

Resiliency research should compel educators to become aggressive in promoting protective factors. The motivation is that students need to gain enough protective factors to offset the risk in their lives. Therefore, a student coming to school with three risk factors needs to obtain several protective factors; however, the student coming with six risk factors needs to gain even more. A common complaint heard from educators is that students from low socioeconomic environments are coming to school with an increasing number of risk factors. Since resiliency research provides educators with a blueprint of what to do, it is incumbent upon them to do everything within reason to promote healthier students.

Many low-income students bring to school biological, psychological, and social issues that alter their brain's normal functioning. These circumstances require a skilled teacher who understands not only how these students can learn but also one who is keenly aware of interventions that can heal a damaged brain. Resiliency research discovered that every protective factor a student gains instills a level of protection against obstacles the child has faced and will endure. Schools that take on the challenge of conferring protective factors will provide a level of protection that will transform the brains of those students today and into the future.

As discussed in the previous chapter, reading on or above grade level is a protective factor that every school serving a low-income student population should incorporate as a targeted focus. Resiliency research shows that when teachers pair quality instruction with a positive relationship, the student's capacity to learn can be maximized. In the late '90s, a reading study focused on students who were labeled emotionally disturbed, receiving special education services, and who were at least two years behind in reading. They were provided one hour of one-on-one reading instruction by a certified reading specialist each school day. They were given a standardized reading test at the beginning and the end of the school year. In addition to the standardized test, both instructor and student independently filled out a relationship index determining the quality of the relationship between the student and teacher.

All students in the study made at least one-grade level gain in reading. However, every student who improved two or more grade levels in reading also had a high relationship rating by both student and instructor (Sanchez, 2008). There are many reasons neuroscience determined the relationships between teacher and student correlate with gains in reading. One reason is that a relationship improves reading scores by lowering cortisol levels, which in turn enhances executive functions in the brain. As mentioned in an earlier chapter, executive function refers to advanced abilities in the areas of self-awareness, inhibition, non-verbal working memory, verbal working memory, emotional self-regulation, self-motivation, and problem-solving. Another reason relationships improve reading ability is that the brain is designed to learn language through interpersonal communication. A recent finding explains how relationships improve reading comprehension. An individual's level of social capacity is directly correlated to the activation in the regions of the brain involved in producing high-level thinking (Wenner, 2009).

Resiliency research discovered that every protective factor a student gains instills a level of protection against obstacles the child has faced and will endure.

The study showed that those who seek social engagement get an increase in brain white matter, strengthening the connections between the striatum and the prefrontal cortex, and increasing the capacity to engage in higher-order thinking. All of these reasons justify why relationships maximize student performance. The reality is that neuroscience has only begun to scratch the surface of the benefits social interaction has on learning. Meltzoff's in-depth study on language acquisition and reading lead her to conclude that social factors play a more critical role in learning than anyone had yet realized. Her research on how infants attain language through the quality of interpersonal interaction and how it is predictive of future reading performance led her to conclude that social engagement holds the key to human learning across domains and throughout everyone's lifetime (Meltzoff et al., 2009).

At that point when schools can teach students how to interact socially in a positive manner, educational agencies are promoting another protective factor. Social skills training for low-income students should include a focus on empathy. Educators should embrace the goal of helping students learn the essential role empathy plays in understanding others and in academic learning. Nature determined that empathy is so vital that it is a hardwired trait in the human brain. However, we now know it is a trait that can be diminished and even lost. Helping students understand the importance of empathy and the steps they can take to maintain it is one of the most critical actions educators can do to produce healthy future citizens.

> The ability to navigate the school experience successfully to the point of high school graduation confers a protective factor.

The ability to navigate the school experience successfully to the point of high school graduation confers a protective factor. This protective factor does not refer to good grades but to the ability to stay in school and complete the academic and behavioral standards set by the institution. Students living in poverty are at high risk of not completing their high school education. Educational institutions face a growing number of low-income students who come to school unmotivated and defeated without the capacity to focus and remain on task. Additional challenges include an increasing number of students who lack the required social skills to survive in large, diverse school settings. The obstacles for these students are becoming even more significant as larger numbers of students are lacking in empathy and finding innovative ways to bully and intimidate one another.

Perhaps the most significant finding in resiliency research is that every individual who overcame the risk in their lives was able to identify at least one long-term relationship with a healthy, positive adult outside of their immediate family. In many cases, the positive relationship was with a teacher. Logically, teachers often become the significant adult relationship outside of parents—almost every child and adolescent encounters teachers from early childhood into young adulthood. In reality, it should be difficult for any student to complete their educational experience and not identify at least one teacher they perceive as a mentor. Every student deserves to have the perception that at least one adult in the school believes in them.

Promoting Resiliency—Part 1

Resiliency Plan

How schools can systematically approach building protective factors is outlined in a three-tier format that most schools can implement. Tier I describes the protective factors to promote across the entire school setting as universal interventions. Tier II identifies additional protective factors to develop in a classroom or small group setting. The goal here is to add extra support for students who seem to require more than what is available through universal interventions. Tier III is an added layer of intervention needed to promote protective factors in a more intensive and individualized manner for students with complex behavioral and academic issues.

Tier I: School-Wide

Universal interventions promote two elements linked to healthy school climates: ritualized environments and healthy relationships. Protective factors related to these two attributes improve the school climate and positively impact every student's neurobiology by improving their chemical balance. A ritualized environment creates a predictable setting to cultivate other protective factors. Promoting a perception of a positive relationship with an adult at school establishes the one universal protective factor found in people who overcame risk in their lives—the belief that an adult outside the family cared about them. Addressing these two areas are validated steps to promoting a climate that improves student academic performance and behaviors. The best thing about focusing on universal interventions is that they advance the performance of every student because they are rooted in the basic neurobiological needs that all humans possess.

School-wide interventions are recommended for all students to maximize their learning potential and to lower impulsive behaviors. Overstimulating the brain reduces the functioning of the prefrontal

Promoting a perception of a positive relationship with an adult at school establishes the one universal protective factor found in people who overcame risk in their lives—the belief that an adult outside the family cared about them.

cortex. The cortex is where formal learning takes place. When emotions elevate, the cortex is less engaged, and individuals are at higher risk for poor cognitive processing and impulsive behaviors (Sanchez, 2008). Therefore, instituting school-wide interventions designed to lower the arousal of the brain can improve academic and behavioral performance. For individuals to maximize their potential, they must maintain optimal chemical balance—homeostasis.

1. Establish an Effective Routine for the Major Transitions

Resiliency research determined that students from every socioeconomic background had better life outcomes when the home had consistent rules, a predictable schedule, and rituals the family engaged in together. Emmy Werner found that students coming from unstructured environments could find the established routines they needed in a safe and predictable school environment (Werner, 1989). Since many students from low-income homes experience unstructured environments and do not adapt well to change, they will often resist adhering to the structure initially. However, if impulsive students succeed in making the school environment unpredictable, they are the ones most negatively affected. Anxiety is the underlying issue related to impulsivity. As a result, when students suffering from anxiety succeed in creating unpredictability in the school environment, they only increase their own chemical imbalance, making their presenting problems more severe. In an unpredictable environment, students at risk for impulsive behaviors experience anxiety and paranoia, leading to extreme actions. Schools should establish routines during times of increased stimuli, which occur during every major transition in the school day. These transitions represent periods of mounting arousal, intensifying impulsive behavior for students suffering from any form of chemical imbalance. If students start to associate adverse events to the school's transitions, each occurrence becomes a source of heightened anxiety negatively influencing the ability to regulate behavior and to learn. Therefore, investing in ritualizing school transitions benefits all students.

How to Establish Effective Routines for a Major Transition

Teachers must be able to describe to students what an effective transition looks like when it is performed correctly. The focus is on practicing desired behaviors and actions rather than emphasizing what not to do. Negative bias makes it hard for individuals to shift their focus from what not to do to desired behaviors. The rationale for modeling and practicing desired behaviors is explained in chapter 8. The brain performs better when the desired action is demonstrated. An added benefit of modeling an action is that the male brain responds better to modeling than to verbal instruction. The goal is to promote repetitive practice for the behavior to become habit forming. It is important to remember that repetitive actions increase the brain's efficiency by supporting chemical balance. Repeated practice is more likely to receive chemical reinforcement, dopamine, which is the critical element for any behavior to become a habit (Pronin et al., 2008).

An effective transition should incorporate non-verbal reminders to prompt and motivate desired behaviors. The emotional brain will process a gesture during times of arousal and is motivated to comply with the cue even in times of crisis (Sanchez, 2008). Also, during times of increased stimuli, the brain is less capable of processing language and can even become agitated by verbal commands. By incorporating gestures to desired behaviors, teachers can then remind students of any element of the transition using a simple cue.

> An effective transition should incorporate non-verbal reminders to prompt and motivate desired behaviors.

Adults should also reinforce student behavior regularly with a gesture that represents "good job" or "thank you." The adults supervising transitions should be on the lookout for opportunities to reinforce students that are performing the transition correctly. Emphasizing success motivates the brain to change behavior faster than correction. When a student requires reminding and complies, the teachers should quickly reinforce the modified behavior to shift immediately back to the success approach of motivating desired practices.

2. Establish a Beginning Class Routine

A routine at the beginning of class will allow something familiar to be done at the start of each class period to help restore homeostasis after the increased stimulus during transitions. The familiarity of the ritual will help restore calm and improve students' cortex function. A beginning class ritual should be easy to do, not time-consuming, and, if possible, interactive. The reason an interactive beginning class ritual is preferred is that it sets the tone for participation at the beginning of each class period. Students are more likely to participate when there is a predictable behavioral pattern that their brains can expect when it will occur. Even for students who do not outwardly take part, research shows that mirror neurons still activate reinforcing the behavior. Mirror neurons activate in the premotor and parietal cortex of the brain regions that prepare the body for movement and attention. Brain scans reveal that we mirror the actions of another person in our minds automatically. However, mirror neurons begin to encode behavior when the same movements are seen repeatedly and done at predictable times.

With any new strategy and intervention, teacher attitude is predictive of effectiveness. The brain is not designed to disguise beliefs and values. Signs of what we feel are always portrayed through subconscious nonverbal cues and unconscious actions. Therefore, if a teacher believes that a strategy will fail, it likely will. Where the science is clear on what students need to succeed, it is incumbent on teachers to put aside any biases that will interfere with the effective implementation of the strategies. For example, some high school teachers might believe that opening class rituals are only for younger students. However, a majority of the high school teacher of the year winners' identified used beginning class rituals.

How to Establish a Beginning Class Routine

The teacher can initiate the classroom ritual with a gesture or phrase or include both a movement and expression. Teachers instruct the students on a response that can also be a gesture, expression, or a combination of both. The best classroom rituals reinforce a desired affirmative action, behavior, or attitude. For example, on the first day of class, the teacher does a lesson on how learning improves the brain's ability to accomplish any future goal. After the lesson, the teacher introduces the opening class ritual and explains why saying it each day will improve the brain's capacity over time. After that, the teacher begins class each day by saying, "We learn," to which the students respond, "to improve our brain." Then the teacher says, "Everything we learn today makes our brain more capable tomorrow." Students hearing these phrases said daily will begin to internalize the positive message.

Educators often forget the influence they have on shaping students' perceptions. Research findings suggest that we judge a viewpoint's prevalence by how familiar it is. Kimberlee Weaver and her colleagues in numerous studies determined that familiarity was the most critical factor in whether subjects considered an opinion to be common knowledge and later accepted (Weaver et al., 2007). Her research shows that the frequency in which we hear a message increases acceptance. It is important to note that it did not matter if a person hears a comment numerous times from one individual or various times from several people; the increase in acceptance of the statement is the same.

The scientific reason why repeated messages are more likely to be accepted may be related to one of the many functions of the amygdala. The amygdala filters information before it reaches the cortex and is alerted to new information. People react to new ideas daily. The level of emotion in their reactions is often based on how familiar an idea is. When the amygdala overreacts to a concept, it will likely not be accepted. On the other hand, themes consistently stated become familiar enough over time, lowering the arousal of the amygdala and increasing acceptance.

Best practice educational programs have taken advantage of establishing consistent positive messages for years. Best practice programs select positive themes that help students develop better behaviors, instill new beliefs, or improve self-esteem. A repeated slogan is especially crucial for schools that have a high population of low-income students. Many studies have shown that students from at-risk backgrounds struggle with self-esteem and confidence. Hart and Risley's research found that children from low SES hear less affirming statements than children from middle-class or affluent homes (Hart & Risley, 1995).

> Best practice programs select positive themes that help students develop better behaviors, instill new beliefs, or improve self-esteem.

One of the most important things schools can do is identify some consistent themes that help promote what they want students to achieve. An effective way to accomplish this is for the school staff to select one or two topics that they think are important and create a catchphrase that appropriately captures the idea. Explain the meaning of the phrase to the students through stories, movies, and other creative examples. Then continually use the phrase. For example, a school in California once had a rich tradition of producing exceptional students. However, the surrounding neighborhood changed, and the tradition faded. A new principal came in and wanted to restore hope to the young inner-city students. She used the catchphrase, "Our students accomplish great things." The school consistently brought in many of its famous graduates and always had them end their life stories with the phrase "Our students accomplish great things." Restoring the tradition of producing successful graduates is a positive theme. A theme by itself is not enough. However, when schools are making a concerted effort to improve instruction and school climate, a catchphrase can expedite the rate of change.

3. Establish a Ritual Associated with a Caring Relationship

As explained earlier, the human brain anchors the perception of caring to concrete actions. Once an action is associated with caring, the perception of concern develops as the behavior is repeatedly done. The feeling of being cared for can release the hormone oxytocin, which lowers stress

(Uvnas-Moberg, 1997). The presence of a perceived relationship releases oxytocin, improving the functions of the cortex and amygdala. An additional benefit to promoting the perception of a caring relationship is that it increases students' capacity to take on challenges (Schnall et al., 2008). The fact that relationships help us overcome challenges might explain why addicts have a better rate of recovery when they have a sponsor. In moments when they desire to relapse, they can find the courage and strength to overcome the urge with the help of their sponsor. The teacher-student bond often helps struggling students believe they can succeed.

How to Establish a Caring Ritual

Develop an action that is associated with caring. Make sure to remind students as to the purpose of the action repeatedly. The teacher should model the appropriate non-verbal cues that denote warmth and caring when doing the action. If someone were to tell you that they care, but their affect appears angry, the incongruence of the message would produce skepticism. Take steps to maintain the practice throughout the school year.

The importance of displaying non-verbal cues that match the sentiment of caring when doing the action cannot be overemphasized. The human brain is hardwired to look for non-verbal signs during every social encounter (Ambady & Rosenthal, 1992). The non-verbal behaviors naturally associated with caring, such as smiling, must accompany the action. At a subconscious level, students develop an intuitive understanding of the teachers' intent (Clayson & Sheffet, 2006; Naftulin et al., 1973). Further, when a teacher has a ritual that the students believe is performed because the instructor cares about them, it sets a social tone for all interpersonal behavior in the classroom. It is important to remember that simple actions can have significant neurobiological implications. For example, a simple pat on the back is seen through fMRI to communicate faster to the amygdala than the spoken word. The amygdala is influenced by the tone of voice used more than the words said. Teachers should be aware that they are communicating at all times.

4. Promote Social Comfort

The part of the human brain that governs emotions is attracted to things that are familiar and alerted to anything unfamiliar. It explains why humans who share commonalities develop *cliques*. However, when stress and anxiety rise, the emotional brain becomes easily agitated to anything different. Students who do not belong to socially accepted groups can experience teasing, pranks, or a range of other negative behaviors.

Promoting social comfort in every class is a step schools can implement to reduce tensions between disparate groups by focusing students on things they share in common. This simple step lowers the arousal of the emotional brain and allows students to develop a tolerance for individuals different from them.

How to Promote Social Comfort

Conduct a survey that has students identify things they like. Then, have students who would not usually interact with one another work cooperatively on small projects because they shared something on the survey in common. It is important to emphasize that the students are being grouped based on something they all have in common. Each survey question should have an accompanying symbol so the visual can be prominently displayed at each group table. Symbols hold a higher value to the amygdala than words and are easy to remember. Repeat this process until all students in the class have had an opportunity to work cooperatively with one another, based on something they share in common. The cooperative activities help the amygdala calm down in diverse social situations because students are focused on what they have in common with their peers. When teachers have students focus on commonalities, stress is less likely to cause division. Remember, neuroimaging studies found that in times of stress, the brain becomes agitated toward individuals who are least like you.

All the universal measures that improve school climate also increase the ability of the school to implement additional educational programs successfully. Schools should consider the investment in the school climate as a strategy for improving the probability of the success of other school initiatives. Research by Zins and Ponti concerning the implementation of new programs revealed that regardless of the quality of the program, success intricately depends on the overall health of the school environment, "Effective programs cannot survive in difficult school climates" (Zins & Ponti, 1990).

Promoting Resiliency

Tier II: Building Capacity by Promoting Identified Protective Factors

The acquisition of the following protective factors will enable students who are at risk of school failure to become more resilient. The protective factors can be developed through a range of interventions: They can be incorporated into character education, Positive Behavioral Support programs, or classroom intervention programs. For students who are

> Promoting social comfort in every class is a step schools can implement to reduce tensions between disparate groups by focusing students on things they share in common.

products of multigenerational poverty, a tier two level of intervention can be required.

The key to promoting any of the following protective factors is to incorporate all the elements identified by science to increase the dopamine reinforcement process in the brain's reward pathway (the nucleus accumbens). The goal is to have the behavior reinforced by dopamine to promote new habits. Dopamine reinforcement is the essential chemical element needed to create a new habit. The following are the five steps that encourage dopamine secretion in the nucleus accumbens:

1. Design age-appropriate modules for each protective factor. Make sure to apply quality brain-based instructional strategies throughout the lesson. New behaviors have to be learned and recalled to occur. The goal is to establish quick recall that is not taxing to the brain.

2. Associate each protective factor to concrete skills that can be consistently practiced during school, and associate it with one of the three values of the amygdala. Humans have automated emotional values that drive their actions. These values have great significance because the amygdala is activated in times of high emotion and it is a monitoring system that dictates immediate reactions when aroused. Thus, only values held in the amygdala are active when our decisions are impulsive. Therefore, amygdala values influence our behaviors in times of crisis and chaos. As a result, behaviors associated with the three values of the amygdala are more likely to influence our decisions even when our emotions override the logical part of the brain.

   These are the three amygdala values:

   • The need to be safe

   • The need to be loved

   • The need to be successful

3. Develop a non-verbal gesture to remind students when they are to engage in the behavior. The amygdala is hardwired to notice gestures. The tendency to notice gestures is so strong that our pre-attentional system, the first thing we tend to look at subconsciously, sees these movements even when our conscious minds miss them. A physical cue rather than a verbal command can also trigger hormones associated with motivation.

4. Practice the action consistently. Consistency is essential in determining the level of importance in the human brain and to creating a habit. Consistency also triggers mirror neurons to play the action happening like a film in the brain before the behavior occurs. A further explanation of mirror neurons can be found under the heading "Demonstrated Ability to Function as a Good Student" later in this chapter.

5. Reinforcement is a critical element for any behavior to be maintained long term. In order to develop a new habit, dopamine has to secrete in the nucleus accumbens. The nucleus accumbens is the part of the brain associated with reward. Teachers can expedite the dopamine process by reinforcing behaviors through praise. However, for dopamine to be triggered, the reinforcement has to be novel; this means praise must be consistent yet randomized. Reward programs that schedule reinforcement do not trigger dopamine because the lack of novelty makes the reward predictable and less valuable to the brain. Consider getting donuts from the principal every Friday for doing a good job. It would be pleasing and appreciated for a short period, but eventually, the reinforcement would lose its impact.

Each of the protective factors listed below is accompanied by the standard established in the research to verify when it has been obtained. In addition to the standards, any neurologic finding that can help better understand why the protective factor is important or how it can be more easily obtained is provided. The teacher can select any protective factor from the following list to help develop a higher level of resiliency. Resiliency researchers found that gaining any protective factor improves life outcomes. It is important to remember it is not which protective factor a student gains that promotes resiliency, but how many. It is highly likely that every protective factor improves brain function. Therefore, gaining protective factors is a strategy for counteracting the impact poverty has on the brain. The best strategy for promoting resiliency might be to select the protective factors the students are most likely to obtain based on their circumstances and capacity.

Protective Factors

Problem-Solving Skills at School Age

This protective factor is demonstrated by the student's ability to handle problems without resorting to physical violence, extreme behaviors, or exhibiting inappropriate emotional responses. Problem-solving is evident in the ability to get along with others.

Schools that teach a universal problem-solving approach that teachers adapt to their classroom curriculum have greater success with students developing this skill. By adopting a specific problem-solving method, schools can have students practice the steps in various settings. Students can use the problem-solving process when resolving academic and interpersonal problems. If a school uses a peer mediation method to resolve conflicts, the same problem-solving process should be incorporated. The lack of knowing how to deal with a problem often leads to impulsive behaviors. However, providing students the opportunity to practice how to respond when problems arise will help internalize a cognitive approach to handling issues. Neuroscience shows that when a person engages in an intellectual exercise to address an emotional situation, it lowers the arousal of the amygdala. Lowering amygdala arousal is vital because high activation overrides the prefrontal cortex ability to think and respond rationally, which results in increased impulsive actions.

Once teachers adopt a standard problem-solving process, they can set up fun opportunities for students to practice the application. Activities ranging from academic problems to real-life scenarios allow students greater comfort with the problem-solving model. Adults often fail to realize that although many teens physically appear to be young adults, they can quickly become overwhelmed by life's problems. Researchers found that when adults are processing emotional situations, they have higher activity in their frontal lobes than do teenagers (Yurgelun-Todd, 2007). The increased activity in the frontal lobes allows adults to solve problems more efficiently, using a fraction of the brain's resources. Adults also have lower activity in their amygdala than do teenagers, ensuring that by comparison, adult decision-making is usually calmer and more thoughtful.

The frontal lobes during early adolescence are undergoing dramatic change. A long-range study using fMRI to scan the brains of nearly 1,000 healthy children and adolescents aged 3 to 18 showed that just before puberty the frontal lobes undergo a second reorganization (Mills et al., 2014). During adolescence, millions of new synapses are forming, but frontal lobe functions are compromised. Following the growth of the frontal lobes is a massive pruning of connections that continues into early adulthood. The restructuring process can cause the brain to become quickly overwhelmed when coping with complex issues. Having a consistent method to think through problems is beneficial for all adolescent students.

The following is an example of a standard problem-solving model.

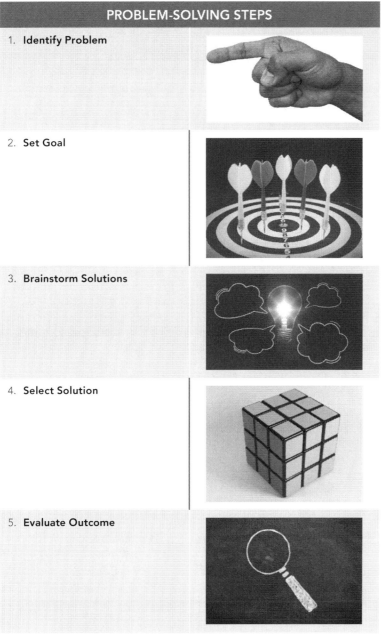

PROBLEM-SOLVING STEPS

1. Identify Problem

2. Set Goal

3. Brainstorm Solutions

4. Select Solution

5. Evaluate Outcome

Pixabay.com

Demonstrated Ability to Function as a Good Student

In resiliency studies, the ability to function as a good student did not mean achieving above-average academic grades but rather the student's ability to understand the organizational constructs of the school environment and have the ability to meet social and academic expectations. Individuals receiving this protective factor think positively about their educational experience. Students must exhibit consistent patterns of success at school for over two years for this protective factor to be considered present. Success is defined as the student avoiding any significant behavioral or academic issues that result in disciplinary separation or academic retention.

A considerable portion of this book is dedicated to assisting schools on how to promote desired practices. When schools can shift the focus from discipline to what is required to be a good student, it mitigates negative behaviors that occur because individuals do not know what is expected of them. Students who come from deprived backgrounds often do not understand what is required of them in the school or classroom setting. Assuming that they all know what it takes to be successful in school is illogical. Many students erroneously perceive that grades determine how well one is doing in school. Although academic learning and performance is a primary desired outcome of education, it constitutes only a portion of the educational experience.

The human brain excels in clarity. When specific behaviors are taught, practiced, and reinforced, the brain will emulate desired procedures. Whenever behaviors are observed consistently, mirror neurons encode those actions and increase the likelihood that the student will be able to demonstrate the behavior in the future (Caggiano et al., 2009). When there is a predictable behavioral pattern, mirror neurons create a visual imprint in the brain that plays like a film whenever the behavior is anticipated. Mirror neurons are the brain's way of teaching social practices. Prevalent behaviors viewed at school are always influencing students' actions. The bad news is schools that fail to promote healthy behavioral patterns increase the likelihood that undesirable behaviors will be emulated. This occurs because a pattern of bad behavior can also be anticipated and played like a film in the brain. What makes a pattern of negative behaviors more significant is that it is imprinted by mirror neurons faster than reoccurring positive actions. We all possess a negative bias as a survival mechanism that makes us weigh negative experiences more than positive ones. As a result, when students become anxious, the amygdala will recall negative experiences associated with the time and place of prior adverse events. Best practice schools improve their climates by increasing positive behavioral patterns that the institution wants students to model. Positive and desired behavioral patterns also promote student self-control and influence the brain better than rules alone.

> The human brain excels in clarity. When specific behaviors are taught, practiced, and reinforced, the brain will emulate desired procedures.

Good Reader

The student must be reading on or above grade level to achieve this protective factor. Reading is the only academic protective factor found in the research. This protective factor was likely identified in the studies because reading on grade level signifies healthy brain function. Some functions of the human body are inexplicably connected—for example, heart disease and depression. Long-term studies have found that people with depression are at a significantly higher risk of heart disease (Wyman et al., 2012). Likewise, people with heart disease are at substantially higher risk for depression. If one of the two factors are treated, both issues improve. The same is valid for reading. People who read proficiently consistently display better overall brain functioning than their counterparts who do not (Kuhl, 2011). Therefore, by promoting reading, one improves a wide range of other brain functions.

Socioeconomic status is independently associated with variability in reading proficiency, brain structure, and brain functions. Recent research shows that quality reading interventions improve the brain structures involved in performing the task. A study looked at children between the ages of six and nine from diverse socioeconomic backgrounds. They assigned some students to an intensive six-week summer reading intervention program. The researchers conducted before and after neural scans to measure the cortical thickness of brain regions highly involved in reading. The children from low SES in the intervention group exhibited both significant improvements in reading and increased cortical thickness in the related brain areas. Students not receiving the summer reading intervention showed no change in cortical thickness (Romeo et al., 2017). The cortical thickness reflected an increase in both white and grey brain matter and indicated improved efficiency in related areas of the brain. These findings confirm that effective reading intervention can produce cortical growth and is an effective intervention with students from low-income backgrounds. However, it is critical to note that this was an intensive reading program that used a proven curriculum and highly qualified instructors. Highly qualified instructors, in this case, refers to two findings in the study. The instructors had a high degree of mastery of the curriculum, which increases the ability to explain the subject matter clearly. Also, the instructors applied many of the strategies identified as principles of good instruction for low SES students. For example, they were more likely to use multisensory strategies when providing instruction.

The Perception That the Student Is Competent at Some Activity

The student needs only to believe that he is competent and consistently engage in activities to improve related skills. Schools looking to promote potential competencies should consider a wide range of skills since there are multiple forms of intelligence. Avoid confusing narcissistic responses by a student as evidence of possessing a competence. Without proof of the student's active participation in developing skills related to the identified ability, the protective factor is not considered to be present.

A logical approach to promoting this protective factor is to recruit and facilitate student participation in extracurricular activities that match their skills or interests. It is important to note that most competencies need to be nurtured in the early stages by encouragement. Gaining a competency is initially challenging, and many individuals who do not receive support give up far too quickly. Too many schools limit participation in extracurricular activities to students who are already proficient in the endeavor. Students talented in music join the band, those skilled at sports make the team, or those gifted in an academic area receive opportunities to take part in related scholastic activities. Schools that put in the effort to recruit students to participate in extracurricular activities and support them until they are confident in their abilities find that the overall climate is significantly enhanced.

Too many schools limit participation in extracurricular activities to students who are already proficient in the endeavor.

There is a movement happening in many progressive schools that afford students the opportunities to develop competencies. One example is hobby clubs. Club activities led by teachers afford students additional opportunities to cultivate new skills based on interest. The student has to maintain participation in the selected club for one semester and, after that, can attempt another activity. Schools also host events like Maker Faire to offer students opportunities to engage in hands-on, creative projects. Maker Faire brings people of all ages who have created anything with their own hands together to one location to display the possibilities of what anyone can build. Often this sparks interest in students attending the fair to produce their own creations. The people involved with Maker Faire provide opportunities, supplies, and even guidance from other experienced builders. The satisfaction of creating something from conceptual design to a finished product promotes self-esteem and confidence. Brain research has clearly shown that being successful at anything paves the way for future achievements. There are fantastic examples of student transformations from the Maker Faire movement. Dale Dougherty, the founder of Maker Media, tells the story of a shy underperforming middle school student who developed a line of miniature robots and now runs a successful company. After developing this one competence, the middle school student was invited to the White House along with other entrepreneurs. His self-confidence also dramatically improved his academic performance at school.

Neuroscience has identified why competencies are so beneficial to the human brain. Anyone who engages in an activity requiring repetition changes their brain structure. The acceleration of white matter and the strengthening of neuron connections are two benefits related to gaining a competency. Students do not have to become proficient in the skill to obtain the improvements to the brain. The student needs only to practice regularly at whatever skill he or she is attempting to cultivate. Encouraging students to build competencies is a proven method of improving the brain's capacity to learn.

Involvement in Extracurricular Activities or Hobbies

Participation in extracurricular activities or hobbies is defined as consistent and frequent involvement. One should not count hobbies that are brief, temporary, or prove to be self-destructive. Educators should be aware that as schools continue to grow in size, the student opportunities to participate will continue to diminish. In a school with five hundred students, a higher percentage of the students are allowed to get involved in extracurricular activities than in a school with two thousand pupils. As schools continue to trend toward building larger facilities, they need to consider developing strategies to compensate for the loss of opportunities for students to participate. The neurobiological benefits identified in developing a competency also apply to extracurricular involvement.

Having a Good Sense of Humor (For additional guidance, see the lesson in Appendix C, "Having a Good Sense of Humor")

Look for the ability to take good-natured ribbing from peers and adults. This protective factor would not include a sense of humor with morbid or sadistic overtones. A healthy sense of humor can be developed. Many schools have begun to educate students on the importance of developing and maintaining a good sense of humor. Several schools schedule lessons and activities to promote humor during national humor month.

Dr. Lee Berk, at Loma Linda University's School of Allied Health and Medicine, found that laughter helps the brain regulate the stress

Many schools have begun to educate students on the importance of developing and maintaining a good sense of humor.

hormones cortisol and epinephrine. Humor can also help the brain increase dopamine levels (Berk et al., 2008). A healthy sense of humor activates dopamine, which can assist with mood stabilization, increased motivation, attention, and learning capacity.

Donald Stuss's research on chemical imbalance showed that persistent stress or exposure to emotionally charged situations could lower the ability for the frontal lobes to control *pathological laughter* (Floden et al., 2008). Pathological laughter is inappropriate laughter occurring at things that are not funny or at other people's pain or misfortune. Individuals from concentrated poverty settings seem to be at higher risk for engaging in pathological laughter. Schools have seen an increase in pathological laughter as more students post negative comments, pictures, and videos about their schoolmates on the internet. The number of students who find these actions funny is evidence that schools should take proactive measures to educate on the importance of a healthy sense of humor. Antonia Damasio's research indicates that pathological laughter does not have any of the positive effects on the brain that wholesome laughter does (Parvizi et al., 2001).

The Adolescent Feels Confident That Life Events Are Under His Control

This protective factor is not based on whether an adolescent feels that he can do great things in the future. The protective factor is assessed on the presence of established indicators that provide an individual with a feeling of control over life. The following are signs to look for: identification and continued development of competencies, engagement in activities that correlate with future goals, the absence of depression, the ability to make and maintain friends, a lack of crisis events resulting from impulsive behavior, and the ability to recognize the consequences of actions.

One of the negative effects of stress related to poverty is that the brain begins to lose future orientation. Students coping with stressful circumstances focus on day-to-day events. When individuals focus on future planning, it has an immediate positive effect on their brain. An essential key to restoring future orientation is the verbalization of future goals. Many schools are asking students to verbalize future goals and highlighting areas of the curriculum relevant to their objectives. Making the curriculum pertinent to the individual motivates learning. Too many students find out later in life that there is a correlation of future success with their past academic performance.

However, many people debate the correlation of life success to academic performance. They cite examples such as Albert Einstein and Bill Gates as people who dropped out of formal education and yet became successful. The benefit of mandatory education is that it provides a structure that compels students to learn. Both Einstein and Gates may have dropped out of school, but they did so to focus their minds on particular areas of academic interests. Unlike Einstein and Gates, most high school dropouts do not dedicate themselves to broadening their minds and advancing their ideas. For the majority of students, the exercise of building their brain's capacity is expedited through the rigors of obtaining a mandatory education. Neuroscience finds that the concentrated focus on learning during childhood and adolescence provides a foundation for expanding the brain's capacity during crucial periods of development. It is the capacity developed during these formative years that sets a trajectory for the brain's future ability.

The Adolescent Has Positive and Realistic Expectations for the Future (For additional guidance, see the lesson in Appendix A, "Goal Setting")

It is important to not define *realistic* to mean low expectations. As it relates to future expectations, *realistic* is defined as actively striving to achieve an identified goal. If the individual is taking clear and measurable steps to achieve the desired goal, this protective factor is present.

One point made earlier when discussing a student's capacity to learn is that the brain focuses on things related to what an individual already knows. What the mind focuses on has real-life implications. Individuals exposed to a broad range of experiences are likely to explore a variety of possibilities. Individuals coming from poverty often limit their future opportunities based on their brain's tendency to focus on what is familiar. Schools that make a concerted effort to expose students to a greater variety of experiences help create new expectations. The ability of schools to expand students' horizons are limited only by their creativity. Many schools invite speakers from diverse professions to address students regularly. Some schools have established clubs that allow students to practice building computers, producing music, developing apps, and designing school attire and even interning at local companies. Public educational institutions that don't have the funding to take field trips can engage in creative fundraising endeavors. Through the advancements in technology, classes in other states or countries can learn together while exposing students to new cultures and ideas. A brain exposed to greater possibilities can make extraordinary ideas become realities.

> The benefit of mandatory education is that it provides a structure that compels students to learn.

The Adolescent Actively Plans for His Future (For additional guidance, see the lesson in Appendix B on hope and expectation for the future)

Actively planning for the future is a protective factor in resiliency studies that is more common among adolescent girls than boys. One of the advantages of a female brain structure is the ability to engage in future planning. Research supports that the female brain structure is more detail oriented than the male brain structure. In addition, the female brain has a larger corpus callosum, which supports planning functions. However, every student can create a long-term plan and achieve desired objectives through a series of short-term goals.

Students should demonstrate an awareness of cause and effect to be able to alter their plans appropriately. An excellent exercise to do with students is for the teacher to identify an event and then have students offer a probable positive or negative outcome. In the activity, students continue to provide the next possible outcome based on the prior event. The teacher instructs each student whether the subsequent event should be a positive or negative one. This activity helps students better understand cause and effect, but more importantly, that any situation can lead to a positive outcome.

Students coming from low-income environments benefit from transition planning at least a year earlier than most schools engage in the practice. Schools usually complete a transition plan with students during the senior year of high school in states that have it as an established standard. However, senior year is often too late for many students from low SES backgrounds. Students living in poverty often do not understand the requirements for college admission. Research proved that early orientation concerning how high school is relevant to college and future employment could have positive ramifications on the actions of students. The vocalization of a future plan, along with continuous monitoring of small measurable short-term goals, are crucial elements for helping students gain this protective factor.

Independent-Minded Adolescent Female

Research shows that independent-minded girls are not as easily pressured to engage in behaviors that are unhealthy or harmful to them. It is interesting to note that there is a direct correlation with involvement in extracurricular activities and the obtaining of this protective factor. Research shows that increased testosterone triggered by participation in competitive sports is one reason more girls are becoming independent-minded. Also, girls who take part in extracurricular activities seem to develop healthier social networks and self-esteem.

The female brain is susceptible to mood disorders beginning in early adulthood. However, researchers are beginning to think that independent-minded girls are at a lower risk of developing mood disorders. The thought is that a healthy self-image seems to improve the functions of the insula, which plays a significant role in establishing an accurate perception of self. Independent-minded girls seem to have an accurate and positive view of who they are. When the insula does not function correctly, self-image can be lowered or even dramatically altered. Girls at risk of developing eating disorders often have an insula that distorts their ability to self-evaluate accurately. A distorted insula begins to explain how a thin girl can perceive herself to be overweight and engage in unhealthy eating practices.

Promoting Resiliency

Tier III: Mentoring Services

Tier III is reserved for students who have severe behavioral or emotional issues requiring an intensive approach to gain the protective factors identified in Tier II. Students from multigenerational poverty seem more able to develop protective factors with the aid of an adult relationship. Based on the emphasis neuroscience and resiliency research place on relationships, it should not be surprising that at-risk students have greater success in obtaining protective factors when working with an adult they trust. Therefore, it is logical that at the highest tier of intervention, the emphasis is on cultivating a relationship with students who often lack the skills to build rapport with an adult on their own.

Mentor Services

Resiliency studies found relationships to be a natural catalyst for promoting protective factors. However, research also shows the more severe the emotional disorder(s), the harder it is to develop and maintain relationships. Therefore, it seems reasonable that there will be a small group of students who will need someone designated to help them learn how to develop relationships and how to use those relationships to attain additional protective factors. Mentorship requires people who are trained to work with students with emotional disorders because the population is so well versed in sabotaging attempts to establish relationships.

The most consistent finding in resiliency studies is that the presence of one long-term positive relationship with an adult helps overcome the existence of multiple risk factors. As discussed earlier, in the presence of a positive relationship with an adult, the brain views challenges as more achievable. It is only logical that individuals with emotional vulnerability need additional support to get through life ordeals. A well-known example of mentorship is the proven practice found in substance use recovery.

Naturally resilient individuals cultivate these relationships easily. Students who are not naturally resilient and come from deprived environments need mentors placed in their lives. Mentors are a bridge to developing a social network. The primary role of a mentor is to unlock the secrets of how to develop and maintain a positive, healthy relationship. In a culture with a divorce rate that has consistently hovered between 40 and 50 percent, it is clear that fewer students are exposed to healthy relationship models in the home. Students from multigenerational poverty are less likely to come from two-parent homes than the rest of the population. In the 2016 census, 64 percent of children in poor families lived with a single parent as opposed to only 26 percent of children in middle- and affluent-income families lived with a single parent (Proctor, Semega, & Kollar, 2016). Mentors will need guidance concerning strategies for working with at-risk students as well as specific objectives to be performed. Schools should provide mentors with an accurate expectation of what each student's negative behaviors are like and methods for effectively managing them. If a school counselor or psychologist is available, these individuals are well qualified to assist the mentors in these areas.

There are also many mentoring models that schools can select to implement a successful program.

> The primary role of a mentor is to unlock the secrets of how to develop and maintain a positive, healthy relationship.

School Staff Mentoring Model

School staff members who are naturally adept at working with challenging students can volunteer to mentor one identified pupil each year. This model seems to have the most success because the educators involved already possess the skills required to be successful with low-income students. The school identifies a process for identifying which students are priorities for mentoring services. The school then allows the staff to choose the student they feel they can work with successfully. Teachers should not pick students who are in their classes because having to make academic demands and address behavioral issues often interfere with the mentoring relationship. Allowing the teachers to select students who they believe they can build a rapport with enables the mentor program to begin with an expectation of success.

Mentoring programs need to be highly structured to be successful. School staff members are busy with daily responsibilities, so unless the mentor program requirements are precise, the programs will wane. Schools should expect mentors to schedule a time to work with their students at least once a week. These meetings should focus on actions that will cultivate specific protective factors. Students should be allowed to check in with their mentors at least three times a week just to touch base or discuss how they are doing. These are brief meetings that can occur during allotted transition times. Mentors should attempt to do one activity early in the mentoring relationship, designed to help cultivate a bond between teacher and student. Mentors can schedule additional events to further develop the bond throughout the mentoring process at the discretion of each staff member.

Volunteer Mentor Model

Community volunteers fill out an application to become a mentor and, after passing a comprehensive background check, are selected to work with identified students. This model seems to be the most difficult to support. Since the volunteers are not employees, they can choose to stop coming, in which case, the program fails. Schools that have the most success with this model usually have strong parent organizations or community partners already in existence. Someone from the parent group or community organization helps coordinate the program with the help of one primary school contact. The mentors will need training, scheduling, and ongoing support.

The information on the mentor application is used to match each volunteer with a student to maximize rapport building. Volunteers are asked to make a formal commitment to work with their identified students for a minimum of one school year. The organization provides mentors with a schedule and a dedicated location where they can meet and work with their appointed students on school grounds. Mentors must be briefed on the student and be prepared for the array of behaviors they might encounter. It is recommended that mentors enroll and complete a comprehensive training program as part of the orientation process. The course can help the mentor know how and what they should do if certain behaviors occur and how to promote recommended protective factors. All volunteers should have a designated contact they check in with regularly to be able to communicate issues or concerns. These issues are discussed with the school contact to maintain comprehensive two-way communication.

Employed Mentor Model

Employed mentors are full-time school employees who may or may not have other duties. However, at least one of their responsibilities is to focus on providing mentoring services to selected students. Unlike the staff model, paid mentors do not choose their students but are appointed a caseload. In some instances, the artificial nature of the connection, in the beginning, can slow the development of a positive relationship. Some students may have difficulty trusting a relationship with the mentor because they perceive that they are paid to work with them. Another concern is that mentors are usually in a low-paying position, and individuals will often lack the skills required to work with students with complex problems.

In this model, each mentor has a schedule with established times and dates to work with each assigned student. It is recommended that the employed mentor complete training on how to work with the population and how to promote protective factors effectively. The mentors should have an on-site supervisor whose role is to provide periodic supervision, develop a schedule, and make sure mentor interactions and activities are designed to promote the acquisition of specific protective factors.

Any of the mentoring models adopted should include some form of ongoing evaluation to determine what protective factors each student is acquiring and how it is impacting school performance. Schools need to embrace data-driven assessment and perceive it as a method for constant improvement rather than an indication of success or failure. Even established programs require ongoing modification because of changing environments and student populations. It is vital that the school leadership frame and treat the evaluation process as opportunities to improve rather than only a program assessment.

Summary

There are many reasons why schools should invest in improving the resiliency of students. The first reason is confidence. Schools can be confident that promoting protective factors will help students address presenting issues. The history of resiliency research founded on longitudinal studies determined the benefits of protective factors. No other validated approach has identified what improves life outcomes for at-risk children and adolescents. The second reason is schools can promote many of the protective factors within the educational setting. Schools have always reinforced protective factors; the key is that the approach must be modified to allow the most vulnerable students the opportunity to obtain a sufficient number. The final reason is that promoting protective factors works regardless of the students' presenting problems. Schools invest sizable amounts of resources on student assessments, and upon gaining the information, they are no closer to identifying a solution. Perhaps it is time to invest in solutions validated by research and supported by neuroscience.

Appendix A

Model Lesson: Goal Setting

The goal-setting process can improve self-regulation and promote brain development. Emerging evidence from neuroscientific studies found that working toward goals during adolescence develops cognitive skills that will enhance brain function throughout the life span (Blakemore & Choudhury, 2006; Giedd, 2004). Goal setting is a validated method to improve an individual's ability to self-regulate (West et al., 2005). It can also positively impact goal-related memories and the belief that you can accomplish what you set your mind to achieve. Resiliency research has demonstrated that goal setting and attainment improves brain function and outcomes. Therefore, goal setting is a critical cognitive exercise for students as it enhances brain function across many regions (Bandura, 1997; Schunk, 2001; Schunk & Zimmerman, 1997).

Research shows that challenging and specific goals produce better task performance than generalized support, such as *do your best,* or than having no objective at all (Locke & Bryan, 1966). We also know that performance improvement is proportional to how challenging or difficult the goal is to obtain; however, when students reach the limits of their abilities, their performance will suffer (Locke & Latham, 1990). Effective goal setting has to be challenging to bring the best out of a student, but it cannot exceed the student's capacity. As a result, teachers might be the best-equipped individuals to take students through a goal-setting process because they can assess cognitive capability to prevent unattainable goals from being established. However, teachers should also guard against the bias of low expectations that often accompany students from lower SES. There is evidence that correlating short-term goals to long-term goals maximizes progress (Frierman et al., 1990). The act of sharing your goal with another person improves the probability that you will attain it (Matthews, 2015). The goal-setting process can substantially help students from poverty to shift their paradigm from the present to the future.

The sample goal-setting lesson outlined below is designed to incorporate elements found in research to facilitate the development of new behavioral habits. The development of protective factors requires discipline and consistency. For example, gaining a competency cannot be achieved without some consistent practice. Neuroscience research reveals that consistent actions get dopamine reinforcement, which motivates the brain to create new habits.

- Associate the protective factor to concrete actions that the student can regularly perform within the school setting.

- Develop non-verbal gestures to remind or trigger the desired actions.

- Consistently reinforce the practice.

- Maintain the action(s) associated with the protective factor to help students internalize the practice.

Teachers should review the following section prior to teaching the goal-setting lesson. It is important for teachers to have a comprehensive knowledge of any subject matter before attempting to provide instruction based on a curriculum. It is this fuller knowledge that aids in making sure that your non-verbal cues to the students project a confident understanding.

Teacher Review

WHY

Why is it imperative that students learn to set and meet goals?

- Once a student consciously sets a goal, he will begin to develop the ability to focus.
  - Early in the goal-setting process, the student's focus will improve only when engaged in goal attainment activities.
  - However, research shows that as students increase their proficiency in setting and attaining goals, their ability to focus will expand to other areas.
  - Improving focus is a crucial skill to achieving greater success academically and in life.

- When an individual sets a goal, the brain will subconsciously filter out distractions of irrelevant information in the environment that are inconsistent with achieving the goal (Vorhauser-Smith, 2011).

- ○ Many students from low SES struggle with filtering out distractions; they need to practice goal attainment to strengthen the brain's ability to ignore irrelevant information.

- Goals can trigger motivation in the human brain. Motivation is a primitive brain pathway related to survival. The motivation to achieve positive outcomes is a sign of a healthy brain (Vorhauser-Smith, 2011).

- ○ Many students living in poverty struggle with self-motivation and, as a result, do not actively strive to attain positive goals.

- ○ Many of these students think life just happens, and they only react to it. This approach produces a sense of loss of control, which results in overreaction, impulsive behavior, and aggression.

- The ability to set and attain goals is an essential component of developing self-regulation. It helps the brain activate and sustain cognitions and behaviors (Schunk & Ertmer, 2000).

- ○ Many students from low SES lack the ability to self-regulate both thoughts and behaviors.

- ○ Goal setting is an active exercise to help develop self-regulation.

Why will students struggle with goal attainment?

- The primary reason many students from low SES struggle with goal attainment is because of poverty-related circumstances that often lead to a history of repeated failures, which creates doubt as to their ability to accomplish anything (Locke & Latham, 2002).

- ○ One of the primary reasons students are unmotivated to attempt goals is the belief that the goals are impossible for them to attain because they have consistently failed in the past (Locke & Latham, 2002).

- ○ Many at-risk students struggle with boredom. Boredom is a product of an unhealthy brain (Hunter & Csikszentmihalyi, 2003). Although a healthy brain can become bored, it will not maintain that state for an extended period of time. A healthy brain will determine some action to engage in that will eliminate the boredom. Goal attainment requires discipline to engage in some behaviors repeatedly to the point of automation. These students often feel boredom in repeated actions, causing them to stop before gaining the level of automation, which improves high-level thinking in related areas.

- Students also fail to set or attain goals because prior experiences and observations of their environments have formed the belief that the likely consequences for focusing on self-improvement are socially negative.
    - In many low-income areas, students are ostracized for striving to obtain positive goals by peers and even adults in the community.
    - It is up to the school and not the students to create a school climate that makes it safe to focus on self-improvement.

- It is easier for the human brain to rationalize existing habits than engage in new ones (Hagger, 2013).
    - Existing habits are less taxing to the brain because we do not have to think about them, and they require less energy than engaging in a new behavior (Wood & Neal, 2007).

- Being able to achieve goals has less to do with willpower than with specific coping skills. Many students coming from poverty have not developed the necessary skills to create attainable goals or to pursue them actively. Poverty emphasizes focusing on the present, reducing future orientation. The act of goal setting is essentially planning for the future.
    - The ability to engage in time management
    - The ability to bounce back after setbacks
    - The ability to begin with modest goals
    - The discipline to practice consistently

- Goal setting does not alter performance in the absence of commitment (Locke & Latham, 1990). Therefore, students who set goals only to meet the requirement of the lesson will not get the motivation the brain produces when short-term objectives are achieved. As a result, getting students to identify an objective they are genuinely committed to is critical.
    - Getting students from low SES to commit to attaining a goal is often difficult, based on all the reasons previously mentioned.
    - Many things influence goal commitment:
        - Skill level
        - Previous performance
        - Social-environmental factors
        - The nature of authority and feedback

WHAT

What is a goal?

A goal is a behavior or outcome that one is consciously trying to perform or attain.

What is goal setting?

Goal setting refers to the process of establishing a behavior or outcome to serve as the aim of one's actions.

Goal setting alone does not produce positive results

Simply having a goal does not automatically benefit a student's performance (Bandura, 1986; Locke & Latham, 1990, 2002). However, never engaging in the process of goal setting results in students being unaware that planning related to the future is how many individuals gain a sense of control over life and direction for their future. Having a goal in the absence of commitment might predict failure, yet learning how to set and plan goals is a skill that can be beneficial in the future.

- Many New Year's resolutions fail because of poor planning.
  - I will get in shape—and impulsively buying a gym membership is not how the goal-setting process is accomplished.
- If a student does not develop the skills required for obtaining goals, confidence building is an empty act.

What are the elements of successful goal setting?

- Short-term objective
  - Short-term goals lead to higher motivation directed toward goal attainment than merely establishing long-term goals (Bandura, 1986). The brain is motivated by success; the act of obtaining a short-term objective stimulates the desire to reach the next goal.
  - Goal-setting research suggests that the key to completing a long-term objective is to divide it into short-term tasks.
- Specific
  - Goals that incorporate precise standards (e.g., complete 20 problems in one hour) are more likely to enhance motivation and learning than are general goals (e.g., do your best). Specific goals better describe the amount of effort needed to succeed.

- Challenging (but achievable)
  - A vital goal property is the level of difficulty or how hard it is to attain the goal. In general, challenging goals (e.g., read a 30-page chapter tonight) boost motivation better than simple goals (e.g., read five pages tonight). Students persist longer and spend considerable effort when they pursue challenging goals.
    - ❖ The goal should be a challenge but must be attainable. If the student is a poor reader, thirty pages in one hour might not be achievable. However, five pages in one hour might be feasible and still challenging.
  - Challenging goals do not raise motivation and learning in the absence of the skills needed to attain them.

- Realistic
  - Many students are not realistic about the steps involved or about how much time is required to complete a goal.
    - ❖ Some of the least skilled students often verbalize goals they think the adults want to hear. Usually, this results in a pattern of unrealistic goal setting and failure.
  - As students gain experience with goal setting, they will be able to set realistic goals on their own.

- Measurable with consistent feedback
  - A specific and measurable goal immediately creates focus and energy toward its achievement.
  - Feedback on goal progress provides students information about their advancement toward objectives and can promote self-efficacy and motivation for students who lack the ability to assess gains.
    - ❖ Many students from low-income backgrounds focus on the negative and cannot identify when they are making progress.
  - Feedback executed poorly or negatively can have adverse effects on motivation.
    - ❖ Teachers need to be cognizant of the fact that a pattern of past failure produces a psyche that can be easily shattered by harsh criticism.

- Automation
  - The target for any goal is to replicate the steps that must be accomplished to reach automation.
  - Automation is evidence that the brain has restructured. If the repeated practice is beneficial, brain function has improved.

HOW

Students need to develop specific skills to increase their opportunities to achieve goals. The following skills are consistently identified in the literature on goal setting as playing a pivotal role in achieving objectives.

- Learn to start with short-term goals. Achievable goals build up their confidence as students move forward.

- Use implementation intentions. Implementation intentions are statements that specify the **how, what, when, and where** of performing goals. When goal setting involves this level of detail, students will be more successful at motivating behavior than merely setting a general goal.

  o For example, if you aspire to eat three servings of vegetables every day, you might tell yourself, "When I go home, I will stop by the grocery store and buy vegetables" (Gollwitzer, 2012).

    ❖ Avoid incorporating rational justifications in the statement because it reduces the automation of behavior. "If I leave work on time, I will buy vegetables at the grocery store."

    ❖ Put the statement in the affirmative.

- Channel factors. Identifying seemingly insignificant details about the environment that can have tremendous effects on behavior is one example.

  o For example, in the 1960s, medical professionals at Yale University wanted to encourage students to go to the student health center and get vaccinated against tetanus. Although most of the students responded favorably and conveyed an interest in receiving the vaccines when told, only 3 percent of the students ended up going to the health center and getting the shot. However, one modest change increased participation to over **25 percent**: providing the students with a map of the campus (on which the health center was circled) and asking them to check their schedules and find the time when they would be near the center and be available to get the shot. Keep in mind that these were all college seniors; they presumably already *knew* where the health center was by that point in their college careers. They also probably knew how to check their schedules before the researchers told them to do so. The point is that identifying one specific element in the environment helps to translate good intentions into healthy actions. The single *channel factor* of noting the next time they will be near the health center made the act seem convenient and manageable. Channel factor is a form of embodied cognition, making an abstract concept concrete.

- Find personal motivation. This can keep you feeling accomplished and in control of your fate. To maximize your chances of sticking to a goal, you need to figure out exactly why you are pursuing the objective in the first place.

- Eliminate negative triggers. This means planning to minimize such situational factors that lead to bad habits that will interfere with a goal's attainment. If you are trying to give up caffeine, for instance, find a route to work that does not take you past your favorite Starbucks.

- Imagine success. What will the successful result of your efforts look like? Visualization helps improve skill levels faster.
  - When possible, have students see the action done at a high level.
  - Your past exposure is predictive of what and how well you can visualize.
  - One way of overcoming cultural and economic factors is having students see the behavior performed correctly.
    - Modeling is a natural form of instruction for the human brain.

- Create new routines. This will make your desired behaviors be as automatic as the negative habits you wish to break.
  - Elements of a routine are designed to produce automation:
    - Make abstract concepts concrete
    - Make the action valuable to the amygdala by aligning the act to one of the core values of the amygdala. Remember that values held in the amygdala are motivators even in times of high arousal. Students who get frustrated while engaging in new activities will need the action to be valued by the emotional brain, which stays engaged even when upset.
      - The core values of the amygdala are the desire to feel safe, wanted, or successful.
    - Establish a visual cue to trigger the behavior.
    - Set a specific time to practice the action.
    - Provide positive feedback—praise and random reinforcement.
  - The steps mentioned above help trigger dopamine in the nucleus accumbens. The brain requires dopamine for a behavior to become repetitive. Many students who lack positive habits suffer from reward deficit syndrome, which means that it takes more

for dopamine to activate in the nucleus accumbens. Therefore, following the above-mentioned steps that promote dopamine activation are strategies essential to promote success.

WHEN

When should students practice goal setting and goal attainment?

- It is initially recommended that teachers provide students specific, brief classroom goals that can be attempted, completed, and evaluated.

- Teachers should model how to design an appropriate short objective that relates to a long-term goal.

- Teachers should also infuse the *Hows* of goal attainment into these brief objectives for students to become more proficient.

- Once students have built confidence in goal attainment, then Phase II and Phase III of the lesson can be taught and implemented.

The following module is for grades 6–12 *(teacher instructions are in italics)*.

Teachers should experience this lesson by setting brief daily goals related to their instruction. The best form of instruction is provided by individuals who have accomplished the lesson to a level of proficiency. The teacher's shared personal experience can help students become more aware of the obstacles and challenges with implementing goal setting. The teacher can establish a goal of consistently implementing a strategy identified in Chapter 8, Principles of Good Instruction for Students from Low SES. Developing a goal to improve the ability to provide effective instruction to low-income students is a perfect exercise for experiencing the goal-setting process.

This lesson helps teachers introduce goal setting in a manner that increases student participation. *The lesson can be taught as one lesson or in sections. The sections delineated in the lesson are merely natural breaks in the information flow but are not hard and fast rules.*

Lesson Goals

1. Learn what is a goal.

2. Learn how to develop a goal.

3. Consistently practice skills that increase goal attainment.

4. Experience the value of goal attainment.

Lesson

Section 1

When you hear the word goal, what is the first thing that comes to your mind?

Allow students the opportunity to process.

Show pictures of some athletic goals: basketball goal, hockey goal, soccer goal, and so on.

Pixabay.com

What do these goals have in common?

The following are examples of the ideas you want your students to identify. You might have to guide students in this direction.

- *Action*

- *Takes skill*

- *Takes a lot of practice*

- *Takes effort*

- *Perform under pressure*

- *You will fail many times*

- *Feels good when you succeed*

Today, I want to introduce you to another type of goal. Show pictures of personal goals: finishing a marathon, climbing a mountain, graduating school, etc.

Pixabay.com

What type of goals do these pictures bring to mind? *The objective is to lead students to see that personal goals and athletic goals are, in many ways, the same. Both require these elements:*

- *Action*
- *Skill*
- *Practice*
- *Effort*
- *Performance under pressure*
- *Failing many times*

Definition of a personal goal

A personal goal is an action or actions that you are willing to do consistently to reach an objective.

Why is it important that we all set goals and persistently attempt to meet them?

Goal setting improves your brain, especially the prefrontal cortex (the front part of your brain). The prefrontal cortex is important because it enables you to grow skills:

- Improve self-control
- Increase focus
- Make better decisions
- Achieve goals
- Be more successful

What does setting a goal do for you?

- It improves your ability to focus.

  Many times students get in trouble or don't complete their work because their brains have problems with focusing.
  - If you set a goal, your brain will help you learn to focus on the target.
    - ❖ If you do not want to meet the goal, your brain cannot help you.
    - ❖ If you want to reach the goal, and you make a plan, your brain will help you to focus.

Show the following picture and emphasize the point that the harder it is to focus, the more the brain has to work to do simple things. This picture is a functional magnetic resonance imaging (fMRI) of the brain scans of people asked to do a simple task. The yellow is a composite example of the brainpower used by people who multitask with technology and the brain activity needed to complete the simple task. Multitasking with technology means you use multiple forms of technology at the same time. For example, an individual attempts to listen to music while texting and surfing sites. The little white dot represents the brainpower used by people who don't multitask with technology consistently, doing the same task. The researchers found that multitasking with technology reduces the brain's ability to focus and makes it work less efficiently. The harder the brain works, the easier it is to become overwhelmed by simple problems in life and respond poorly. Goal setting is one exercise that helps the brain regain focus.

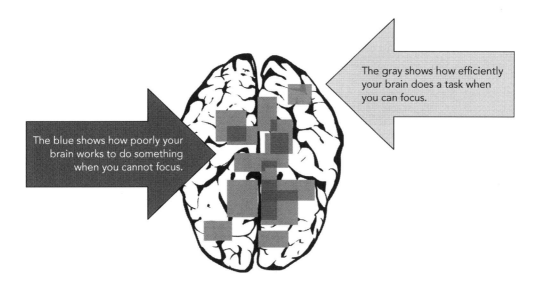

The gray shows how efficiently your brain does a task when you can focus.

The blue shows how poorly your brain works to do something when you cannot focus.

- o If your brain is working this hard to do simple things, you will avoid working on more challenging tasks.

- When you set a goal, the subconscious brain (the part of the brain that works automatically) helps filter out distractions.
  - o The best working brains have learned to focus on one thing at a time.
  - o You can improve how your brain works by just learning to set goals and trying to reach them.

- Goals can help motivate your brain to do things you did not think you could do.
  - A motivated brain is a sign of a mind that is working well.
  - A brain that gets bored is a sign of a mind that is not working well.
  - The good news is that the brain is like a muscle, and you can build it up and make it work better! *The brain is like a muscle is an important point.*
- Maybe the best thing about setting and achieving goals is that it helps the brain gain control over how you think and how you behave. Self-regulation is performed by the area in the front of your brain called the prefrontal cortex.
  - So if you have ever wished that you could control your behaviors more, setting and reaching a goal is something you want to practice.

If you want your brain to focus better, avoid being so easily distracted, improve motivation to accomplish what you want, and increase self-control; then learn to set and achieve goals. The practice of goal setting gives you a way that you can gain more control over your own life.

Section 2

How do you design a goal so that you can achieve it?

Goals need these qualities:

1. **Short-term**
   - Meeting short-term goals leads to higher motivation and the ability to achieve long-term goals (Bandura, 1986).
   - Completing long-term goals is attaining a range of short-term goals that lead to your long-term goals.

2. **Specific**
   - The term *specific* in this context explains what, when, where, and how.
   - The brain is better motivated by a specific goal than by a general objective.

3. **Challenging (but achievable)**

- If it is too easy, the brain will not view it as a goal.

- If it is too hard, the brain might not believe it can do it.

- Goals have to be challenging to raise motivation.

- You still need to develop the skills required to reach your goal.

4. **Realistic**

- Avoid the temptation of targeting something too big before being able to reach short-term goals consistently.

- As you meet short-term goals, you will be able to make progress toward long-term goals.

5. **Measurable with Feedback**

- When you know that you have achieved a goal, you get energy for the next one.

- When you get feedback and improve, the brain can become more efficient.

6. **Automatic**

- Practice will make achieving goals more automated to the brain. When you do a specific task repeatedly and successfully, the subconscious brain tells you that you should have similar success in the future. However, if you repeatedly fail to meet objectives, your subconscious will tell you to expect failure.

Pixabay.com

Is there any reason to remember the six steps for designing a reachable goal? *Have students do a pro/con chart on the whiteboard. The following is an example of what you want the outcome of this exercise to produce.*

Pros and Cons for Remembering Six Steps for Designing a Reachable Goal	
PRO	**CON**
• When you remember something, it is easier to do.	• More work
• If you learn the steps, you can use the steps on your own.	• Don't like memorization
• The brain is better able to apply the information it can recall quickly.	• Why remember them if you can look them up?
• These steps are something you might use for the rest of your life, so you need to remember them.	

It seems that there are more advantages to remembering the steps than not remembering the steps. Fortunately, there are tricks to remembering things faster.

The part of the brain that determines what you will remember, the hippocampus, pays attention to some things more closely than words alone. *The teacher can decide if she would like to teach the students the formal name for that part of the brain—hippocampus.* It pays attention to these things:

- Pictures (that is why there is a picture associated with each step)

- Movements (movements improve not only memory but comprehension too)

- Rhythm (that is why it is easier to remember songs)

- Repetition (this is the primary way the brain identifies what is critical)

The following pictures represent each step in the goal-setting process. Describe why the pictures represent each step: 30 seconds for short term, a bullseye for specific, a difficult rock climb for challenge, your reflection for realistic, a tape measure for measurable, and as predictable as a timepiece for automatic. Have students repeat the steps aloud while focusing on each image. After repeating the process three times, remove the words, and see if students can recall the steps by seeing the pictures alone.

1. **Short-term**

2. **Specific**

3. **Challenging (but achievable)**

4. Realistic

5. **Measurable with Feedback**

6. Automatic

Pixabay.com

To further improve recall, have students add a movement to each step. *The following are examples that the teacher can use or just use to spark ideas.*

1. Short-term—the thumb and index finger slightly separated

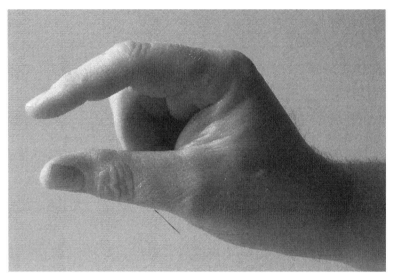

Pixabay.com

2. Specific—pointing

Pixabay.com

3. Challenge—a hand reaching out to grab something

Pixabay.com

4. Realistic—fist bump

Pixabay.com

5. Measurable—two arms spread apart, measuring a distance

https://www.istockphoto.com/portfolio/filistimlyanin

6. Automatic—typing on a laptop

Pixabay.com

Once students have learned the steps, set specific times to review. The consistent review of the steps prioritizes the importance of the information to the brain, improving recall. When information is remembered efficiently, it becomes less taxing to the brain, freeing the mind to focus on application.

We will use the goal-setting model when we begin class projects. Each time we use the goal-setting model, we can review the steps to improve efficient recall. The review process means that students will get enough repetition, so the brain will know that it is important.

If students are motivated, you could allow them to think of a rap or song to help them remember the steps even quicker.

Has anyone in the class ever really wanted to do something and failed? *A rhetorical question.*

- You wanted to play an instrument but did not practice.

- You wanted money but were not motivated to find a job.

- You wanted to get in shape but did not go to the gym regularly.

- You wanted to lose weight but could not stop eating foods that cause weight gain.

- You wanted to make the team but did not practice enough.

- You wanted to stop doing something but found yourself doing it anyway.

I think everyone here, including me, has wanted to reach a goal and failed. There are ways that we can improve our chances of meeting our goals. There has been lots of research done on how people can best reach their goals. The research has identified specific skills that increase the probability of achieving your goals. The key to successfully reaching our goals is to know and practice these skills.

Section 3

What can we do to help us reach our goals?

Simply put, you need to develop specific skills to reach your goals. Remember, personal goals are not different from other objectives; they take steps:

- Action

- Skill

- Lots of practice

- Effort

- Performance under pressure

- Willingness to fail many times

When the above elements are practiced, the opportunity for successfully achieving a goal is increased. Once you reach a goal, the brain will reinforce the practice with dopamine. The result is that remembering how good it feels after achieving a goal becomes a source of future motivation.

Six Skills to Achieving Goals

1. **Learn to establish and regularly meet goals.** We have already learned the steps for establishing a goal:
   - Short-term
   - Specific
   - Challenging
   - Realistic
   - Measurable
   - Automatic

Check to see if the following goals meet the six steps for designing a reachable goal.

- I struggle to practice the piano because I wait until the end of the day, and by that time, I am either too tired or just don't feel like practicing. Goal: Every day after I have my snack when I get home from school at 4:00 p.m., I will practice the piano for 20 minutes.
  - *Is it short term? No, it says every day.*
  - *Is it specific? Yes, after a snack at 4 p.m. for 20 minutes.*
  - *Is it challenging? Yes.*
  - *Is it realistic? No, because of saying every day.*
  - *Is it measurable? Yes, you can check for everyday practice and 20 minutes of practice duration.*

- I have problems doing my homework at my house because there are five younger brothers and sisters always running around, making noise and bothering me. Goal: During September, I will get off at the Ninth Street bus stop after school, walk to the library, and do homework for one hour before going home.
  - *Is it short term? Yes, one month.*
  - *Is it specific? Yes, get off at the Ninth Street bus stop after school and do homework at the library for one hour.*
  - *Is it challenging? Yes, 30 days.*
  - *Is it realistic? Yes, just 30 days, only weekdays, only one hour.*
  - *Is it measurable? Yes, Monday through Friday, one hour, one month*

Let's try to create our own short-term goal. I will give you a problem, and you write a short-term goal that meets the first five steps of designing a reachable goal.

- Ken said, "I want to try out for the basketball team, but I know my jump shot has to improve." Design a workable goal for Ken.

OR

- Brianna said, "I want to be a singer, but my music teacher, who is giving me free lessons, says he will drop me in one month unless he can tell that I have been doing my voice drill daily."

2. **Set up something in your environment to trigger meeting your goal.** Think of the many things in our environment that trigger behaviors:

Pixabay.com

- Morning alarm clock

Pixabay.com

- Stop light

Pixabay.com

- Police sirens

Pixabay.com

- A school bell

Since we know things in the environment can trigger behaviors, then we can set up something in our environment that will help us do the action we want to achieve. What kinds of things could we use right here at school to trigger a reaction? *The key here is for the teacher to help students understand that simple things in the environment can help them achieve their goals. The teacher can provide examples of something small in the environment that helps change behavior.*

Here are additional examples of effective environmental triggers *(implementation intentions)*:

Goal: Lose weight.

- Environmental trigger: Smaller plate
  - When I have dinner at home, I will use a smaller plate to reduce the size of my portions.

Goal: Drink more water.

- Environmental trigger: Place the water bottle on the desk at the beginning of each class.
  - Each time I place the water bottle on the desk, I will take a small drink of water.

Below are some possible ideas that your students should come up with:

- A school bell

- An image on the data projector

- A gesture by the teacher

- A music clip on a cell phone alarm

3. **Tell yourself what exactly you will do and when you will do it.** Your brain is more likely to reach a goal if you say, "I will do fifty push-ups right before I shower Monday through Friday," than if you say, "I will do push-ups every day."

What happens to the brain if you tell it a specific thing to do and when to do it?

- Just saying a specific action triggers the part of the brain responsible for physical movement. Those neurons fire like they are doing the activity.

- Mirror neurons are a set of neurons that activate when you execute a movement and when you see someone else performing the same action. If you do the action consistently when the brain expects the movement, mirror neurons play a film of you doing the action in your mind. The act replaying in your mind helps it become automated. Mirror neurons help us learn new behaviors faster to develop habits.

- Hearing yourself say the action over and over, produces belief in the human brain that you can do it.

- If you can picture yourself doing the action, the brain will help you get better at the action faster.

So there are concrete reasons to say what we will do, when we will do it, and to repeat the phrase over and over to ourselves.

4. **Tell yourself why it is essential that you meet a short-term goal.** Think about the things we learned concerning the benefits of goal setting and pick one that is important to you.

   - I need to meet short-term goals because I want to be able to focus better.
   - I need to meet short-term goals because I want to stop being so easily distracted.
   - I need to meet short-term goals because I want to feel motivated.
   - I need to meet short-term goals because I want to feel like I have self-control.
   - If you have a specific personal reason that is important to you, it will be even more meaningful for your brain.

5. **Eliminate negative triggers.** A student that wants to stop eating sweets should not go down the dessert aisle in the cafeteria.

   - Avoid walking past the bakery on the way to school.
   - Stop stashing sweets in your bedroom.
   - Ask your mom to stop buying your favorite cookies.
   - Don't stay up on weekends watching movies because this is when you binge.

Show the clip from the movie Flight *where Denzel Washington plays an alcoholic who was on the wagon until he sees a minibar in a hotel room.*

https://www.youtube.com/watch?v=yZbvbWznmaM

So when you set a goal, it is helpful to identify anything or anyone who might get in your way of achieving the objective; then, make a plan on how you can avoid or better handle the situation before it happens.

6. **Imagine success.** What would it look like if you achieve the goal? What will it feel like if you reach the goal? What other long-term goals will be closer?

Too many people plan for failure. They think of all the things that can go wrong. Assuming you can achieve changes the brain's chemistry and improves your opportunity to succeed. The mind automatically justifies whatever you are feeling. Often the term *realist* is merely the brain rationalizing negative thinking. Since the brain identifies every time your realistic fear comes through, the realist never wants to change. The brain counts all the times that being a realist is valuable and then forgets or never realizes when being realistic limits dreams from occurring. This process is called confirmation bias. The brain tends to notice things in the environment that support your beliefs and will overlook the things that contradict what you believe. The outcome is that our points of view often become entrenched with only partial information. However, you can be a realist and still strive to achieve challenging goals; just plan for actual obstacles, then believe in your plan and see yourself being successful.

Create new routines. Every goal requires practice. Practice makes things automated. Once something is automatic, it is easier for the brain to perform. Remember that with most new goals, there is a progression:

New	New things are usually harder to do in the beginning. Think about when you first learned to play a sport or ride a bike.
Slow	When you do something a few times, you assume that it will get easier faster than it usually does. The initial slow stage of progression is called *growing pains*—remember: you crawl, walk, run, and then run faster.
Average	You will reach a level when you can do something pretty well. Becoming reasonably good is the stage that most people become content because it takes a lot more effort to become highly skilled. The average level is the *push through stage*; you can get better, but you have to want it.
Good	The feeling of satisfaction—you can do the action so well now that it seems fairly effortless. The next stage is reserved for a select few, which is why many people rationalize not trying.
Great	When you put in extra time and your skills refine to the point where you are consistently better than good, it becomes more *automatic for you* than for most people.

Do not be discouraged if it is hard during the new and slow stage. Celebrate when you become average, but push through to good and then even to excellent. Every time your brain gets good at a new skill, it becomes stronger.

Show the film clip, What It Takes to Succeed.

https://www.youtube.com/watch?v=lsSC2vx7zFQ

Phase I—Practicing and Consistently Achieving Brief Goals

The teacher explains to students that she will establish some short-term goals for students to practice achieving. The goals will meet the six elements and incorporate the skills that will improve the opportunity to be successful.

Section 4

The following is an example of a brief classroom goal. The teacher should explain to students that the primary measure of goal attainment is for students to complete the problems without distraction; however, over time, students should also see academic improvement. When describing the measurable feedback, stress that students should not get frustrated or feel like they are not meeting the goal if the problems completed are not correct. If they consistently work on the objective of not being distracted, academic improvement will naturally occur.

What are the elements of successful goal setting?

During the month of September, we will begin math class with five problems on the board. The goal is to complete the five problems without being distracted and before doing anything else.

- Short-term goal
  - One month
- Specific
  - Five problems
- Challenging (but achievable)
  - Without being distracted (by anyone or anything)
- Realistic
  - Students will complete five problems at the beginning of the class for one month.
- Measurable with consistent feedback
  - Each day, I will provide you with an index card that has two scores from the day before:
    - ❖ Number of problems completed correctly

STANDARD	
Average	Three problems consistently correct
Good	3 to 4 problems consistently correct
Great	4 to 5 problems consistently correct

❖ Score on the ability to focus without distractions

➤ Students during this exercise have to become conditioned to self-evaluation. The majority of the personal goals they will set can be measured only by them. No teacher can monitor all forms of distraction that can take place since some can occur in the student's mind. The teacher needs to emphasize that students cannot experience the goals of this exercise unless they can be honest with themselves. Students are evaluating if their level of focus is improving and if the outcomes are evident in their academic performance. Get students conditioned to immediately make a small mark each time they lose focus during the exercise.

STANDARD	
Average	1 or 2 brief distractions with the ability to get back on track without adult intervention consistently
Good	0 or 1 brief distraction with the ability to get back on track without adult intervention consistently
Great	0 distractions consistently

- Automation
  - One month of practicing focusing without distraction will build confidence in the ability to achieve short-term goals.

Incorporate elements to improve students' opportunity to be successful

- Make sure all the components for designing a good short-term goal are present.
  - Short-term
  - Specific
  - Challenging
  - Realistic
  - Measurable
  - Automatic

- Set up something in your environment to trigger meeting your goal.
  - Use a music clip *(use the sound clip; the students will eventually associate with preparing to begin the goal-directed activity)*
  - I will have it play for about 20 seconds to trigger the actions needed to begin the short-term goal.
- Tell yourself exactly what you will do and when you will do it.
  - Each time the song plays, the following phrase will come up on the screen:
    - "When I hear the music, I will begin the five math problems and not be distracted until completed."
- Tell yourself why it is vital that you practice meeting the short-term goal.
  - *Have each student identify a personal reason they want to practice meeting the goal.*
    - I need to meet short-term goals because I want to be able to focus better.
    - I need to meet short-term goals because I want to stop being so easily distracted.
    - I need to meet short-term goals because I want to feel motivated.
    - I need to meet short-term goals because I want to feel like I have self-control.
    - Other personal reasons
- Eliminate negative triggers
  - *Have students write and put into an envelope anything that might hamper them from meeting their goal, and then seal it and turn it in.*
    - *Set a time to meet with each student to help them develop strategies for eliminating any negative triggers.*
    - *The students are placing the negative triggers into envelopes in case a negative trigger is a classmate or something confidential.*
    - *The meeting with the students will be private with the promise that whatever is discussed will be held in confidence.*
      - *Be careful not to discuss with other adults who are not in the classroom.*

- Imagine success
  - *Show a video of what it looks like when students are attending to an assignment.*
  - *Have students write what it will feel like when they are successful. Also, have students write what bigger goal or goals they would like to achieve.*

- Create new routines
  - *Honor time and ritual consistently.*
  - *Remind students periodically of phase expectations when they are at a new phase, slow phase, average phase, good phase, and great phase.*
  - *When students move from the new to slow phase, provide praise.*
  - *When students get to the average phase, do something special.*
  - *If they achieve the good or great phase, have a special celebration.*
    - ❖ Remember to establish standards and hold to them.

The teacher should create a new goal each month.

Note: Teachers will be tempted to increase the number of problems or the length of a task when students are successful. When learning to focus, it requires a high level of brain energy. Students must build the skill over time, or else the brief goal will be beyond their capacity, and they will lose motivation. Also, avoid using the short-term goal-setting, skill-building activities as merely a strategy to keep students on task during independent work times. The overuse might have the unintended outcome of destroying motivation. Make sure enough of the short-term goals are fun interactive activities.

Once students are consistently excelling in achieving short-term goals, introduce the module in Appendix B, titled "Promoting Hope and Expectation." In this module, you will introduce students to long-term goals and help them design a sequence of related short-term goals. When a student is working on a series of short-term goals related to a future long-term goal, they are working on obtaining a few protective factors:

- *Having a positive and realistic expectation for the future.*

- *Actively planning for the future.*

- *Feeling confident that life events are under her control, rather than controlled by luck or fate.*

Appendix B

Model Lesson: Promoting Hope and Expectation

The acquisition of hope and expectation is a protective factor that enables students who are vulnerable to poor life outcomes to shift their perspective from the present to the future. Many students from low SES do not engage in long-term planning, which results in reactionary behaviors. The absence of hope for the human brain is debilitating, and it causes a lack of motivation in activities such as school and a refusal to consider positive possibilities. Resiliency research determined that hope and expectation for the future are essential in at-risk students overcoming challenging environments to attain academic and vocational success.

The promoting of hope and expectation for the future can be accomplished in character education programs or any other model for teaching citizenship. This lesson incorporates elements found in the research that promote new long-term habits:

- Associate the protective factor to concrete actions that are done within the school setting.

- Develop non-verbal gestures to trigger desired behaviors.

- Consistently reinforce the practice.

- Maintain the action(s) associated with the protective factor to help students internalize the practice.

The adolescent has positive and realistic expectations for the future—standard for the protective factor being present:

It is important not to equate realistic to low expectations. Realistic expectations are objectives that one is actively striving to achieve. If the individual is taking clear and measurable steps to achieve desired goals, this protective factor is present. Clear, quantifiable measures are a sequence of short-term goals that enable the student to reach an identified long-term goal. When students are attaining short-term goals that relate to a long-term goal, they begin to embody future orientation. When a student from low SES starts to plan for the future, it helps combat the disparity and the lack of motivation often produced by poverty.

If this lesson is taught and consistently reinforced, it has the potential to help students acquire two protective factors:

1. The student has positive and realistic expectations for the future.

2. The student actively plans for the future.

━━━ ━━━ ━━━

The following module is for grades 9–12; however, it can successfully be used in upper middle school grades (*teacher instructions are in italics*).

Lesson Goals

- To learn that actions performed today can have a positive or negative impact on the future
  - Students often cannot see how achieving small steps toward a goal can have a profound impact on their future success.

- To provide a concrete approach for students to learn how to plan for the future

- To focus on developing concrete skills related to identified goals

Main Points

1. Life is cause and effect.

2. Small actions can have significant ramifications on life.
   - Small actions can include implementation intentions, channel factors, and short-term goals.
     - Implementation intentions support a goal by setting out in advance when, where, and how. For example, each time I check my cell phone, I will review one SAT word on the vocabulary list.
     - A channel factor is a stimulus that supports obtaining a goal or outcome—for example, consistently being the first person to show up for work because the boss always comes in early, will help in your bid for promotion.

3. It is imperative to be doing even small actions related to your goals.
   - Many initial steps toward achieving a long-term goal are small actions.
   - Small actions often aid skill development.
     - Planning where and when an action is done seems insignificant but can play a significant role in skill development.
     - A trigger in the environment to alert you to do an action is another small but essential step.
     - Imagining yourself completing the goal is another small action that improves the odds of being successful.

4. The most successful people adapt plans to ever-changing circumstances.
   - Life circumstances often cause many people to give up on their goals; however, some of the most successful individuals were fueled by failure or adapted their goals based on changing events.

The key to this module is helping students identify a long-term goal to shift the focus from the present to the future. The concrete skills will include planning and achieving short-term goals. Students should have established a pattern of meeting short-term goals based on the previous lesson on goal setting in Appendix A. *Remind students that achieving long-term goals is merely the ability to accomplish a sequence of short-term goals, which they have already established. When students think that they will be successful, the brain subconsciously supports the belief.*

Lesson

Life is cause and effect

It's like the domino effect—one event impacts another and then another.

Anything in life, from small to big actions, illustrates cause and effect. *It is recommended that the teacher either use a picture of dominoes along with a video of dominoes falling, or line up a set of dominoes and have students watch them fall in succession to demonstrate this point in an embodied cognition activity to enhance the lesson.*

A player makes a move, and another player attempts to make a countermove. *Find and show a video of a basketball player feigning a move and another player reacting to provide an illustration for this point.*

- Cause and effect

Someone spills some water on the restaurant floor, causing the waiter to slip and drop his drinks.

• Cause and effect

A boy chases a ball out into the street and gets hit by a car.

• Cause and effect

Exercise

The purpose of this exercise is for students to validate that life is cause and effect.

Give the class the first scenario. Then call upon students randomly to provide a possible subsequent event stemming from the prior situation. This process continues with the teacher occasionally dictating to a student when an effect has to be positive or negative. The reason a teacher wants to go back and forth from positive outcomes to adverse outcomes is to illustrate that cause does not dictate if an effect is ultimately positive or negative. Students need to believe that it is what they do in response to an event that will often determine how an incident will influence them.

Example:

> The teacher says, "A drunk driver runs a red light."
>
> The teacher then selects a student to provide an effect. The first student says, "And hits a family of five."
>
> The next student says, "The drunk driver lives."
>
> The following student says, "Only the two children in the other car live."
>
> The next student says, "The drunk driver is sent to prison."
>
> The teacher tells the next student, "Your effect has to be a positive effect resulting from the incident"; the student says, "A loving family adopts the two children."
>
> This pattern continues with the teacher occasionally dictating when a positive or a negative effect must be stated.

After the exercise, the teacher stresses the following point:

• *So you have proven that life is cause and effect.*

- *The universal law of cause and effect states that life doesn't just happen. Every action leads to another reaction.*

- *Most importantly, you have proven that we can make an adverse event into something positive!*

Rules for Planning for the Future

Rule 1—Life is cause and effect

Even small actions taken today can have a significant impact on the future.

During World War II, the Japanese often made distress calls claiming to be U.S. ships in trouble in the hope of luring ships into a trap. The United States began to ignore all such calls from areas where Japanese submarines had been sighted.

In 1945, the USS *Indianapolis* left Guam to ship to Leyte in the Philippines. A torpedo from a Japanese submarine hit it. It sank in twelve minutes; 896 men survived and made several distress calls. However, they were ignored because the U.S. Navy thought the calls were coming from the Japanese. Most of the survivors of the torpedo attack died from shark bites during the next four days. By the time they were rescued, only 317 men were alive.

In the 18th century, during the peak of the smallpox epidemic, a British scientist named Edward Jenner overheard a milkmaid say that people who had cowpox never seem to get smallpox. Cowpox was a harmless infection often suffered by children. Jenner then experimented. He infected an eight-year-old boy with cowpox and then exposed him to smallpox. That is how the smallpox vaccine was discovered.

After this section, the teacher should drive home the following points: Even small actions like a prank call or overhearing a casual observation made by a milkmaid can make a significant impact on the future.

- Little actions can have a big impact.
- Help students make the correlation that it is small goals that lead to big goals.
- Many initial goals are small and are not glamorous.

Rules for Planning for the Future

Rule 1—Life is cause and effect

Rule 2—Little actions can have a big impact

Got to be doing something *(This phrase is a play on words from a Michael Jackson song that can be used when covering this point.)*

While Alexander Fleming was working on how to treat the flu, he noticed that mold was growing in one of his petri dishes. Upon closer inspection, he realized that the area with the mold had no bacteria. After running some tests, Fleming discovered that mold was the key to fighting bacteria. Penicillin was born, and we still use it today to treat pneumonia, ear, skin, and throat infections. Fleming never discovered a cure for the flu.

After this section, the teacher drives home the following point: Great things happen while you are doing something, even if it has nothing to do with what you think your ultimate goal will be.

- **You got to be doing something**

Show a video clip that states that success is overcoming setbacks. An example is the Michael Jordan video, Why I Succeed.

Michael Jordan: Most people wouldn't believe that a man often lauded as the best basketball player of all time was cut from his high school basketball team. Luckily, Jordan didn't let this setback stop him from playing the game. He stated,

> *I have missed more than 9,000 shots in my career. I have lost almost 300 games. On 26 occasions I have been entrusted to take the game-winning shot, and I missed. I have failed over and over and over again in my life. And that is why I succeed.*

https://www.youtube.com/watch?v=JA7G7AV-LT8

Remind students that they already know this because when they learned to achieve a goal, they were taught to plan for obstacles and setbacks. "You got to be doing something" refers to the importance of continuing to work on short-term goals even if they seem small. Michael Jordan worked for hours on layups, dribbling, and jump shots despite initial failures. It was these small actions that helped him be able to make game-winning shots. When it comes to achieving goals, the key is always to be doing something. Achieving goals requires some grit. Show a video on the importance of grit in achieving goals. An example is, The Power of Grit—The Motivation Minute.

https://www.youtube.com/watch?v=EXE2mwZfmIc

Rules for Planning for the Future

> Rule 1—Life is cause and effect
>
> Rule 2—Little actions can have a big impact
>
> Rule 3—You have to be doing something

Survivors adapt to what life throws at them

- *The teacher should pose the question "Are you a survivor?" in a manner that students want to verbally or in writing respond "yes."*

Survivors adapt—you can change your plan, but you cannot fail to plan (you got to be doing something). People don't achieve goals while doing nothing toward those goals.

Survival of the fittest is the idea that species **adapt** to what is best suited to their situation.

Successful people adapt.

- The best chess players adapt to their opponent's moves.

- The best teams adapt to the opposing teams' defenses and offense.

- The best plans adapt to ever-changing situations.

Life is ever changing. We know this because of cause and effect. However, you have all proven that an adverse event can have a positive outcome. The key is that we always adapt. So you never avoid planning, because it is better to be doing something, no matter how small. As life changes, so will your plan, but the most successful people in life do not wait or just hope, they plan and they engage in actions that will help make their strategies a reality.

Remind students, they get to their long-term goal by reaching a sequence of short-term goals. Each short-term goal is valuable by itself because it ensures that we are learning and improving our brains. What happens if, on the way to being a singer, you learn to produce music and discover that you are good at it? You might not become a singer, but you have stumbled on a career that you love. Good things come when you are taking little steps to be successful. "Survivors adapt."

Rules for Planning for the Future

> Rule 1—Life is cause and effect
>
> Rule 2—Little actions can have big impacts

Rule 3—You have to be doing something

Rule 4—Survivors adapt

1. Soichiro Honda: Honda wanted to engineer motorcycles. He interviewed at several places, including Toyota Motor Corporation, for a job, and they all turned him down. After being unemployed for some time, he began building scooters at home. That led to him starting his own business. Today he is the founder of the billion-dollar company that is Honda.

2. Akio Morita: You may not have heard of Morita, but you've undoubtedly heard of his company, Sony. Sony's first product was a rice cooker that unfortunately didn't cook rice so much as burn it. A list of other failed inventions followed this. These setbacks didn't stop Morita from pushing forward to create a multi-billion dollar company.

3. Harland David Sanders: Perhaps he is better known as Colonel Sanders of Kentucky Fried Chicken. Sanders had a hard time selling his chicken at first. His famous secret chicken recipe was rejected 1,009 times before a restaurant accepted it.

A good rule for life is "survive and advance."

Exercise

Step 1

Before students can identify long-term vocational goals, they should experience exposure to a few options. Many students from low SES struggle to identify long-term professional goals because of a lack of exposure to possibilities. There is a difference between immediate employment opportunities and long-term vocation. Many surveys help students identify career options based on their skills and interests. It is also vital that students are exposed to a few long-term career opportunities before they identify a long-term vocational goal. The best way to achieve this is by having people who represent a range of career options speak to the students directly. These individuals should address some consistent information in addition to their personal story of what brought them to their profession when speaking to the class:

- How did you become interested in this profession?

- What makes it rewarding?

- What kind of person succeeds in this field?

- What are the qualifications?

- Where did you train, and how long did it take?

- How much did your education and training cost you?

- What is the average entry salary?

If getting individuals to address students is not possible, then use videos to inform students. Dedicate one or two weeks for short videos on different careers. The videos below provide an example of career videos. *Be sure to frame and anchor the experience.*

Framing, according to many psychologists, linguists, and cognitive scientists, is a process used to facilitate the thinking process (Goffman, 1974; Nelson et al., 1997, pp. 221–246). It is a process used to invoke a particular image or idea and attach it to another. Examples of framing are all around us, from politics to television. The term "liberal spending Democrats" was used by the Republicans to frame the fiscal policies of their rivals. This association became so strong that many people failed to take note that in a Republican-controlled government, spending was often higher. Polls showed that the general public associated two concepts linked, liberal spending to Democrats. When a teacher can introduce a new concept and associate it with something students feel positive about, it allows the brain to be more open to the idea.

Another technique teachers should utilize is anchoring. Anchoring is the technique that helps the brain value what has been framed. This step allows something that has just been introduced to gain internal importance to the brain (Krugman et al., 1985, p. 526). Anchoring is a psychological term used to describe the brain's tendency to use emotional values when making decisions. During the normal decision-making process, individuals rely on related information and values to reach daily conclusions. It is emotional values that influence behavioral patterns the most. Therefore, the decision-making process can be adjusted to consider new information if it is emotionally anchored to something students value. It has been established that the amygdala, the emotional brain, has three inherent values: safety, love, and success. Anchoring is the ability to help students feel like what has been framed makes them safer or successful. It is recommended that the teacher anchor to one of the universal values held by the amygdala because personal values vary.

Frame

For the next two weeks, we will be doing a series on professional careers. At the beginning of each class, we will watch a video on different types of jobs so you can get a better understanding of these vocations. Knowledge is power; the more you know, the more informed your decisions can be.

"Learning about professions empowers your future."

Anchor

One of the fascinating things in these videos is that many people began their careers by accident. They were doing an entry-level job and were allowed to learn or observe a profession and then became invested. When it comes to life achievements, we have already learned good things happen to people who are doing something. Anchoring is best achieved by an activity that helps students internalize a point.

Take students through a visualization exercise where they close their eyes and imagine three scenarios, and then have students write what they envisioned as the outcome for each one. The first scenario is what you will be doing four years from now if you have no life goal and make little effort in achieving any goal for your life. The second scenario is what you will be doing four years from now if you have a life goal, but you made no plan, and your effort in achieving it was not diligent. The third scenario is what you will be doing four years from now if you have a life goal, a good plan, and have done everything in your power to follow the plan to obtain your goal. Lead students in a brief discussion on which scenario they envisioned gave the best life outcome. The discussion should lead the students to conclude that having a plan with short-term objectives increases the belief that good things will happen.

Find videos of different professions if getting professionals to speak to the class is not appropriate. Below are merely examples of videos that expose students to various professions. Attempt to not limit the type of professions you expose students to. *The teacher may want to survey students on the professions they are interested in learning about in order to select relevant videos of interest.*

Chef

https://www.youtube.com/watch?v=YUtZzMGctdM

Auto technician

https://www.youtube.com/watch?v=b8ieaIfZKy4

Music producer

https://www.youtube.com/watch?v=R1S4KBwAjXE

Nurse

https://www.youtube.com/watch?v=cQoTnihTk0g

- Have students brainstorm and research possible long-term career goals.

- Then have each student submit in writing their long-term goal.

Step 2

The teacher should review student goals and obtain resources to help students research their identified objectives at a later date. Once the materials are in place, help students understand their goals better and identify specific skills and requirements that they will need.

- What
  - What do I have to accomplish in high school to qualify for my desired vocational objective?
  - What is the long-term goal?
  - What are the qualifications and requirements?
  - If a specific vocation is the identified goal, what is the average starting salary?
- When
  - By when can you achieve this goal?
- Where
  - If the goal requires education or training, where can you get it?
- How
  - How will you make this a reality? Include strategies for achieving academic qualifications, application completion, cost, and other expenses.

Please see an example of a completed form below:

Name: Randy Samos

- What is the long-term goal?
  - To become a chef

- What are your current academic objectives?
  - Improve math skills because cooking requires mathematical calculations to adapt recipes
  - Obtain enough credits to qualify for the senior year work release program
  - Graduate from high school on time
- What are the qualifications and requirements?
  - Although some people can work their way up in the restaurant business, some cooks own a restaurant and become chefs without formal training. There is also the customary way into the profession, which is to complete a culinary arts program.
  - I have selected to attend a culinary arts school.
- If a vocation is the identified goal, what is the average starting salary?
  - Chefs and head cooks earned a median annual salary of $48,460 in 2018, according to the U.S. Bureau of Labor Statistics (Bureau of Labor Statistics, 2018). On the low end, chefs and head cooks earned a salary of $26,320, and on the high end they earned $81,150. Because of the popularity of cooking networks, the number of chefs in America has been steadily increasing and is estimated to reach 154,000 by 2026. Full-time chefs often receive benefits such as medical and life insurance, paid days off, sick time, and retirement benefits.
- By when can you achieve this goal?
  - It is usually a two-year culinary arts program, but it might take three if you have to work while going to school.
- If the goal requires education or training, where can you get it?
  - The top five culinary schools that I am interested in are
    - Culinary Institute of America at Hyde Park, Hyde Park, NY
    - Institute of Culinary Education, New York, NY
    - International Culinary Center, New York, NY
    - Auguste Escoffier School of Culinary Arts, Austin, TX
    - L'Académie de Cuisine, Gaithersburg, MD
- How will you make this a reality: include strategies for cost and other expenses
  - Obtain my high school diploma
  - Complete the application and save up the submission fee of $500

- ○ Apply for tuition assistance because it is $21,600 per year
- ○ Set up a meeting with the student financial aid officer to learn more about financial aid options
- ○ If I do not get enough financial aid to attend, I can explore one of the many programs available for people who work during the day and attend nights and weekends.

Step 3

Once the teacher has assisted students with identifying and researching their long-term goal, students should follow the steps below:

Step (1) If I work toward this goal, where do I think I will be four years from now?

- Try to describe a destination, situation, or position, so you know where you are going.

Step (2) Why do I want to be there?

- Take into consideration your talents and desires, and try to identify what fits best.

Step (3) How can I get there?

- Identify the initial short-term goal to move toward your long-term goal. Once you have identified the initial step, put together a series of steps that will make a comprehensive plan.
- Don't forget that proper planning requires monitoring the progress regularly.

Step (4) What are the additional skills or training you will gain in the short term to make your long-term goal a reality?

- Growth can come only from learning new things.

Step (5) Who can help me get there?

- Role model
- Mentor—a mentor can offer objective feedback, advice, and support.

Example

Name: Randy Samos

Step (1) If I work toward this goal, where do I think I will be three years from now?

- Completing my culinary arts degree

Step (2) Why do I want to be there?

* Cooking is something I like to do, and I am good at it. A famous quote says do what you love for a living and never work a day in your life.

Step (3) How can I get there?

* Follow my plan and begin with the first short-term goal.

Step (4) Are there additional skills or training you will need to obtain in the short term?

* Complete high school (improve math skills, which is my weak subject)
* Get entry-level restaurant experience
* Learn money management

Step (5) Who can help me get there?

* My teacher
* Job specialist

* *Help students learn the difference between skills and qualifications.*

* *Teach students a concrete process for researching the skills and qualifications related to their goals.*

* *Give the assignment and collect completed work.*

Step 4

Activity

Materials

Magazines

Masking tape

Cornhole sets with bags (several)

Step 1

Have students who have identified a long-term goal look through magazines and identify a picture associated with their objective.

Step 2

Have students cut out the selected picture and glue it at the top of a sheet of paper, leaving enough room to write below the image.

Step 3

Have each student number one to five under the picture.

Step 4

Have students write five short-term goals that they can work on to achieve their long-term goals. The first short-term goal should be related to school so that the teacher can monitor it.

Example

GOOD EXAMPLE	POOR EXAMPLE
Name: Randy Samos	Name: Randy Samos
1. Work on completing math assignments in January. (Math is my worst subject and might prevent me from graduating from high school.)	1. Finish high school
2. For the next month, whenever I finish my English assignment, I will work on my culinary art school application and essay.	2. Apply to a culinary arts school
3. I will secure work release time from school for Wednesday (insert date) to meet with the financial aid advisor for college applicants.	3. Meet with the financial aid advisor
4. I will meet with the job placement officer at the high school on Tuesday after lunch to discuss getting a job at a local restaurant.	4. Get a job in a restaurant
5. When accepted, I will begin the culinary arts program in September of this coming fall.	5. Complete the culinary arts program

Pixabay.com

Support Plan for the First Short-Term Goal

Students who do not have self-regulation struggle to meet objectives. A history of not following through can establish a pattern of subconscious expectation of failure. As a result, the smallest setback can cause them to quit. Therefore, a plan that will help them follow through is advisable. The following are structured steps for supporting a plan to help students better meet their objectives.

- Set up something in your environment to trigger meeting your goal.
  - I will set the alarm on my watch to prompt me to begin my math homework.
  - When I hear the buzz tone, I will focus on math for one hour without distractions, in January.
- Tell yourself exactly what you will do and when you will do it.
  - When math class starts, I will focus on not being distracted.
  - If I do not understand a problem, I will request help from the teacher or aide.
  - I will begin math at 4:15 p.m. every day, Monday through Friday during January, and focus on assignments for one hour.
- Tell yourself why it is essential that you practice meeting short-term goals.
  - I am motivated to do better in math, so I can graduate and get into a cooking school.
- Eliminate negative triggers
  - I will not sit next to Josh during math class because I play around too much when I am next to him.
- Imagine success
  - I see myself getting my math homework back with scores of 85 or better in January.
- Create new routines
  - Action—work on math homework when the alarm goes off.
  - Valued by the amygdala—focusing on my academic weakness will make me more successful in math.
  - Visual cue—set the alarm on my watch with the picture of an A+ to signal when to begin my math homework.

   ○ Predictable and consistent practice—begin math homework at 4:15 p.m. during January.

   ○ Praise and reinforcement—I will treat myself to something from the school store every time I get a grade of "B" or better on a math assignment during January.

Final Activity

Once students complete their assignments, set up cornhole sets at one end of the room. Then tape five lines at two-yard intervals from the cornhole set. Have each student write their five short-term goals on individual index cards. Then have students take turns placing one goal on each line. The first short-term goal to complete should be set on the line ten yards away. Each line signifies a short-term objective in reaching the long-term goal. *Students will attempt to toss the beanbag into the hole first from 10 yards, then 8, 6, 4, and 2. The activity is an embodied cognition exercise designed to make concrete the abstract concept that attempting to reach a long-term goal without steps that get you closer is difficult.* The purpose of the activity is that as you accomplish each short-term goal, your long-term goal is closer and more attainable. Even if some students get the beanbag in from the farther distance, the odds are lower, and it involves luck. Make sure that each student attempts the shot at each yard marker and record the number that went in or missed at each yard mark.

Process Concrete Applications of Activity With Students

- Some students might be successful from 10 yards away, but it is hard to achieve a goal from that far away consistently.

   ○ The difficulty of meeting a long-term objective is why students worked on meeting a set of short-term goals to work toward a long-term objective (Appendix A—Goal Setting). Students should have learned not to shoot at a long-term goal from far away because it is harder to attain. The odds of success continue to increase the more short-term goals you achieve. Eventually, your long-term goal is directly in front of you, and you will be confident of success.

- As students toss the beanbag from 8 yards, then 6, then 4, then 2, what will happen is that the closer they get to the goal, the easier it is to achieve.

o People who focus on setting and meeting short-term goals are always progressing. Before they know it, they are closer to their goals. Individuals who just set long-term goals without a plan, often experience many failures because they want their goal immediately.

o All goals seem more attainable when closer to them.

Conclusion

The verbalization of future goals helps counteract the hopelessness present with many students from low SES. Therefore, the best use of this lesson is to have students review goals regularly and update what they have achieved and what is next.

Appendix C

Model Lesson: Having a Good Sense of Humor

The acquisition of the following protective factor enables students who are vulnerable to poor life outcomes to gain the capacity to improve their educational experience. Research demonstrates that every protective factor a student attains improves their ability to achieve better results in school and the community.

The promotion of protective factors can be a part of a character education program or any other model for teaching citizenship. This lesson incorporates elements found in the research that promote long-term behavioral change:

- Associate the protective factor to concrete actions that can be done within the school setting.

- Develop non-verbal gestures to remind or trigger desired behaviors.

- Consistently reinforce the practice.

- Maintain the action(s) associated with the protective factor to help students internalize the practice.

Having a Good Sense of Humor

Having a good sense of humor refers to an age-appropriate demonstration of a sense of humor. Look for the ability to take good-natured ribbing from peers and adults. A good sense of humor does not include morbid or sadistic qualities.

Teaching the lesson with consistent follow-up offers students the potential to acquire one protective factor and promote two others:

1. The student demonstrates a good sense of humor.
2. The student demonstrates empathy, caring behavior, and sensitivity to the feelings of others.
   - The ability to laugh with others is a form of empathy.
3. The student is generally considered likable by most people.
   - The ability to laugh with others is a trait that increases likability.

The following module is for grades 9–12; however, it can successfully be used in middle school grades as well *(teacher instructions are in italics)*.

The vocabulary mentioned below can be formally taught to assist with references in the lesson but is not required to teach the lesson.

Lesson Goals

- Learn why we laugh
- Understand the benefits laughter has on the human brain
- Learn why some people do not laugh as much as others
- Learn how to develop a healthy sense of humor

VOCABULARY WORDS		
Philosopher	Offers theories on questions in ethics, metaphysics, and logic	
Researcher	Systematically investigates a subject to discover facts, theories, and applications	

VOCABULARY WORDS		
Anthropologist	Studies the origins, cultural development, and social customs of humanity	
Behaviorist	Analyzes quantifiable behaviors to determine mental states	
Neuroscientist	Studies the structure and function of the nervous system	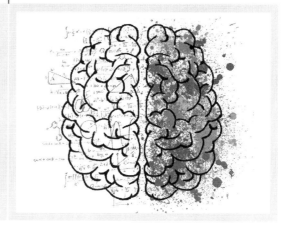

Pixabay.com

Show the following video or another video example of diverse people laughing. All videos in this lesson are merely examples that the teacher should view to see if appropriate for students or alternative film clips that the instructor prefers can be substituted.

https://www.youtube.com/watch?v=yLmd0100T9g

Lesson

Why Do We Laugh?

Key points:

- We laugh from birth to death.
- Laughing is a natural response.
- Most people laugh.

Philosopher

A philosopher named John Morreall believes that humans first laughed as a response to relieve tension after escaping danger. A person experiences a form of relaxation as a result of laughter because it lowers the level of arousal in the part of the brain responsible for "fight or flight" (amygdala; Morreall, 2009).

Researchers

Many researchers believe that the purpose of laughter is related to making and strengthening human connections.

Anthropologist

When people laugh together, they bond quicker, and it helps build trust, says cultural anthropologist Mahadev Apte. The bond it creates might be why laughter is contagious (Apte, 1985).

Behaviorist

Robert Provine believes that laughter, like a bird's song, functions as a kind of social signal. Other studies have confirmed the theory by proving that people are thirty times more likely to laugh in social settings than when they are alone. Even nitrous oxide, laughing gas, loses much of its effect when taken in solitude, says German psychologist Willibald Ruch (Provine, 2000).

The research of Greengross and Miller from the University of New Mexico shows that laughing "may be one of the most important traits for humans seeking mates." The ability to make another person laugh increases their attractiveness (Greengross & Miller, 2008).

Neuroscience

All of these reasons are good, but science has proven that we need to laugh to be healthy. How laughter improves health is the primary focus of the remainder of the lesson.

Is Laughing Good for You?

Relieves Stress

Dr. Lee Berk, at Loma Linda University's School of Allied Health and Medicine, found that laughter helps the brain regulate the stress hormones cortisol and epinephrine. Laughter also produces antibodies and endorphins, the body's natural painkillers (Berk et al., 1989).

In the 21st century, we have become a serious society with a culture that is polarized by politics, religion, and race. It is hard to make a joke without running the risk that someone will become offended. The American Association for Therapeutic Humor states that individuals often store negative emotions, such as anger, sadness, and fear, rather than expressing them. Laughter provides a way for these emotions to be harmlessly released.

Stress (Cortisol) Causes

- Exposure to stress can produce a state of fearfulness.
- Stress can impair physical development. Studies of the brains of abused children showed that physical growth is stunted during periods of mistreatment.
- Excessive cortisol levels contribute to hypervigilance, a state of paranoia that results in anxiety.
- Stress contributes to poor emotional intelligence; lowering the inability to read social cues accurately causes social awkwardness.
- Persistently elevated cortisol results in depression, which is a chemical state producing sadness, lack of motivation, and even anger.
- Stress increases the risk of acquiring a wide range of emotional disorders.
- Stress hurts the brain's ability to file information accurately, form long-term memories, and process the senses correctly.
- High levels of cortisol damage the hippocampus, which is the part of the brain responsible for initial memory and learning.

1. Laughing   Stress

Reduces

Pixabay.com

Have students repeat the four benefits of laughing. Begin with benefit number one. During each review, add a benefit, and remove the word under the picture of the prior benefit. Students will remember the word because of the visual cue.

Do You Think Society Has Become Too Serious?

Lead a discussion on whether society has become too serious. Then, introduce the concept of polarization and emphasize that whenever you focus the brain on differences, it leads to conflict.

Stabilizes Moods, Increases Attention, and Helps in Learning

Humor also helps to regulate the brain's dopamine levels (Mobbs et al., 2003). Dopamine is a hormone in the brain known as the reward hormone that helps stabilize mood, improve motivation, and increase attention and learning.

A Stanford team examined the brains of sixteen people as they viewed cartoons and rated them as either funny or not funny. The funny videos activated a crucial area of the brain involved in regulating dopamine. At the time of the study, there was no method available to track dopamine levels in the brain. However, they knew that when dopamine increased, it elevated the beta-endorphin hormone levels, which increases pain tolerance. This led them to measure pain tolerance and found that individuals watching funny video clips displayed increased pain tolerance. However, when individuals watching funny videos within a group laughed, their pain tolerance *significantly* increased.

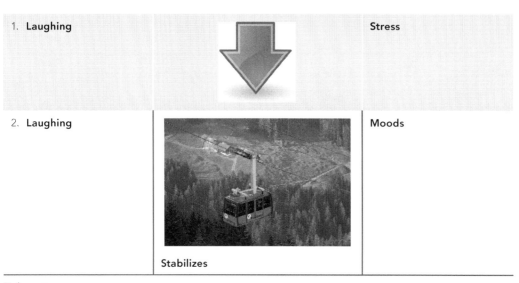

1. **Laughing**

Stress

2. **Laughing**

Moods

Stabilizes

Improves Health

Scientists at Loma Linda University had volunteers watch a twenty-minute video of a funny movie or a stand-up routine. Researchers found that laughing, along with some lighthearted comedy, lowered volunteers' blood pressure.

Laughing one hundred times is equal to ten minutes on the rowing machine or fifteen minutes on an exercise bike. Laughing can be a total body workout: it gives our diaphragm and abdominal, respiratory, facial, leg, and back muscles a workout. That is why you often feel exhausted after laughing too long.

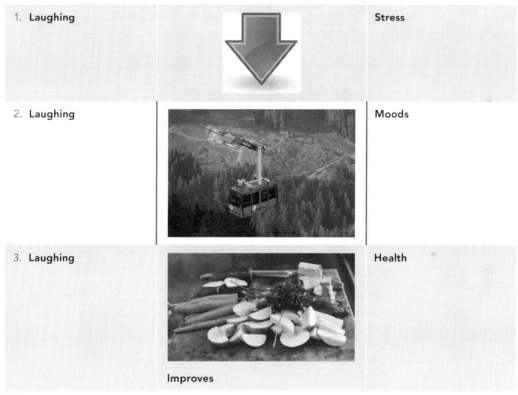

1. Laughing   Stress

2. Laughing   Moods

3. Laughing   Health

Improves

Pixabay.com

Aids in Recovery

A review of numerous studies suggests that humor and laughter can improve clinical outcomes in inflammatory disorders, asthma, cancer, and heart disease by reducing the physiological stress response (Hassed, 2001). Stress has more than physiological effects; it has psychological consequences as well. While there is sufficient evidence that laughter aids health and recovery, it should be noted that the claims that laughter can dramatically heal physical disease have not been validated by studies seeking to replicate their findings.

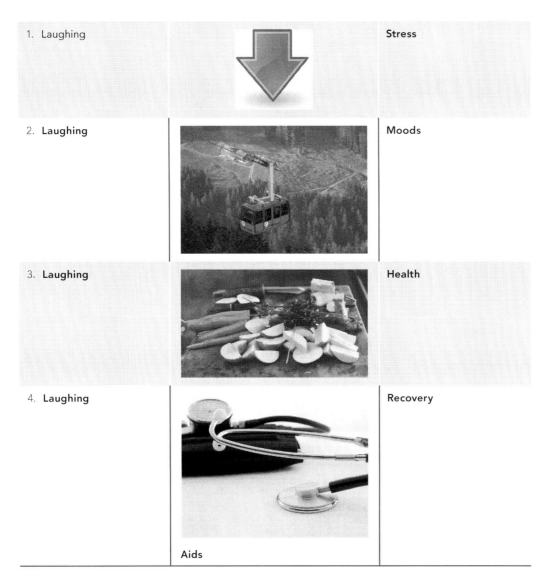

1. Laughing		Stress
2. Laughing		Moods
3. Laughing		Health
4. Laughing		Recovery
	Aids	

Pixabay.com

Pose the following question to students. Do you think laughing is good for you?

Why Do Some People Seldom Laugh or Laugh at the Wrong Things?

Laughter has an environmental, cultural, and experiential base. Comedians often draw on their life experiences to craft jokes. Most people who grew up in the inner city would struggle to relate to Jeff Foxworthy's "You Might Be a Redneck" comedy routine or humor made popular by Foxworthy that describes growing up as a poor, rural white southerner because of a lack of exposure. Some people who grew up in stressful circumstances condition themselves over time to laugh less.

While our environment, culture, and experience shape our sense of humor, it should not reduce our ability to laugh. People throughout history faced many life and death struggles; however, their ability to laugh kept them sane and stable.

Show the following video

Show a comedy video that focuses on humor related to a particular cultural or racial group. The exercise demonstrates how humor develops from our experiences and that a lack of understanding can alter the brain's ability to interpret something as funny. Example: Lewis Black's Christian interpreting the Tanakh (the Hebrew Bible) at https://www.youtube.com/watch?v=SC-nz71kmWE&t=4s

The teacher should emphasize the point that if a student did not find the video funny, their cultural awareness or personal experience is different from that of a Jewish person.

Pathological Laughter

Donald Stuss noticed that chemical imbalance, resulting from persistent stress or exposure to emotionally charged situations, lowers the ability of the frontal lobes to remain in charge, therefore producing what is called *pathological laughter* (Stuss & Benson, 1983). Pathological laughter is inappropriate laughter at things that are not funny or at other people's pain and misfortune. Antonia Damasio's research shows that pathological laughter does not have the positive effect on the brain that healthy laughter does (Damasio & Carvalho, 2013).

Can You Learn to Laugh More or at the Right Things?

Laugh Therapy

Dr. Madan Kataria states that replicating fake laughter like "ho, ho—ha, ha, ha" repeatedly has many of the same benefits of natural laughter (Kataria, 2002).

Show the following video as an example

Show a video on laugh therapy. Example: *Laugh With Me Session* by Bianca Spears at https://www.youtube.com/watch?v=wtoXb6_oxck

Consistently Expose Yourself to Opportunities for Laughter

People laugh more often when they are in groups. Groups that engage in activities designed to increase laughter increase their sense of humor, improve their brain's health, and socially get along better.

- It is essential to tell yourself it is OK to laugh.
  - People who don't frequently laugh often tell themselves not to laugh. Some individuals even take pride in the fact that other people are laughing, and they are not. They think laughing is a sign of weakness. The truth is, laughing is a sign of a healthy brain.

Show the following video as an example

Show a video about someone who does not seem to laugh. The goal is for students to see that most people known for not laughing appear to be scowling most of the time. Example: *Kevin Hart: Ice Cube Never Laughs* at https://www.youtube.com/watch?v=ltcS5ZtBymQ

Opportunities for laughter

- Watch funny videos, television shows, or movies
  - Degree of difficulty low—because it is passive, and you just have to react.

Show the following video as an example

Show a funny video. Example: *Key & Peele—Mr. Nostrand's Big Mistake* at https://www.youtube.com/watch?v=18t5V3gvfa4

- Tell jokes aloud to a group
  - Degree of difficulty moderate—telling a joke takes practice: how you say things and when you say something often determines if it is funny.
  - When you deliver a joke in a manner that makes people laugh, it requires the right timing.

Show the following video as an example

Show a video of a stand-up comedy show where the comedian demonstrates timing. Example: *Hard Working Indians/Bank Robbery* at https://www.youtube.com/watch?v=Tu_m5diSk4k

- Fake laugh out loud
  - Degree of difficulty high—you can't be self-conscious; just do it and keep on doing it (it gets easier and eventually can become fun).

Show the following video as an example

Show a video of someone doing laughter therapy. Example: *Laughter Therapy* by GloZell at https://www.youtube.com/watch?v=4ecfhEBIKWw

Let students know that it is crucial to set aside time for laughter. Making time to laugh is an easy way to ensure that you will have enough laughter in your life. As a result, we will set aside some mornings for laughter. The class will watch videos, read jokes, and even practice fake laughter.

Review the benefits

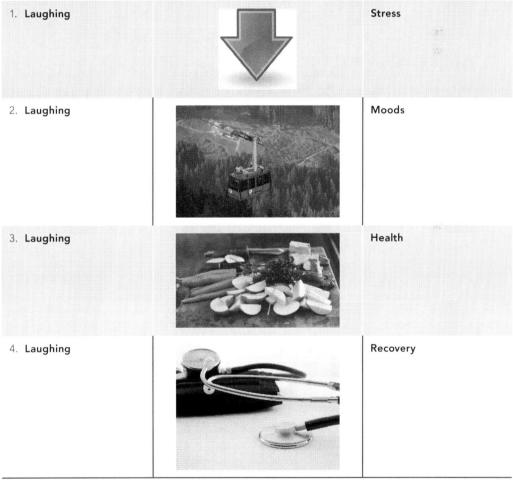

1. **Laughing**		Stress
2. Laughing		Moods
3. **Laughing**		Health
4. Laughing		Recovery

Pixabay.com

References

Adolphs, R. (2013). The biology of fear. *Current Biology*, *23*, R79–93.

Akalis, S., Banaji, M. R., & Kosslyn, S. M. (2008). Crime alert! How thinking about a single suspect automatically shifts stereotypes toward an entire group 1. *Du Bois Review*, *5*(2), 218.

Alexander, M. (2012). *The new Jim Crow: Mass incarceration in an age of color blindness*. New York, NY: New Press.

Almeida, D. M., Neupert, S. D., Banks, S. R., & Serido, J. (2005). Do daily stress processes account for socioeconomic health disparities? [Special issue] *The Journals of Gerontology. Series B: Psychological Sciences and Social Sciences*, *60*(2), 34–39.

Ambady, N., & Rosenthal, R. (1992). Thin slices of expressive behavior as predictors of interpersonal consequences: A meta-analysis. *Psychological Bulletin, 111*(2), 256–274. https://doi.org/10.1037/0033-2909.111.2.256

American Academy of Pediatrics. (1999). Early brain development and childcare. *Healthy Child Care America*, *3*, 5–8.

Apte, Mahadev L. (1985). *Joking relationships. In humor and laughter. An anthropological approach* (pp. 29–66). Ithaca, NY: Cornell University Press.

Bahník, Š., & Vranka, M. A. (2017). Growth mindset is not associated with scholastic aptitude in a large sample of university applicants.

Bailey, C. (2007). Cognitive accuracy and intelligent executive function in the brain and in business. *Annals of the New York Academy of Sciences*, *1118*, 122–141. 10.1196/annals.1412.011

Bailey, J. A., Hill, K. G., Oesterle, S., & Hawkins, J. D. (2009). Parenting practices and problem behavior across three generations: Monitoring, harsh discipline, and drug use in the intergenerational transmission of externalizing behavior. *Developmental Psychology*, *45*(5), 1214–1226. https://doi.org/10.1037/a0016129

Bandura, A. (1986). *Social foundations of thought and action: A social cognitive theory*. Englewood Cliffs, NJ: Prentice Hall.

Bandura, A. (1997). *Self-efficacy: The exercise of control*. New York: Freeman.

Bandura, A., & Schunk, D. H. (1981). Cultivating competence, self-efficacy, and intrinsic interest through proximal self-motivation. *Journal of Personality and Social Psychology*, *41*, 586–598.

Barber, B. K., & Harmon, E. L. (2002). Violating the self: Parental psychological control of children and adolescents. In B. K. Barber (Ed.), *Intrusive parenting: How psychological control affects children and adolescents* (pp. 15–52). Washington, DC: American Psychological Association. https://doi.org/10.1037/10422-002

Barnes, G. M., Hoffman, J. H., Welte, J. W., Farrell, M. P., & Dintcheff, B. A. (2006). Effects of parental monitoring and peer deviance on substance use and delinquency. *Journal of Marriage and Family*, *68*(4), 1084–1104. https://doi.org/10.1111/j.1741-3737.2006.00315.x

Baron, A. S., & Banaji, M. R. (2006). The development of implicit attitudes: Evidence of race evaluations from ages 6, 10 & adulthood. *Psychological Science*, *17*, 53–58.

Barr, M. S. (2012). Introduction. In: Barr M. S. (Ed.). *No slack: The financial lives of low-income Americans*. Washington, DC: Brookings Institution Press.

Bartlett, J. (1968). *Familiar quotations* (14th ed., revised and enlarged, p. 454). Boston, MA: Little, Brown.

Bean, R. A., Bush, K. R., McKenry, P. C., &
    Wilson, S. M. (2003). The impact of paren-
    tal support, behavioral control, and psycho-
    logical control on the academic achievement
    and self-esteem of African American and
    European American adolescents. *Journal of
    Adolescent Research*, 18(5), 523–541. https://doi
    .org/10.1177/0743558403255070

Beek, L.V., Ghesquière, P., Lagae, L., & Smedt, B.D.
    (2014). Left fronto-parietal white matter cor-
    relates with individual differences in children's
    ability to solve additions and multiplications: A
    tractography study. *NeuroImage*, 90, 117–127.

Bell, N. (2007). *Seeing stars*. San Luis Obispo, CA:
    Gander.

Berk, L. S., Tan, L., & Tan, S. (2008). Mirthful
    laughter, as adjunct therapy in diabetic care,
    attenuates catecholamines, inflammatory cyto-
    kines, C-RP, and myocardial infarction occur-
    rence. *FASEB Journal*, 22, 1226.2–1226.2.
    doi:10.1096/fasebj.22.1_supplement.1226.2

Berk, L. S., Tan, S. A., Fry, W. F., Napier, B. J., Lee,
    J. W., Hubbard, R. W., Lewis, J. E., & Eby,
    W. C. (1989). Neuroendrocrine and stress hor-
    mone changes during mirthful laughter. *American
    Journal of the Medical Sciences*, 298(6), 390–396.

Bernstein, M. J., Young, S. G., & Hugenberg, K. (2007).
    The cross category effect: Mere social categorization
    is sufficient to elicit an own-group bias in face rec-
    ognition. *Psychological Science*, 18, 706–712.

Berry, Christopher. (2004). School inflation. *Education
    Next*, 56–58.

Bettinger, E. P., Long, B., Oreopoulos, P., & Sanbonmatsu,
    L. (2012). The role of application assistance and
    information in college decisions: Results from the
    H&R Block FAFSA experiment. *Quarterly Journal
    of Economics*, 127(3), 1205–1242.

Birckhead, T., R. (2012). Delinquent by reason of
    poverty. *Washington University Journal of Law &
    Public Policy*, 38. Retrieved from http://works
    .bepress.com/tamar_birckhead/17/

Blackmon, D. A. (2008). *Slavery by another name: The
    re-enslavement of Black people in America from
    the Civil War to World War II*. New York, NY:
    Doubleday.

Blair, C. (2002). School readiness: Integrating
    cognition and emotion in a neurobiological
    conceptualization of child functioning at school
    entry. *American Psychologist*, 57(2), 111–127.

Blair, C., Granger, D. A., Willoughby, M., Mills-
    Koonce, R., Cox, M., Greenberg, M. T., . . .
    Fortunato, C. K. (2011). Salivary cortisol
    mediates effects of poverty and parenting on
    executive functions in early childhood. *Child
    Development*, 82(6), 1970–1984. https://doi.org/
    10.1111/j.1467-8624.2011.01643.x

Blair, C., & Raver, C. C. (2012). Child develop-
    ment in the context of adversity: Experiential
    canalization of brain and behavior. *American
    Psychologist*, 67(4), 309–318. https://doi.org/
    10.1037/a0027493

Blair, C., & Raver, C. C. (2014). Closing the achieve-
    ment gap through modification of neurocogni-
    tive and neuroendocrine function: Results from a
    cluster randomized controlled trial of an innova-
    tive approach to the education of children in kin-
    dergarten. *PLoS One*, 9:e112393. doi:10.1371/
    journal.pone.0112393

Blair, C., & Razza, R. P. (2007). Relating effortful
    control, executive function, and false belief
    understanding to emerging math and literacy
    ability in kindergarten. *Child Development*,
    78, 647–663. doi:10.1111/j.1467-8624.2007
    .01019.x

Blair, R. J. (2005). Applying a cognitive neurosci-
    ence perspective to the disorder of psychopathy.
    Developmental Psychopathology, 17, 865–891.

Blakemore, S. J., & Choudhury, S. (2006). Develop-
    ment of the adolescent brain: Implications for
    executive function and social cognition. *Journal
    of child psychology and psychiatry, and allied
    disciplines*, 47(3-4), 296–312. https://doi.org/
    10.1111/j.1469-7610.2006.01611.x

Blank, R. M., & Barr, M. S. (2009). *Insufficient funds:
    Savings, assets, credit, and banking among low-
    income households*. New York, NY: Russell Sage
    Foundation.

Boakes, N. (2009). The impact of origami-
    mathematics lessons on achievement and spatial
    ability of middle-school students. In *Origami4:
    Fourth International Meeting of Origami Science,
    Mathematics, and Education* (pp. 471–481). Boca
    Raton, FL: CRC Press

Bogira, S. (1987, September). They came in through
    the bathroom mirror: A murder in the projects.
    Chicago Reader, 16 (46), 2.

Booth, J. R., Burman, D. D., Meyer, J. R., Gitelman,
    D. R., Parrish, T. B., & Mesulam, M. M. (2003).

Relation between brain activation and lexical performance. *Human Brain Mapping, 19*(3), 155–169. https://doi.org/10.1002/hbm.10111

Booth, J. R., Burman, D. D., Meyer, J. R., Gitelman, D. R., Parrish, T. B., & Mesulam, M. M. (2004). Development of brain mechanisms for processing orthographic and phonologic representations. *Journal of Cognitive Neuroscience, 16*(7), 1234–1249. https://doi.org/10.1162/0898929041920496

Booth, J. R., Burman, D. D., Van Santen, F. W., Harasaki, Y., Gitelman, D. R., Parrish, T. B., & Marsel Mesulam, M. M. (2001). The development of specialized brain systems in reading and oral-language. *Child Neuropsychology, 7*(3), 119–141. https://doi.org/10.1076/chin.7.3.119.8740

Borman, G. D., & Overman, L. T. (2004). Academic resilience in mathematics among poor and minority students. *The Elementary School Journal, 104*(3), 177–195.

Borofsky, L. A., Kellerman, I., Baucom, B., Oliver, P. H., & Margolin, G. (2013). Community violence exposure and adolescents' school engagement and academic achievement over time. *Psychology of Violence, 3*(4), 381–395. https://doi.org/10.1037/a0034121

Bradshaw, C. P., Mitchell, M. M., & Leaf, P. J. (2010). Examining the effects of schoolwide positive behavioral interventions and supports on student outcomes: Results from a randomized controlled effectiveness trial in elementary schools. *Journal of Positive Behavior Interventions, 12*(3), 133–148.

Brainerd, C. J. (1978). The stage question in cognitive-developmental theory. *Behavioral and Brain Sciences, 1*(2), 173–182.

BrainyQuote.com. (n.d.). *Norman Vincent Peale quotes.* Retrieved from https://www.brainyquote.com/quotes/norman_vincent_peale_159750

Bransford, J. D., & Johnson, M. K. (1972). Contextual prerequisites for understanding: Some investigations of comprehension and recall. *Journal of Verbal Learning and Verbal Behavior, 11*(6), 717–726.

Brito, N. H., Fifer, W. P., Myers, M. M., Elliott, A. J., & Noble, K. G. (2016). Associations among family socioeconomic status, EEG power at birth, and cognitive skills during infancy.

Developmental Cognitive Neuroscience, 19, 144–151. https://doi.org/10.1016/j.dcn.2016.03.004

Brochard, R., Dufour, A., & Després, O. (2004). Effect of musical expertise on visuospatial abilities: Evidence from reaction times and mental imagery. *Brain and Cognition, 54*, 103–109.

Brody, G. H., Kim, S., Murry, V. M., & Brown, A. C. (2005). Longitudinal links among parenting, self-presentations to peers, and the development of externalizing and internalizing symptoms in African American siblings. *Development and Psychopathology. 17*, 185–205.

Brody, G. H., Murry, V. M., Gerrard, M., Gibbons, F. X., Molgaard, V., McNair, L. D., Brown, A. C., Wills, T. A., Spoth, R., Luo, Z., Chen, Y., & Neubaum-Carlan, E. (2004). The Strong African American Families Program: Translating research into prevention programming. *Child development, 75*(3), 900–917.

Brophy, J. (1999). Toward a model of the value aspects of motivation in education: Developing appreciation for. *Educational Psychologist, 34*(2), 75–85.

Brophy, J., & Good, T. L. (1985). Teacher behavior and student achievement. In M. C. Wittrock (Ed.), *Third handbook of research on teaching.* New York, NY: Macmillan.

Brown, R. (n.d.). *Extracurricular activity: How does participation encourage positive youth development?* [Fact Sheet 99-32]. Retrieved November 15, 2008, from www.unce.unr.edu/publications/files/cy/other/fs9932.pdf

Brown, S. A., Tapert, S. F., Granholm, E., & Delis, D. C. (2000). Neurocognitive functioning of adolescents: Effects of protracted alcohol use. *Alcoholism: Clinical and Experimental Research, 24*(2), 164–171. https://doi.org/10.1111/j.1530-0277.2000.tb04586.x

Brown, T. E., & Landgraf, J. M. (2010). Improvements in executive function correlate with enhanced performance and functioning and health-related quality of life: Evidence from 2 large, double-blind, randomized, placebo controlled trials in ADHD. *Postgraduate Medicine, 122* (5), 42–51. doi:10.3810/pgm.2010.09.2200

Brown, T. T., Lugar, H. M., Coalson, R. S., Miezin, F. M., Petersen, S. E., & Schlaggar, B. L. (2005). Developmental changes in human cerebral functional organization for word generation. *Cerebral Cortex*, *15*(3), 275–290. https://doi .org/10.1093/cercor/bhh129

Brüning, F., Noya, S. B., Bange, T., Koutsouli, S., Rudolph, J. D., Tyagarajan, S. K., Cox, J., Mann, M., Brown, S. A., & Robles, M. S. (2019). Sleep-wake cycles drive daily dynamics of synaptic phosphorylation. *Science*, *366*(6462), eaav3617.

Bruns, B., De Gregorio, S., & Taut, S. (2016). *Measures of effective teaching in developing countries* (RISE Working Paper Series). https://doi .org/10.35489/BSG-RISE-WP_2016/009

Bryson, D. (2016, January 23). Family and home, impact of the Great Depression on. In Robert S. McElvaine (Ed.), *Encyclopedia of the Great Depression* (Vol. 1: U.S. History in Context, pp. 310–315). New York: Macmillan Reference USA (2004).

Bugos, J. A., & DeMarie, D. (2017). The effects of a short-term music program on preschool children's executive functions. *Psychology of Music*, *45*(6), 855–867. doi:10.1177/0305735617692666

Buhl-Wiggers, J., Kerwin, J. T., Smith, J. A., & Thorton, R. (2017). *The impact of teacher effectiveness on student learning in Africa*. Centre for the Study of African Economies Conference, Oxford, England.

Burden, P. R., & Byrd, D. M. (2010). *Methods for effective teaching: Meeting the needs of all students* (5th ed.). Boston, MA: Allyn & Bacon.

Bushman, B., & Anderson, C. (2009). Comfortably numb: Desensitizing effects of violent media on helping others. *Psychological Science*, *20*(3), 273–277. doi:10.1111/j.1467-9280.2009.02287.x

Buu, A., & Dipiazza, C., Wang, J., Puttler, L., & Fitzgerald, H., Zucker, R. (2009). Parent, family, and neighborhood effects on the development of child substance use and other psychopathology from preschool to the start of adulthood. *Journal of Studies on Alcohol and Drugs*, *70*, 489–498. 10.15288/jsad.2009.70.489.

Cacioppo, J. T., & Berntson, G. G. (1994). Relationship between attitudes and evaluative space: A critical review, with emphasis on the separability of positive and negative substrates. *Psychological Bulletin*, *115*(3), 401–423.

Caggiano, V., Fogassi, L., Rizzolatti, G., Thier, P., & Casile, A. (2009). Mirror neurons differentially encode the peripersonal and extrapersonal space of monkeys. *Science*, *324*(5925), 403–406. https:// doi.org/10.1126/science.1166818

Caillois, R. (1965). *Au coeur du fantastique*. Paris, France: Éditions Gallimard.

Capron. C., & Duyme, M. (1989). Assessment of effects of socio-economic status on IQ in a full crossfostering study. *Nature*, *340*, 552–554.

Carlson, S. M. (2005). Developmentally sensitive measures of executive function in preschool children. *Developmental Neuropsychology*, *28*, 595–616. doi:10.1207/s15326942dn2802_3

Carr, L., Iacoboni, M., Dubeau, M.-C., Mazziotta, J., & Lenzi, G. (2003). Neural mechanisms of empathy in humans: A relay from neural systems for imitation to limbic areas. *Proceedings of the National Academy of Sciences, USA*, *100*, 5497–5502. 10.1073/pnas.0935845100.

Carstensen, L. L., Pasupathi, M., Mayr, U., & Nesslroade, J. R. (2000). Emotional experience in everyday life across the adult lifespan. *Journal of Personality and Social Psychology*, *79*, 644–655.

Case, G. A., & Brauner, D. J. (2010). Perspective: The doctor as performer: A proposal for change based on a performance studies paradigm. *Academic Medicine: Journal of the Association of American Medical Colleges*, *85*(1), 159–163.

Casey, P., Goolsby, S., Berkowitz, C., Frank, D., Cook, J., Cutts, D., Black, M. M., Zaldivar, N., Levenson, S., Heeren, T., & Meyers, A. (2004). Maternal depression, changing public assistance, food insecurity, and child health status. *Pediatrics*, *113*(2), 298–304.

Center on the Developing Child. (2013). *The science of neglect* (InBrief). Retrieved from http://www .developingchild.harvard.edu

Centers for Disease Control and Prevention. (2016). *ACEs in young children involved in the child welfare system*. Retrieved from http://www.flcourts .org/core/fileparse.php/517/urlt/ACEsInYoung ChildrenInvolvedInTheChildWelfareSystem .pdf and https://www.flcourts.org/content/ download/215886/file/ACEsInYoungChildren InvolvedInTheChildWelfareSystem.pdf

Champagne, F., & Meaney, M. (2006). Stress during gestation alters postpartum maternal care and the development of the offspring in a rodent model. *Biological psychiatry*, *59*, 1227–1235. 10.1016/j .biopsych.2005.10.016.

Chan, A., Ho, Y. C., & Cheung, Mei-chun. (1998). Music training improves verbal but not visual memory. *Nature, 396,* 128. 10.1038/24075.

Chan, S. (2006). Alum profile: Mollie Orshansky, June '31. *Alumnotes, 32*(3), 4–5.

Charles, S. T., Reynolds, C. A., & Gatz, M. (2001). Age-related differences and change in positive and negative affect over 23 years. *Journal of Personality and Social Psychology, 80*(1), 136–151.

Chavez, L. (2005, June 12). We were poor, but I didn't know it [Editorial]. *The New York Times* online. Retrieved from http://www.nytimes.com

Chetty, R., Friedman, J. N., & Rockoff, J. E. (2014). Measuring the impacts of teachers II: Teacher value-added and student outcomes in adulthood. *American Economic Review, 104*(9), 2633–2679.

Chomsky, N. (1959). On certain formal properties of grammars. *Information and Control, 2*(2), 137–167.

Christenson, S., Reschly, A. L., & Wylie, C. (2012). *Handbook of research on student engagement.* New York, NY: Springer.

Christian Advocate, The. (1945). They starve that others may be fed. *The Christian Advocate,* 1945. pp. 788–790.

Chu, M., Meyer, A., Foulkes, L., & Kita, S. (2014, April). Individual differences in frequency and saliency of speech-accompanying gestures: The role of cognitive abilities and empathy [published correction appears in *Journal of Experimental Psychology: General,* 143(2), 709]. *Journal of Experimental Psychology: General, 143*(2), 694–709. doi:10.1037/a0033861

Cikara, M., Bruneau, E. G., & Saxe, R. R. (2011). Us and them: Intergroup failures of empathy. *Current Directions in Psychological Science, 20,* 149–153. doi:10.1177/0963721411408713

Clayson, D. E., & Sheffet, M. J. (2006). Personality and the student evaluation of teaching. *Journal of Marketing Education, 28*(2), 149–160.

Clearinghouse, W. W. (2009). *READ 180.* What Works Clearinghouse Intervention Report. What Works Clearinghouse. See https://ies.ed.gov/ncee/wwc/

Collins, K., Connors, K., Davis, S., Donohue, A., Gardner, S., Goldblatt, E., Hayward, A., Kiser, L., Strieder, F., & Thompson, E. (2010). *Understanding the impact of trauma and urban poverty on family systems: Risks, resilience, and interventions.* Baltimore, MD: Family Informed

Trauma Treatment Center. http://nctsn.org/nccts/nav.do?pid=ctr_rsch_prod_ar and http://fittcenter.umaryland.edu/WhitePaper.aspx

Connor, C. M., Ponitz, C. C., Phillips, B. M., Travis, Q. M., Glasney, S., & Morrison, F. J. (2010). First graders' literacy and self-regulation gains: The effect of individualizing student instruction. *Journal of School Psychology, 48*(5), 433–455. http://dx.doi.org/10.1016/j.jsp.2010.06.003

Corballis, M. C. (2003). From hand to mouth: The gestural origins of language. In M. H. Christiansen & S. Kirby (Eds), *Language Evolution: The States of the Art* (pp. 199–260). New York, NY: Oxford University Press.

Corno, L. Y. N. (2008). On teaching adaptively. *Educational Psychologist, 43*(3), 161–173.

Covey, H. C., Menard, S., & Franzese, R. J. (2013). Effects of adolescent physical abuse, exposure to neighborhood violence, and witnessing parental violence on adult socioeconomic status. *Child Maltreatment, 18*(2), 85–97. https://doi.org/10.1177/1077559513477914

Cunningham, W. A., Johnson, M. K., Raye, C. L., Gatenby, J. C., Gore, J. C., & Banaji, M. R. (2004). Separable neural components in the processing of black and white faces. *Psychological Science, 15,* 806–813.

Daley, A., & Leahy, J. (2003). Self-perceptions and participation in extracurricular physical activities. *The Physical Educator, 60*(2), 13–19.

Damasio, A., & Carvalho, G. B. (2013). The nature of feelings: Evolutionary and neurobiological origins. *Nature Reviews Neuroscience, 14*(2), 143–152.

D'Argembeau, A., Ruby, P., Collette, F., Degueldre, C., Balteau, E., Luxen, A., Maquet, P., & Salmon, E. (2007). Distinct regions of the medial prefrontal cortex are associated with self-referential processing and perspective taking. *Journal of Cognitive Neuroscience, 19,* 935–944.

Davey, B. (1983). Think aloud: Modeling the cognitive processes of reading comprehension. *Journal of Reading, 27*(1), 44–47.

Davis, E. P., Bruce, J., & Gunnar, M. R. (2002). The anterior attention network: Associations with temperament and neuroendocrine activity in 6-year-old children. *Developmental Psychobiology, 40*(1), 43–56. https://doi.org/10.1002/dev.10012

Davis, J. C., Marra, C. A., Najafzadeh, M., & Liu-Ambrose, T. (2010). The independent contribution of executive functions to health related quality of life in older women. *BMC Geriatrics 10*, 16. doi:10.1186/1471-2318-10-16

Deci, E. L., & Ryan, R. M. (1985). *Intrinsic motivation and self-determination in human behavior*. New York, NY: Plenum Press.

Decker, D. M., Dona, D. P., & Christenson, S. L. (2007). Behaviorally at-risk African American students: The importance of student–teacher relationships for student outcomes. *Journal of School Psychology*, *45*(1), 83–109.

de Gelder, B., Snyder, J., Greve, D., Gerard, G., & Hadjikhani, N. (2004). Fear fosters flight: A mechanism for fear contagion when perceiving emotion expressed by a whole body. *Proceedings of the National Academy of Sciences of the United States of America*, *101*, 16701–16706.

de Jong, P. (2014). *Effects of training working memory in adolescents with a below average IQ*. Poster session at the workshop on Enhancing Executive Functions in Education in Nijmegen, Netherlands.

DeParle, J. (1990, September 3). In rising debate on poverty, the question: Who is poor? *The New York Times*, p. 10.

Diamond, A. (2014). Want to optimize executive functions and academic outcomes? *Minnesota Symposia on Child Psychology*, *37*, 205–232.

Diamond, A. (2016). Why improving and assessing executive functions early in life is critical. In J. A. Griffin, P. McCardle, & L. S. Freund (Eds.), *Executive function in preschool-age children: Integrating measurement, neurodevelopment, and translational research* (pp. 11–43). Washington, DC: American Psychological Association.

Diamond, A., & Lee, K. (2011). Interventions shown to aid executive function development in children 4–12 years old. *Science*, *333*, 959–964. doi:10.1126/science.1204529

Dichter, B. K., Breshears, J. D., Leonard, M. K., & Chang, E. F. (2018). The control of vocal pitch in human laryngeal motor cortex. *Cell*, *174*(1), 21–31.e9. https://doi.org/10.1016/j.cell.2018.05.016

Diego-Balaguer, R. D., Martinez-Alvarez, A., & Pons, F. (2016). Temporal attention as a scaffold for language development. *Frontiers in Psychology*, *7*, 44.

Dilworth-Bart, J., Poehlmann, J., Hilgendorf, A. E., Miller, K., & Lambert, H. (2010). Maternal scaffolding and preterm toddlers' visual-spatial processing and emerging working memory. *Journal of Pediatric. Psychology*, *35*, 209–220. doi:10.1093/jpepsy/jsp048

DiMatteo, M. R., Giordani, P. J., Lepper, H. S., & Croghan, T. W. (2002). Patient adherence and medial treatment outcomes: A meta-analysis. *Medical Care*, *40*(9), 794–811. https://doi.org/10.1097/00005650-200209000-00009

Dubow, E. F., & Ippolito, M. E. (1994). Effects of poverty and quality of the home environment on changes in the academic and behavioral adjustment of elementary school-age children. *Journal of Clinical Child Psychology*, *23*(4), 401–412.

Dubrow, N. F., & Garbarino, J. (1989). Living in the war zone: Mothers and young children in a public housing development. *Child Welfare: Journal of Policy, Practice, and Program*, *68*(1), 3–20.

Duggal, D., Sacks-Zimmerman, A., & Liberta, T. (2016). The impact of hope and resilience on multiple factors in neurosurgical patients. *Cureus*, *8*(10), e849. doi:10.7759/cureus.849

Duncan, G. J., Brooks-Gunn, J., & Klebanov, P. K. (1994). Economic deprivation and early childhood development. *Child Development*, *65*(2), 296–318. https://doi.org/10.2307/1131385

Duncan, G., Yeung, Wei-Jun, Brooks-Gunn, J., & Smith, J. (1998). How much does childhood poverty affect the life chances of children? *American Sociological Review*, *63*, 406–423. 10.2307/2657556

Dunham, Y., Baron, A. S., & Banaji, M. R. (2006). From American city to Japanese village: A cross-cultural investigation of implicit race attitudes. *Child Development*, *77*, 1268–1281.

Dunlosky, J., Rawson, K. A., Marsh, E. J., Nathan, M. J., & Willingham, D. T. (2013). Improving students' learning with effective learning techniques: Promising directions from cognitive and educational psychology. *Psychological Science in the Public Interest*, *14*(1), 4–58.

Durlak, J. A., Weissberg, R. P., Dymnicki, A. B., Taylor, R. D., & Schellinger, K. B. (2011). The impact of enhancing students' social and emotional learning: A meta-analysis of school-based universal interventions. *Child Development*, *82*, 405–432. https://doi.org/10.1111/j.1467-8624.2010.01564.x

Dweck, C. S. (2006). *Mindset: The new psychology of success*. New York, NY: Ballantine Books.

Eaton, W. J. (1970, April 4). The poverty line. *The New York Post*, p. 24.

Eberhardt, J. L., Goff, P. A., Purdie, V. J., & Davies, P. G. (2004). Seeing Black: Race, crime, and visual processing. *Journal of Personality and Social Psychology, 87*, 876–893.

Edin, K., & Lein, L. (1997). *Making ends meet: How single mothers survive welfare and low-wage work.* New York, NY: Russell Sage Foundation.

Egeland, B., Pianta, R., & O'Brien, M. A. (1993). Maternal intrusiveness in infancy and child maladaptation in early school years. *Development and Psychopathology, 5*(3), 359–370. https://doi.org/10.1017/S0954579400004466

Ehri, L., Nunes, S., Willows, D., Schuster, B., Yaghoub-Zadeh, Z., & Shanahan, T. (2001). Phonemic awareness instruction helps children learn to read: Evidence from the National Reading Panel's meta-analysis. *Reading Research Quarterly, 36*, 250–287. 10.1598/RRQ.36.3.2.

Eisman, A. B., Stoddard, S. A., Heinze, J., Caldwell, C. H., & Zimmerman, M. A. (2015). Depressive symptoms, social support, and violence exposure among urban youth: A longitudinal study of resilience. *Developmental Psychology, 51*(9), 1307–1316. https://doi.org/10.1037/a0039501

Elder, G. H. (1974). *Children of the Great Depression: Social change in life experience.* Chicago: IL: University of Chicago Press.

Elliott, G., Stock, J., & Rothenberg, T. (1996). Efficient tests for an autoregressive unit root. *Econometrica, 64*, 813–836. 10.2307/2171846.

Ensign, L. R., Overberg, P., & Andriotis, A. (2016, June 1). *Banks' embrace of jumbo mortgages means fewer loans for Blacks, Hispanics.* Retrieved from https://www.wsj.com/articles/banks-embrace-of-jumbo-mortgages-means-fewer-loans-for-blacks-hispanics-1464789752#comments_sector

Ensminger, M. E., Juon, H. S., & Fothergill, K. E. (2002). Childhood and adolescent antecedents of substance use in adulthood. *Addiction, 97*(7), 833–844. https://doi.org/10.1046/j.1360-0443.2002.00138.x

Evans, D. K., & Yuan, F. (2017). *Economic returns to interventions that increase learning* (Background paper, World Development Report 2018). Washington, DC: World Bank.

Evans, G. W. (2004). The environment of childhood poverty. *American Psychology 59*, 77–92. doi:10.1037/0003-066X.59.2.77

Evans, G. W. (2006). Child development and the physical environment. *Annual Review of Psychology, 57*, 423–451.

Evans, G. W., & Kim, P. (2007). Childhood poverty and health: Cumulative risk exposure and stress dysregulation. *Psychological Science 18*(11), 953–957.

Evans, G. W., & Schamberg, M. A. (2009). Childhood poverty, chronic stress, and adult working memory. *Proceedings of National Academy of Science USA, 106*(16), 6545–6549.

Evertson, C. M., Anderson, C. W., Anderson, L. M., & Brophy, J. E. (1980). Relationships between classroom behaviors and student outcomes in junior high mathematics and English classes. *American Educational Research Journal, 17*(1), 43–60.

Falconnier, L. & Elkin, I. (2008). Addressing economic stress in the treatment of depression. *American Journal Orthopsychiatry, 78*(1), 37–46.

Fallon, J. H. (2006). Neuroanatomical background to understanding the brain of the young psychopath. *Ohio State Journal of Criminal Law, 3*(2), 341–367.

Fang, X., Brown, D. S., Florence, C. S., & Mercy, J. A. (2012). The economic burden of child maltreatment in the United States and implications for prevention. *Child Abuse & Neglect, 36*(2), 156–165. https://doi.org/10.1016/j.chiabu.2011.10.006

Farah, M. J., Shera, D., Savage, J. H., Betancourt, L. M., & Hurt, H. (2006). Childhood poverty: Specific associations with neurocognitive development. *Brain Research, 1110*, 166–174.

Fecteau, S., Belin, P., Joanette, Y., & Armony, J. (2007). Amygdala responses to non-linguistic vocalizations. *NeuroImage, 36*, 480–487. 10.1016/j.neuroimage.2007.02.043.

Fehr, E. (2018, November). *Behavioral foundations of corporate culture* (UBS Center Public Paper Series No. 7), University of Zurich, Switzerland, UBS International Center of Economics in Society.

Feld, J., & Zolitz, U. (2017). Understanding peer effects: On the nature, estimation, and channels of peer effects. *Journal of Labor Economics, 35*(2), 387–428.

Fernald, A., Marchman, V. A., & Weisleder, A. (2013). SES differences in language processing skill and vocabulary are evident at 18 months. *Developmental Science*, *16*(2), 234–248. doi: 10.1111/desc.12019

Fernald, L., & Gunnar, M. (2009). Poverty-alleviation program participation and salivary cortisol in very low-income children. *Social Science & Medicine*, *68*(12), 2180–2189. 10.1016/j.socscimed.2009.03.032

Finn, J. D. (1993). *School engagement and students at risk*. Washington, DC: National Center for Education Statistics.

Fisher, G. M. (1992a). Poverty guidelines for 1992. *Social Security Bulletin 55*(4), 43–46. Retrieved from http://aspe.hhs.gov/poverty/papers/background-paper92.shtml

Fisher, G. M. (1992c). *The development of the Orshansky poverty thresholds and their subsequent history as the official U.S. poverty measure* (Unpublished paper). Retrieved from http://www.census.gov/hhes/www/povmeas/papers/orshansky.html

FitzGerald, S. (2013, July 22). "Crack baby" study ends with unexpected but clear result. *Philadelphia Inquirer*. Retrieved from http://articles.philly.com/2013-07-22/news/40709969_1_hallam-hurt-so-called-crack-babies-funded-study

Fitzpatrick, C., McKinnon, R. D., Blair, C. B., & Willoughby, M. T. (2014). Do preschool executive function skills explain the school readiness gap between advantaged and disadvantaged children? *Learn. Instruct*, *30*, 25–31. doi:10.1016/j.learninstruc.2013.11.003

Fitzpatrick, C., & Pagani, L. S. (2012). Toddler working memory skills predict kindergarten school readiness. *Intelligence 40*, 205–212. doi: 10.1016/j.intell. 2011.11.007

Flaisch, T., Hacker, F., Renner, B., & Schupp, H. T. (2011). Emotion and the processing of symbolic gestures: An event-related brain potential study. *Social, Cognitive and Affective Neuroscience*, *6*, 109–118.

Floden, D., Alexander, M. P., Kubu, C. S., Katz, D., & Stuss, D. T. (2008). Impulsivity and risk-taking behavior in focal frontal lobe lesions. *Neuropsychologia*, *46*(1), 213–223. https://doi.org/10.1016/j.neuropsychologia.2007.07.020

Francis, D. D., Champagne, F. C., & Meaney, M. J. (2000). Variations in maternal behaviour are associated with differences in oxytocin receptor levels in the rat. *Journal of Neuroendocrinology*, *12*, 1145–1148. doi:10.1046/j.1365-2826.2000.00599.x

Friderici, A. Villringer, A. Weiskopf, N. & Doeller, C. (Eds.). (2020, January). *Research Report 2017–2019*. Leipzig, Germany: Max Planck Institute for Human Cognitive and Brain Science.

Frierman, Frierman, S. H., Weinberg, R. S., & Jackson, A. (1990). The relationship between goal proximity and specificity in bowling: A field experiment. *The Sport Psychologist*, *4*(2), 145–154.

Fry, A. F., & Hale, S. (1996). Processing speed, working memory, and fluid intelligence: Evidence for a developmental cascade. *Psychological Science*, *7*(4), 237–241. https://doi.org/10.1111/j.1467-9280.1996.tb00366.x

Fullan, M. (2007). *The new meaning of educational change*. New York, NY: Routledge.

Gaillard, W. D., Balsamo, L. M., Ibrahim, Z., Sachs, B. C., & Xu, B. (2003). fMRI identifies regional specialization of neural networks for reading in young children. *Neurology*, *60*(1), 94–100. https://doi.org/10.1159/000067831 and doi:10.1212/wnl.60.1.94. PMID: 12525725

Gaillard, W. D., Hertz-Pannier, L., Mott, S. H., Barnett, A. S., LeBihan, D., & Theodore, W. H. (2000). Functional anatomy of cognitive development: fMRI of verbal fluency in children and adults. *Neurology*, *54*(1), 180–185. https://doi.org/10.1212/wnl.54.1.180

Garber, J., Robinson, N. S., & Valentiner, D. (1997). The relation between parenting and adolescent depression: Self-worth as a mediator. *Journal of Adolescent Research*, *12*(1), 12–33. https://doi.org/10.1177/0743554897121003

Gaser, C., & Schlaug, G. (2003). Brain structures differ between musicians and non-musicians. *Journal of Neuroscience*, *23*, 9240–9245.

Gasser, L., Grütter, J., Buholzer, A., & Wettstein, A. (2018). Emotionally supportive classroom interactions and students' perceptions of their teachers as caring and just. *Learning and Instruction*, *54*, 82–92. http://dx.doi.org/10.1016/j.learninstruc.2017.08.003

Gershoff, E., Aber, J., Raver, C., & Lennon, M. C. (2007). Income is not enough: Incorporating material hardship into models of income associations with parenting and child development.

Child Development, *78*, 70–95. 10.1111/j.1467-8624.2007.00986.x

Gianaros, P. J., Horenstein, J. A., Cohen, S., Matthews, K., Brown, S., Flory, J., Critchley, H., Manuck, S., & Hariri, A. (2007). Perigenual anterior cingulate morphology covaries with perceived social standing. *Social, Cognitive and Affective Neuroscience*, *2*, 161–173.

Gianaros, P. J., Horenstein, J. A., Hariri, A. R., Sheu, L. K., Manuck, S. B., Matthews, K. A., & Cohen, S. (2008). Potential neural embedding of parental social standing. *Social Cognitive & Affective Neuroscience*, *3*, 91–96.

Gianaros, P. J., Jennings, J. R., Sheu, L. K., Greer, P. J., Kuller, L. H., & Matthews, K. A. (2007). Prospective reports of chronic life stress predict decreased grey matter volume in the hippocampus. *Neuroimage 35*, 795–803.

Gianaros, P. J., Manuck, S. B., Sheu, L. K., Kuan, D. C., Votruba-Drzal, E., Craig, A. E., & Hariri, A. R. (2011). Parental education predicts corticostriatal functionality in adulthood. *Cerebral Cortex*, *21*(4), 896–910.

Giedd, J. N. (2004). Structural magnetic resonance imaging of the adolescent brain. *Annals of the New York Academy of Sciences*, *1021*, 77–85. https://doi.org/10.1196/annals.1308.009

Giedd, J. N., & Rapoport, J. L. (2010). Structural MRI of pediatric brain development: What have we learned and where are we going? *Neuron*, *67*(5), 728–734.

Giedd, J. N., Snell, J. W., Lange, N., Rajapakse, J. C., Casey, B. J., Kozuch, P. L., Viatuzis, A. C., Vauss, Y. C., Hamburger, S. D., Kaysen, D., & Rapoport, J. L. (1996). Quantitative magnetic resonance imaging of human brain development: Ages 4–18. *Cerebral Cortex*, *6*, 551–560.

Gilliam, W. S., D., Maupin, A. N., Reyes, C. R., Accavitti, M., & Shic, F. (2016). Do early educators' implicit biases regarding sex and race relate to behavior expectations and recommendations of preschool expulsions and suspensions? *Yale University Child Study Center*, *9*(28), 2016.

Gilmore, J. H., Shi, F., Woolson, S. L., Knickmeyer, R. C., Short, S. J., Lin, W., & Shen, D. (2012). Longitudinal development of cortical and subcortical gray matter from birth to 2 years. *Cerebral Cortex*, *22*(11), 2478–2485. https://doi.org/10.1093/cercor/bhr327

Gluck, M. A., Mercado, E., & Myers, C. (2008). *Learning and memory: From brain to behavior*. New York, NY: Worth.

Goffman, E. (1974). *Frame analysis: An essay on the organization of experience*. Cambridge, MA: Harvard University Press.

Gogtay, N., Giedd, J. N., Lusk, L., Hayashi, K. M., Greenstein, D., Vaituzis, A. C., Nugent, T. F., Herman, D. H., Clasen, L. S., Toga, A. W., Rapoport, J. L., & Thompson, P. M. (2004). Dynamic mapping of human cortical development during childhood through early adulthood. *Proceedings of the National Academy of Sciences of the USA*, *101*(21), 8174–8179.

Goldin-Meadow, S. (2003). Hearing gesture: *How our hands help us think*. Cambridge, MA: Harvard University Press.

Goldin-Meadow, S., Cook, S. W., & Mitchell, Z. A. (2009). Gesturing gives children new ideas about math. *Psychological Science*, *20*(3), 267–272.

Gollwitzer, P. (2012). Mindset theory of action phases. In *Handbook of Theories of Social Psychology: Vol. 1*. 10.4135/9781446249215.n26

Good, T. L., Biddle, B. J., & Brophy, J. E. (1975). *Teachers make a difference*. New York: Holt, Rinehart and Winston.

Good, T. L., & Grouws, D. A. (1977). Teaching effects: A process-product study in fourth-grade mathematics classrooms. *Journal of Teacher Education*, *28*(3), 49–54.

Goodwyn, S. W., Acredolo, L. P., & Brown, C. A. (2000). Impact of symbolic gesturing on early language development. *Journal of Nonverbal Behavior*, *24*(2), 81–103.

Gordon M. F. (1992). The development and history of the poverty. *Social Security Bulletin*, *55*(4), 3–14.

Goswami, U. (2015). *Children's cognitive development and learning*. New York, NY: Cambridge Primary Review Trust.

Gou, Z., Choudhury, N., & Benasich, A. A. (2011). Resting frontal gamma power at 16, 24 and 36 months predicts individual differences in language and cognition at 4 and 5 years. *Behavioural Brain Research*, *220*(2), 263–270. doi: 10.1016/j.bbr.2011.01.048

Gould, E., Cooke, T., Davis, A., & Kimball, W. (2015a). *Family budget calculator*. Washington, DC: Economic Policy Institute.

Grabe, H. J., Lange, M., Wolff, B., Volzke, H., Lucht, M., Freyberger, H. J., John, U., & Cascorbi, I. (2005). Mental and physical distress is modulated by a polymorphism in the 5-HT transporter gene interacting with social stressors and chronic disease burden. *Molecular Psychiatry*, *10*, 220–224.

Green, A. R., Carney, D. R., Pallin, D. J., Ngo, L. H., Raymond, K. L., Iezzoni, L., & Banaji, M. R. (2007). Implicit bias among physicians and its prediction of thrombolysis decisions for Black and white patients. *Journal of General Internal Medicine*, *22*, 1231–1238.

Greengross, G., & Miller, G. F. (2008). Dissing oneself versus dissing rivals: Effects of status, personality, and sex on the short-term and long-term attractiveness of self-deprecating and other-deprecating humor. *Evolutionary Psychology*, *6*(3), 393–408.

Griffin, K. W., Botvin, G. J., Scheier, L. M., Diaz, T., & Miller, N. L. (2000). Parenting practices as predictors of substance use, delinquency, and aggression among urban minority youth: Moderating effects of family structure and gender. *Psychology of Addictive Behaviors*, *14*(2), 174–184. https://doi.org/10.1037/0893-164X.14.2.174

Gromko, J. E., & Poorman, A. S. (1998). The effect of music training on preschoolers' spatialtemporal task performance. *Journal of Research in Music Education*, *46*, 173–181.

Gross, A. L., & Ballif, B. (1991). Children's understanding of emotion from facial expressions and situations: A review. *Developmental Review*, *11*(4), 368–398. https://doi.org/10.1016/0273-2297(91)90019-K

Gu, X., Liu, X., Guise, K. G., Naidich, T. P., Hof, P. R., & Fan, J. (2010). Functional dissociation of the frontoinsular and anterior cingulate cortices in empathy for pain. *Journal of Neuroscience*, *30*, 3739–3744.

Gunnar, M. R., Porter, F. L., Wolf, C. M., Rigatuso, J., & Larson, M. C. (1995). Neonatal stress reactivity: Predictions to later emotional temperament. *Child Development*, *66*, 1–13.

Guo, G. (1998). The timing of the influences of cumulative poverty on children's cognitive ability and achievement. *Social Forces*, *77*(1), 257–287.

Gvirsman, S. D., Huesmann, L. R., Dubow, E. F., Landau, S. F., Boxer, P., & Shikaki, K. (2016). The longitudinal effects of chronic mediated exposure to political violence on ideological beliefs about political conflicts among youths. *Political Communication*, *33*(1), 98–117. http://doi.org/10.1080/10584609.2015.1010670

Hackman, D., Farah, M., & Meaney, M. (2010). Socioeconomic status and the brain: Mechanistic insights from human and animal research. *Nature Reviews Neuroscience*, *11*, 651–659. https://doi.org/10.1038/nrn2897

Hadjikhani, N., & de Gelder, B. (2003). Seeing fearful body expressions activates the fusiform cortex and amygdala. *Current Biology*, *13*, 2201–2205.

Hadnot, I. J. (1999). The politics of poverty. *Dallas Morning News*, November 28.

Hagger, M. S. (2013). The opportunity cost model: Automaticity, individual differences, and self-control resources. *The Behavioral and Brain Sciences*, *36*(6), 687–726. https://doi.org/10.1017/S0140525X1300099X

Hair, N. L., Hanson, J. L., Wolfe, B. L., & Pollak, S. D. (2015). Association of child poverty, brain development, and academic achievement. *JAMA Pediatrics*, *169*(9), 822–829.

Hales, C. M., Fryar, C. D., Carroll, M. D., Freedman, D. S., Ogden, C. L. (2018). Trends in obesity and severe obesity prevalence in US youth and adults by sex and age, 2007–2008 to 2015–2016. *JAMA*, *319*(16), 1723–1725. doi:10.1001/jama.2018.3060

Halle, T., Forry, N., Hair, E., Perper, K., Wandner, L., Wessel, J., & Vick, J. (2009). *Disparities in early learning and development: Lessons from the early childhood longitudinal study-birth cohort* (ECLS-B). Washington, DC: Child Trends.

Hamre, B. K., & Pianta, R. C. (2005). Can instructional and emotional support in the first-grade classroom make a difference for children at risk of school failure? *Child Development*, *76*(5), 949–967.

Hanushek, E. A, Kain, J. F., Markman, J. M., & Rivkin, S. G. (2003). Does peer ability affect student achievement? *Journal of Applied Econometrics*, *18*(5), 527–544.

Harnad, S. R., Steklis, H. D., & Lancaster, J. (Eds.). (1976). Origins and evolution of language and speech. In *Annals of the New York Academy of*

Sciences (p. 280). New York, NY: New York Academy of Sciences.

Hart, B., & Risley, T. R. (1995). *Meaningful differences in the everyday experience of young American children*. Baltimore, MD: Paul H. Brookes.

Hassed, C. (2001). How humour keeps you well. *Australian Family Physician, 30*(1), 25–28.

Hassler, M., Birbaumer, N., & Feil, A. (1985). Musical talent and visual-spatial ability: A longitudinal study. *Psychology of Music, 13*, 99–113.

Hattie, J. (2009). *Visible learning: A synthesis of over 800 meta-analyses relating to achievement*. New York, NY: Routledge.

Hattie, J., & Timperley, H. (2007). The power of feedback. *Review of Educational Research, 77*(1), 81–112.

Hattie, J., & Yates, G. (2014). *Visible learning and the science of how we learn*. London, England: Routledge, Taylor & Francis Group.

Hayashi, T., Ko, J. H., Strafella, A. P., & Dagher, A. (2013). Dorsolateral prefrontal and orbitofrontal cortex interactions during self-control of cigarette craving. *Proceedings of the National Academy of Sciences of the USA, 110*, 4422–4427. PMID 23359677 doi:10.1073/pnas.1212185110

Heintzelman, S. J., Trent, J., & King, L. A. (2013). Encounters with objective coherence and the experience of meaning in life. *Psychological Science, 24*(6), 991–998. https://doi.org/10.1177/0956797612465878

Herbert, B. (1993, December 12). *A sea change on crime* [Jackson quote]. *The New York Times Archive*, Section 4, pp. 14–15. https://www.nytimes.com/1993/12/12/opinion/in-america-a-sea-change-on-crime.html

Herrmann, D., & Guadagno, M. A. (1997). Memory performance and socio-economic status. *Applied Cognitive Psychology, 11*(2), 113–120. https://doi.org/10.1002/(SICI)1099-0720(199704)11:2<113::AID-ACP424>3.0.CO;2-F

Hertzman, C., & Boyce, T. (2010). How experience gets under the skin to create gradients in developmental health. *Annual Review of Public Health, 31*, 329–347.

Hetland, L. (2000). Learning to make music enhances spatial reasoning. *Journal of Aesthetic Education, 34*, 179–238. doi:10.2307/3333643

Hewes, G. W., Andrew R. J., Carini L., Choe H., Gardner R. A., . . . Kortlandt, A. (1973). Primate communication and the gestural origin of language [and comments and reply]. *Current Anthropology, 14*, 5–24. 10.1086/201401.

Ho, Y.-C., Cheung, M.-C., & Chan, A. S. (2003). Music training improves verbal but not visual memory: Cross-sectional and longitudinal explorations in children. *Neuropsychology, 17*(3), 439–450. http://dx.doi.org/10.1037/0894-4105.17.3.439

Hoff, E. (2003). Causes and consequences of SES related differences in parent-to-child speech. In M. H. Bornstein & R. H. Bradley (Eds.), *Socioeconomic status, parenting and child development* (pp. 145–160). Mahwah, NJ: Lawrence Erlbaum.

Hoffman, M. L. (1982). Development of prosocial motivation: Empathy and guilt. *The Development of Prosocial Behavior, 281*, 313.

Hojat, M., Vergare, M. J., Maxwell, K., Brainard, G., Herrine, S., Isenberg, G., Veloski, J., & Gonnella, J. (2009). The devil is in the third year: A longitudinal study of erosion of empathy in medical school. *Academic Medicine, 84*, 1182–1191.

Holland, S. K., Plante, E., Weber Byars, A., Strawsburg, R. H., Schmithorst, V. J., & Ball, W. S. Jr. (2001, October). Normal fMRI brain activation patterns in children performing a verb generation task. *Neuroimage, 14*(4), 837–843. doi: 10.1006/nimg.2001.0875. PMID: 11554802.

Holmes, J., Hilton, K. A., Place, M., Alloway, T. P., Elliott, J. G., & Gathercole, S. E. (2014). Children with low working memory and children with ADHD: Same or different? *Frontiers in Human Neuroscience, 8*, 976. doi:10.3389/fnhum.2014.00976

Hughes, C., & Ensor, R. (2007). Executive function and theory of mind: Predictive relations from ages 2 to 4. *Developmental Psychology, 43*, 1447–1459. doi: 10.1037/0012-1649.43.6.1447

Hughes C., & Ensor, R. (2008). Does executive function matter for preschoolers' problem behaviors? *Journal of Abnormal Child Psychology, 36*, 1–14.

Hunter, J., & Csikszentmihalyi, M. (2003). The positive psychology of interested adolescents. *Journal of Youth and Adolescence, 32*, 27–35.

Hurt, H., Malmud, E., Braitman, L. E., Betancourt, L. M., Brodsky, N. L., & Giannetta, J. M. Inner-city achievers: Who are they? (1998). *Archives of Pediatric Adolescent Medicine, 152,* 993–997.

Huttenlocher, J., Waterfall, H., Vasilyeva, M., Vevea, J. L., & Hedges, L. V. (2010). Sources of variability in children's language growth. *Cognitive Psychology, 61,* 343–365.

Ispa, J., Fine, M. A., Halgunseth, L. C., Harper, S. A., Robinson, J., Boyce, L.A., Brooks-Gunn, J., & Brady-Smith, C. (2004). Maternal intrusiveness, maternal warmth, and mother-toddler relationship outcomes: Variations across low-income ethnic and acculturation groups. *Child Development, 75*(6), 1613–1631.

Jack, B. W., Chetty, V. K., Anthony, D., Greenwald, J. L., Sanchez, G. M., Johnson, A. E., Forsythe, S. R., O'Donnell, J. K., Paasche-Orlow, M. K., Manasseh, C., Martin, S., & Culpepper, L. (2009). A reengineered hospital discharge program to decrease rehospitalization: A randomized trial. *Annals of Internal Medicine, 150*(3), 178–187. https://doi.org/10.7326/0003-4819-150-3-200902030-00007

Jaschke, A. C., Honing, H., & Scherder, E. J. A. (2018). Longitudinal analysis of music education on executive functions in primary school children. *Frontiers in Neuroscience, 12,* 103. doi:10.3389/fnins.2018.00103

Jason, J. M., & Jarvis, W. R. (1987). Infectious disease: Preventable causes of infant mortality. *Pediatrics, 80,* 335–341.

Jennings, P. A., & Greenberg, M. T. (2009). The prosocial classroom: Teacher social and emotional competence in relation to student and classroom outcomes. *Review of Educational Research, 79*(1), 491–525.

Jha, A. P., Stanley, E. A., Kiyonaga, A., Wong, L., & Gelfand, L. (2010). Examining the protective effects of mindfulness training on working memory capacity and affective experience. *Emotion, 10,* 54–64. pmid:20141302

Ji, L. J., Nisbett, R., & Su, Y. (2001). Culture, change, and prediction. *Psychological Science, 12,* 450–456.

Jeynes, W., & Littell, S. (2000). A meta-analysis of studies examining the effect of whole language instruction on the literacy of low-SES students. *Elementary School Journal 101*(1), 21–33.

Johnson, M. H. (2001). Functional brain development in humans. *Nature Reviews Neuroscience, 2*(7), 475–483. doi:10.3389/fnins.2018.00103

Johnson, M. H., Halit, H., Grice, S. J., & Karmiloff-Smith, A. (2002). Neuroimaging of typical and atypical development: A perspective from multiple levels of analysis. *Development and Psychopathology, 14*(3), 521–536. https://doi.org/10.1017/s0954579402003073

Johnson, T. C., Stoner, G., & Green, S. K. (1996). Demonstrating the experimenting society model with classwide behavior management interventions. *School Psychology Review, 25*(2), 199–214.

Jones, A. P., Laurens, K., & Herba, C., Barker, G., & Viding, E. (2008). Amygdala hypoactivity to fearful faces in boys with conduct problems and callous-unemotional traits. *The American Journal of Psychiatry, 166,* 95–102. 10.1176/appi.ajp.2008.07071050.

Jones, J. (1985). *Labor of love, labor of sorrow: Black women and work and the family, from slavery to the present.* New York, NY: Vintage Books.

Just, M. A., Cherkassky, V. L., Keller, T. A., & Minshew, N. J. (2004). Cortical activation and synchronization during sentence comprehension in high-functioning autism: Evidence of underconnectivity. *Brain: A Journal of Neurology, 127*(Pt. 8), 1811–1821. https://doi.org/10.1093/brain/awh199

Kail, R., & Ferrer, E. (2007). Processing speed in childhood and adolescence: Longitudinal models for examining developmental change. *Child Development, 78,* 1760–1770. 10.1111/j.1467-8624.2007.01088.x.

Kalisch, R., Wiech, K., Critchley, H. D., & Dolan, R. J. (2006). Levels of appraisal: A medial prefrontal role in high-level appraisal of emotional material. *Neuroimage, 30*(4), 1458–1466.

Kaplan, J. (2020). *The genius of women.* New York, NY: Penguin Random House.

Karssen, A., Her, Song, Li, J., Patel, P., Meng, F., Bunney, W., Jones, E., Watson, S., Akil, H., Myers, R., Schatzberg, A., & Lyons, D. (2008). Stress-induced changes in primate prefrontal profiles of gene expression. *Molecular Psychiatry, 12,* 1089–1102. 10.1038/sj.mp.4002095.

Karter, A. J., Parker, M. M., Moffet, H. H., Ahmed, A. T., Ferrara, A., Liu, J. Y., & Selby, J. (2004). Missed appointments and poor glycemic control: An opportunity to identify high-risk diabetic patients. *Medical Care, 42,* 110–115.

Kataria, M. (2002). *Laugh for no reason* (2nd ed.). Mumbai, India: Madhuri International (ISBN 978-81-87529-01-9).

Katz, S. J., & Hofer, T. P. (1994). Socioeconomic disparities in preventive care persist despite universal coverage: Breast and cervical cancer screening in Ontario and the United States. *JAMA, 272*(7), 530–534.

Katznelson, I. (2013). *Fear itself: The new deal and the origins of our time.* New York, NY: Norton.

Keenan, J. P., Thangaraj, V., Halpern, A. R., & Schlaug, G. (2001). Absolute pitch and planum temporale. *Neuroimage, 14*(6), 1402–1408.

Kelm, Z., Womer, J., Walter, J. K., & Feudtner, C. (2014). Interventions to cultivate physician empathy: A systematic review. *BMC Medical Education, 14,* 219.

Kerkshaw, P., Irwin, L., Trafford, K., & Hertzman, C. (2005). *The British Columbia atlas of child development: Human early learning partnership* (1st ed.). Vancouver, BC, Canada: Victoria.

Keys, A., Brozek, J., Henshel, A., Mickelson, O., & Taylor, H. L. (1950). *The biology of human starvation* (Vols. 1–2). Minneapolis: University of Minnesota Press.

Keysers, C., Kaas, J. H., & Gazzola, V. (2010). Somatosensation in social perception. *Nature Reviews Neuroscience, 11,* 417–428.

Kim, J., Sorhaindo, B., & Garman, E. T. (2006). Relationship between financial stress and workplace absenteeism of credit counseling clients. *Journal of Family and Economic Issues, 27,* 458–478.

Kindermann, T. A. (2007). Effects of naturally existing peer groups on changes in academic engagement in a cohort of sixth graders. *Child Development, 78*(4), 1186–1203.

King, S., Mancini-Marie, A., Brunet, A., Walker, E., Meaney, M. J., & Laplante, D. P. (2009). Prenatal maternal stress from a natural disaster predicts dermatoglyphic asymmetry in humans. *Developmental Psychopathology, 21,* 343–353.

Kirchhoff, B. A., & Buckner, R. L. (2006). Functional-anatomic correlates of individual differences in memory. *Neuron, 51,* 263–274.

Kishiyama, M. M., Boyce, W. T., Jimenez, A. M., Perry, L. M., & Knight, R. T. (2009). Socioeconomic disparities affect prefrontal function in children. *Journal of Cognitive Neuroscience, 21,* 1106–1115.

Klingner, J., Tversky, B., & Hanrahan, P. (2011). Effects of visual and verbal presentation on cognitive load in vigilance, memory, and arithmetic tasks. *Psychophysiology, 48*(3), 323–332.

Knapp, M. S., Shields, P. M., & Turnbull, B. J. (1995). Academic challenge in high-poverty classrooms. *Phi Delta Kappan, 76*(10), 770.

Kochanska, G., Murray, K., & Coy, K. C. (1997). Inhibitory control as a contributor to conscience in childhood: From toddler to early school age. *Child Development, 68,* 263–277. doi: 10.2307/1131849

Koestner, R., Zuckerman, M., & Olsson, J. (1990). Attributional style, comparison focus of praise, and intrinsic motivation. *Journal of Research in Personality, 24,* 87–100.

Kolb, B., Wilson, B., & Taylor, L. (1992). Developmental changes in the recognition and comprehension of facial expression: Implications for frontal lobe function. *Brain and Cognition, 20*(1), 74–84. https://doi.org/10.1016/0278-2626(92)90062-q

Konrath, S. H., O'Brien, E., & Hsing, C. (2011). Changes in dispositional empathy in American college students over time: A meta-analysis. *Personality and Social Psychology Review, 15,* 180–198.

Kramarski, B., & Zeichner, O. (2001). Using technology to enhance mathematical reasoning: Effects of feedback and self-regulation learning. *Educational Media International, 38*(2–3), 77–82.

Kraus, M. W., Torrez, B., Park, J. W., & Ghayebi, F. (2019). Evidence for the reproduction of social class in brief speech. *Proceedings of the National Academy of Sciences of the USA, 116*(46), 22998–23003. https://doi.org/10.1073/pnas.1900500116

Krugman, M. E., Kirsch, I., Wickless, C., Milling, L., Golicz, H. J., & Tóth, A. (1985). Neuro-linguistic programming treatment for anxiety: Magic or myth? *Journal of Consulting and Clinical Psychology, 53*(4), 526–30.

Krugman, Paul. (2008, February 18). Poverty is poison. *The New York Times.* http://www.nytimes.com/2008/02/18/opinion/18krugman.html

Kuhl, P. K. (2010). Brain mechanisms in early language acquisition. *Neuron, 67*(5), 713–727. pmid:20826304. 10.1016/j.neuron.2010.08.038

Kuhl, P. (2011). Early language learning and literacy: Neuroscience implications for education. *Mind, Brain and Education: The Official Journal of the International Mind, Brain, and Education Society*, 5(3), 128–142. https://doi.org/10.1111/j.1751-228X.2011.01121.x

Kuzawa, C. W., & Sweet, E. (2013). Epigenetics and the embodiment of race: Developmental origins of U.S. racial disparities in cardiovascular health. In T. A. LaVeist & L. A. Isaac (Eds.), *Race, ethnicity, and health: A public health reader* (pp. 175–212). San Francisco, CA: Jossey-Bass.

Lamborn, S. D., Brown, B. B., Mounts, N. S., & Steinberg, L. (1992). Putting school in perspective: The influence of family, peers, extracurricular participation, and part-time work on academic engagement. In *Student engagement and achievement in American secondary schools* (Chapter 6). New York, NY: Teachers College Press.

Landry, S. H., Smith, K. E., & Swank, P. R. (2006). Responsive parenting: Establishing early foundations for social, communication, and independent problem-solving skills. *Developmental Psychology*, 42, 627–642. http://dx.doi.org/10.1037/0012-1649.42.4.627

Lane, K. L., Wehby, J., Menzies, H. M., Doukas, G. L., Munton, S. M., & Gregg, R. M. (2003). Social skills instruction for students at risk for antisocial behavior: The effects of small-group instruction. *Behavioral Disorders*, 28(3), 229–248.

Laplante, D. P., Brunet, A., Schmitz, N., Ciampi, A., & King, S. (2008). Project ice storm: Prenatal maternal stress affects cognitive and linguistic functioning in 5 1/2-year-old children. *Journal of the American Academy of Child and Adolescent Psychiatry*, 47, 1063–1067.

Lawson, G. M., & Farah, M. J. (2017). Executive function as a mediator between SES and academic achievement throughout childhood. *International Journal of Behavioral Development*, 41, 94–104. doi: 10.1177/0165025415603489

LeDoux, J. E. (2014). Coming to terms with fear. *Proceedings of the National Academy of Sciences*, 111, 2871–2878.

Lemov, D. (2015). *Teach like a champion 2.0: 62 techniques that put students on the path to college.* Hoboken, NJ: Wiley & Sons.

Leonard, J. A., Mackey, A. P., Finn, A. S., & Gabrieli, J. D. (2015). Differential effects of socioeconomic status on working and procedural memory systems. *Frontiers in Human Neuroscience*, 9, 554.

Leslie, K., Johnson-Frey, S., & Grafton, S. (2004). Functional imaging of face and hand imitation: Towards a motor theory of empathy. *NeuroImage*, 21, 601–607. 10.1016/j.neuroimage.2003.09.038.

Leventhal, T., & Brooks-Gunn, J. (2000). The neighborhoods they live in: The effects of neighborhood residence on child and adolescent outcomes. *Psychology Bulletin*, 126(2), 309–337.

Levin, D. T., & Banaji, M. R. (2006). Distortions in the perceived lightness of faces: The role of race categories. *Journal of Experimental Psychology: General*, 135, 501–512.

Levin, T., with Long, R. (1981). *Effectiveness instruction.* Washington, DC: Association for Supervision and Curriculum Development.

Lavy, V. (2010). *Do differences in schools' instruction time explain international achievement gaps? Evidence from developed and developing countries* (No. w16227). Cambridge, MA: National Bureau of Economic Research.

Light, J. (2013, September 18). Why is the federal poverty line so far off? *Moyers on Democracy.* Retrieved from http://billmoyers.com/2013/09/18/why-is-the-federal-poverty-line-so-low/

Lipina, S. J., & Colombo, J. A. (2009). *Poverty and brain development during childhood: An approach from cognitive psychology and neuroscience.* Washington, DC: American Psychological Association. Retrieved from http://psycnet.apa.org/books/11879

Lo, Y. Y., Loe, S. A., & Cartledge, G. (2002). The effects of social skills instruction on the social behaviors of students at risk for emotional or behavioral disorders. *Behavioral Disorders*, 27(4), 371–385.

Locke, E., & Bryan, J. (1966). The effects of goal-setting, rule-learning, and knowledge of score on performance. *The American Journal of Psychology*, 79(3), 451–457. doi:10.2307/1420886

Locke, E. A., & Latham, G. P. (1990). *A theory of goal setting and task performance.* Englewood Cliffs, NJ: Prentice Hall.

Locke, E. A., & Latham, G. P. (2002). Building a practically useful theory of goal setting and task motivation: A 35-year odyssey. *American Psychologist*, 57, 705–717.

Lu, M., & Halfon, N. (2003). Racial and ethnic disparities in birth outcomes: A life course perspective. *Maternal and Child Health Journal, 7,* 13–30. 10.1023/A:1022537516969.

Luby, J., Belden, A., Botteron, K., Marrus, N., Harms, M., Babb, C., Nishino, T., & Barch, D. (2013). The effects of poverty on childhood brain development: The mediating effect of caregiving and stressful life events. *JAMA Pediatrics, 167.* 10.1001/jamapediatrics.2013.3139

Luders E., Gaser, C., Jancke, L., & Schlaug, G. (2004). A voxel-based approach to gray-matter asymmetries. *NeuroImage, 22,* 656–664.

Lunkenheimer, E. S., Shields, A. M., & Cortina, K. S. (2007, May). Parental emotion coaching and dismissing in family interaction. *Social Development,* 232–248. doi:10.1111/j.1467-9507 .2007.00382.x

Lupien, S., King, S., Meaney, M., & McEwen, B. (2001). Can poverty get under your skin? Basal cortisol levels and cognitive function in children from low and high socioeconomic status. *Development and Psychopathology, 13,* 653–676. 10.1017/S0954579401003133

Johnson, L. B. (1964, January 8). *Annual Message to the Congress on the State of the Union.* [See *Online* by Gerhard Peters & John T. Woolley (1999)]. The American Presidency Project. http://www .presidency.ucsb.edu/ws/?pid=26787 And https:// www.presidency.ucsb.edu/documents/annual-message-the-congress-the-state-the-union-25

MacMillan, H. L., Boyle, M. H., Wong, M. Y., Duku, E. K., Flemming, J. E., & Walsh, A. (1999). Slapping and spanking in childhood and its association with a lifetime prevalence of psychiatric disorders. *CMAJ: Canadian Medical Association Journal, 161,* 805–809.

Magai, C., Cosedine, N. S., Krivoshekova, Y., S., Kudadjic-Gyamfi, E., & McPherson, R. (2006). Emotion experience and expression across the adult life span: Insights from a multimodal assessment study. *Psychology and Aging, 21*(2), 303–317.

Mani, A., Mullainathan, S., Shafir, E., & Zhao, J. (2013). Poverty impedes cognitive function. *Science, 341,* 976–980. 10.1126/science.1238041

Marsh, A. A., & Ambady, N. (2007). The influence of the fear facial expression on prosocial responding. *Cognition & Emotion, 21,* 225–247.

Marsh, A. A., Ambady, N., & Kleck, R. E. (2005). The effects of fear and anger facial expressions on approach- and avoidance-related behaviors. *Emotion, 5,* 119–124.

Marsh, A. A., Finger, E. C., Fowler, K. A., Adalio, C., Jurkowitz, I. T., Schechter, J. C., Pine, D. S., Decety, J., & Blair, R. J. (2013). Empathic responsiveness in amygdala and anterior cingulate cortex in youths with psychopathic traits. *Journal of Child Psychology and Psychiatry and Allied Disciplines, 54*(8), 900–910.

Marsh, A., Finger, E., Mitchell, D., Schneider, M., Sims, C., Kosson, D., Towbin, K., Leibenluft, E., Pine, D., & Blair, R. (2008). Reduced amygdala response to fearful expressions in children and adolescents with callous-unemotional traits and disruptive behavior disorders. *The American Journal of Psychiatry, 165,* 712–720. 10.1176/ appi.ajp.2007.07071145

Marstaller, L., & Burianová, H. (2013). Individual differences in the gesture effect on working memory. *Psychonomic Bulletin & Review, 20,* 496–500. 10.3758/s13423-012-0365-0.

Mason, K. (2017). *Executive function skills in deaf children: An intervention study* (Doctoral dissertation). University College London, England. Retrieved from https://discovery.ucl.ac.uk/id/ eprint/1553334

Mather, M., & Knight, M. (2006). Angry faces get noticed quickly: Threat detection is not impaired among older adults. *Journals of Gerontology, Series B: Psychological Sciences and Social Sciences, 61,* P54–P57.

Matthews, G. (2015). *Goal Research Summary.* Paper presented at the 9th Annual International Conference of the Psychology Research Unit of Athens Institute for Education and Research (ATINER), Athens, Greece.

Mazzocco, P. J., Brock, T. C., Brock, G. J., Olson, K. R., & Banaji, M. R. (2006). The cost of being Black: White Americans' perceptions and the question of reparations. *DuBois Review, 3,* 261–297.

McEwen, B. (2000). The neurobiology of stress: From serendipity to clinical relevance (2000, November 22). *Brain Research, 886*(1–2), 172–189.

McEwen, B. S. (1998). Protective and damaging effects of stress mediators. *New England Journal of Medicine, 338*(3), 171–179.

McEwen, B., & Gianaros, P. (2010). Central role of the brain in stress and adaptation: Links to socio-economic status, health, and disease. *Annals of the New York Academy of Sciences, 1186*, 190–222. 10.1111/j.1749-6632.2009.05331.x.

McEwen, B. S., & Wingfield, J. C. (2003). The concept of allostasis in biology and biomedicine. *Hormones and Behavior, 43*(1), 2–15. https://doi.org/10.1016/S0018-506X(02)00024-7

McLoyd, V. C. (1998). Socioeconomic disadvantage and child development. *American Psychologist, 53*(2), 185–204. https://doi.org/10.1037/0003-066X.53.2.185

McNamara, E., Evans, M., & Hill, W. (1986). The reduction of disruptive behaviour in two secondary school classes. *British Journal of Educational Psychology, 56*(2), 209–215.

McNeill, D. (1985). So you think gestures are nonverbal? *Psychology Review, 92*, 350–371.

Meltzoff, A. N., Kuhl, P. K., Movellan, J., & Sejnowski, T. J. (2009). Foundations for a new science of learning. *Science, 325*(5938), 284–288. https://doi.org/10.1126/science.1175626

Mensebach, C., Wingenfeld, K., Driessen, M., Rullkoetter, N., Schlosser, N., Steil, C., Schaffrath, C., Bulla-Hellwig, M., Markowitsch, H., Woermann, F., & Beblo, T. (2009). Emotion-induced memory dysfunction in borderline personality disorder. *Cognitive Neuropsychiatry, 14*, 524–541. 10.1080/13546800903049853.

Miendlarzewska, E. A., & Trost, W. J. (2014). How musical training affects cognitive development: Rhythm, reward and other modulating variables. *Frontiers in Neuroscience, 7*, 279. doi: 10.3389/fnins.2013.00279

Milam, A. J., Furr-Holden, C. D. M., & Leaf, P. J. (2010). Perceived school and neighborhood safety, neighborhood violence and academic achievement in urban school children. *The Urban Review, 42*(5), 458–467. https://doi.org/10.1007/s11256-010-0165-7

Miles, L., Nind, L., & Macrae, C. (2010). Moving through time. *Psychological Science, 21*, 222–223. doi:10.1177/0956797609359333

Mills, K., Goddings, A.-L., & Clasen, L., Giedd, J., & Blakemore, S.-J. (2014). The developmental mismatch in structural brain maturation during adolescence. *Developmental Neuroscience, 36*. doi:10.1159/000362328

Mobbs, D., Greicius, M. D., Abdel-Azim, E., Menon, V., & Reiss, A. L. (2003). Humor modulates the mesolimbic reward centers. *Neuron, 40*, 1041–1048.

Moffitt, T. E., Arseneault, L., Belsky, D., Dickson, N., Hanco, R. J., & Harrington, H. L. (2011). A gradient of childhood self-control predicts health, wealth, and public safety. *Proceedings of the National Academy of Sciences, 109*, 84–89.

Molina, E., Fatima, S. F., Trako, I., & Wilichowksi, T. M. (2018). *Teaching practices in Philippines.* (Policy Paper). Washington, DC: World Bank.

Morhenn, V. B., Beavin, L. E., & Zak, P. J. (2012). Massage increases oxytocin and reduces adrenocorticotropin hormone in humans. *Alternative therapies in health and medicine, 18*(6), 11–18.

Morreall, J. (2009). *Comic relief: A comprehensive philosophy of humor* (pp. 1–187). Oxford, England: Wiley-Blackwell. 10.1002/9781444307795

Morrison, F. J., Ponitz, C. C., & McClelland, M. M. (2010). Self-regulation and academic achievement in the transition to school. In S. D. Calkins & M. A. Bell (Eds.), *Child development at the intersection of emotion and cognition* (pp. 203–224). Washington, DC: American Psychological Association. doi:10.1037/12059-011

Morrison, I., Lloyd, D. M., Pellegrino, G., & Roberts, N. (2004). Vicarious responses to pain in anterior cingulate cortex: Is empathy a multisensory issue? *Cognitive, Affective, & Behavioral Neuroscience, 4*, 270–278.

Mulder, H., Verhagen, J., Van der Ven, S. H. G., Slot, P. L., & Leseman, P. P. M. (2017). Early executive function at age two predicts emergent mathematics and literacy at age five. *Frontiers in Psychology, 8*, 1706. doi: 10.3389/fpsyg.2017.01706

Murakami, E., & Young, J. Y. (1997). *Daily travel by persons with low income.* Paper presented at the NPTS symposium in Bethesda, Maryland, October 29–31. Washington, DC: Federal Highway Administration, U.S. Department of Travel.

Murphey, D., Cooper, M., & Forry, N. (2013). *The youngest Americans: A statistical portrait of infants and toddlers in the United States.* Washington, DC: Child Trends.

Naftulin, D. H., Ware, J. E., & Donnelly, F. A. (1973). The Doctor Fox lecture: A paradigm of educational seduction. *Journal of Medical Education, 48*, 630–635.

Najman, J., Clavarino, A., McGee, T., Bor, W., Williams, G., & Hayatbakhsh, M. (2010). Timing and chronicity of family poverty and development of unhealthy behaviors in children: A longitudinal study. *The Journal of Adolescent Health: Official Publication of the Society for Adolescent Medicine, 46*(6), 538–544.

National Research Council, Bransford, J., Pellegrino, J. W., & Donovan, S. (2001). *How people learn: Bridging research and practice.* Washington, DC: National Academies Press.

Neal, R. D., Lawlor, D. A., Allgar, V., Colledge, M. A., Ali, S., Hassey, A., Portz, C., & Wilson, A. (2001). Missed appointments in general practice: Retrospective data analysis from four practices. *The British Journal of General Practice: The Journal of the Royal College of General Practitioners, 51*(471), 830–832.

Nelson, T. E., Oxley, Z. M., & Clawson, R. A. (1997). Toward a psychology of framing effects. *Political Behavior, 19*, 221–246.

Neville, H. J., Stevens, C., Pakulak, E., Bell, T. A., Fanning, J., Klen, S., & Isbell, E. (2013). Family-based training program improves brain function, cognition, and behavior in lower socioeconomic status preschoolers. *Proceedings of the National Academy of Science, 110*, 12128–12143.

Newman, S. D., Just, M. A., Keller, T. A., Roth, J., & Carpenter, P. A. (2003). Differential effects of syntactic and semantic processing on the subregions of Broca's area: Brain research. *Cognitive Brain Research, 16*(2), 297–307. https://doi.org/10.1016/s0926-6410(02)00285-9

Nicol, D. J., & Macfarlane-Dick, D. (2006). Formative assessment and self-regulated learning: A model and seven principles of good feedback practice. *Studies in Higher Education, 31*(2), 199–218. doi:10.1080/03075070600572090

Niebuhr, R. (1956). Intellectual autobiography of Reinhold Niebuhr. In C. W. Kegley & R. W. Bretall (Eds.), *Reinhold Niebuhr: His religious, social, and political thought* (pp. 1–24). New York, NY: Macmillan.

Niedenthal, P., Winkielman, P., & Mondillon, L., & Vermeulen, N. (2009). Embodiment of emotion concepts. *Journal of Personality and Social Psychology, 96*, 1120–1136. 10.1037/a0015574

Nisbett, R. E. (2009). *Intelligence and how to get it: Why schools and cultures count.* New York, NY: Norton.

Noble, K. G., Engelhardt, L. E., Brito, N. H., Mack, L. J., Nail, E. J., Angal, J., Barr, R., Fifer, W. P., & Elliott, A. J. (2015). Socioeconomic disparities in neurocognitive development in the first two years of life. *Developmental Psychobiology, 57*(5), 535–551.

Noble, K. G., & McCandliss, B. (2005). Reading development and impairment: Behavioral, social, and neurobiological factors. *Journal of Developmental and Behavioral Pediatrics 26*, 370–378. 10.1097/00004703-200510000-00006

Noble, K. G., McCandliss, B., & Farah, M. (2007). Socioeconomic gradients predict individual differences in neurocognitive abilities. *Developmental Science 10*, 464–480. 10.1111/j.1467-7687.2007.00600.x

Noble, K. G., Norman, M., & Farah, M. (2005). Neurocognitive correlates of socioeconomic status in kindergarten children. *Developmental Science, 8*, 74–87. 10.1111/j.1467-7687.2005.00394.x

Noble, K. G., Tottenham, K. G., & Casey, K. G. (2005). Neuroscience perspectives on disparities in school readiness and cognitive achievement. *The Future of Children, 15*, 71–89.

Noble, K. G., Wolmetz, M., Ochs, L., Farah, M., & McCandliss, B. (2006). Brain-behavior relationships in reading acquisition are modulated by socioeconomic factors. *Developmental Science, 9*, 642–654. 10.1111/j.1467-7687.2006.00542.x

Nordsletten, A. E., Larsson, H., Crowley, J. J., Almqvist, C., Lichtenstein, P., & Mataix-Cols, D. (2016). Patterns of nonrandom mating within and across 11 major psychiatric disorders. *JAMA Psychiatry, 73*(4), 354–361.

Normandeau, S., & Guay, F. (1998). Preschool behavior and first-grade school achievement: The mediational role of cognitive self-control. *Journal of Educational Psychology, 90*(1), 111–121.

Noya, S. B., Colameo, D., Brüning, F., Spinnler, A., Mircsof, D., Opitz, L., Mann, M., Tyagarajan, S. K., Robles, M. S., & Brown, S. A. (2019). The forebrain synaptic transcriptome is organized by clocks but its proteome is driven by sleep. *Science, 366*(6462), eaav2642. https://doi.org/10.1126/science.aav2642

O'Brennan, L. M., Waasdorp, T. E., & Bradshaw, C. P. (2014). Strengthening bullying prevention through school staff connectedness. *Journal of Educational Psychology, 106*(3), 870.

Office of Juvenile Justice and Delinquency Prevention [OJJDP]. *Statistical briefing book.* (2017). U.S. Department of Justice. Retrieved from http://www.ojjdp.gov/ojstatbb/court/qa06206.asp?qaDate=2014

Okonofua, J. A., & Eberhardt, J. L. (2015). Two strikes: Race and the disciplining of young students. *Psychological Science, 26,* 617–624. doi:10.1177/0956797615570365

Oliveira, V. (2016). *The food assistance landscape: FY 2016 Annual Report* [EIB-169. U.S. Department of Agriculture]. Retrieved from https://www.ers.usda.gov/webdocs/publications/82994/eib-169.pdf?v=0

Olofsson, J. K., Nordin, S., Sequeira, H., & Polich, J. (2008). Affective picture processing: An integrative review of ERP findings. *Biological Psychology, 77,* 247–65.

Orshansky, M. (1957). Food consumption of families today. *Nutrition Committee News* (Institute of Home Economics, Agricultural Research Service, U.S. Department of Agriculture), March-April, pp. 1–8.

Orshansky, M. (1963, July). Children of the poor. *Social Security Bulletin, 26*(7), 3–13 (Reprinted in Orshansky, 1977, pp. 5–15).

Orshansky, M. (1965, January). Counting the poor: Another look at the poverty profile. *Social Security Bulletin, 28*(1), 3–29 (Reprinted in *Social Security Bulletin, 51*(10), October 1988, pp. 25–51).

Ostrom, T. M., Carpenter, S. L., Sedikides, C., & Li, F. (1993). Differential processing of in-group and out-group information. *Journal of Personality & Social Psychology, 64,* 21–34.

Ottmar, E. R., Rimm-Kaufman, S. E., Berry, R. Q., & Larsen, R. A. (2013). *The Responsive Classroom Approach increases the use of standards-based mathematics teaching practices.* Retrieved from http://curry.virginia.edu/uploads/resourceLibrary/CASTL_Research_Brief-Ottmar_et_al._(2013)_ESJ.pdf

Parvizi, J., Anderson, S. W., Martin, C. O., Damasio, H., & Damasio, A. R. (2001). Pathological laughter and crying: A link to the cerebellum. *Brain: A Journal of Neurology, 124*(9), 1708–1719. https://doi.org/10.1093/brain/124.9.1708

Patterson, R., & Stewart-Patterson, C. (2001). The well-made bed: An unappreciated public health risk. *CMAJ: Canadian Medical Association Journal, 165*(12), 1591–1592.

Peters, G., & Woolley, J. T. (*Online,* 1999). Johnson, L.B. (1964, January 8). *Annual Message to the Congress on the State of the Union.* The American Presidency Project. http://www.presidency.ucsb.edu/ws/?pid=26787 and https://www.presidency.ucsb.edu/documents/annual-message-the-congress-the-state-the-union-25

Peterson, G. W., Southworth, L. E., & Peters, D. F. (1983). Children's self-esteem and maternal behavior in three low-income samples. *Psychological Reports, 52*(1), 79–86. https://doi.org/10.2466/pr0.1983.52.1.79

Pharo, H., Sim, C., Graham, M., Gross, J., & Hayne, H. (2011). Risky business: Executive function, personality, and reckless behavior during adolescence and emerging adulthood. *Behavioral Neuroscience, 125*(6), 970–978.

Phillips, L. H., Henry, J. D., Hosie, J. A., & Milne, A. B. (2006). Age, anger regulation and well-being. *Aging & Mental Health, 10*(3), 250–256.

Piaget, J. (1952). *The origins of intelligence in children* (M. Cook, Trans.). New York, NY: Norton. doi:10.1037/11494-000.

Piaget, J. (1977). *The development of thought: Equilibration of cognitive structures* (A. Rosin, Trans). Oxford, England: Viking.

Pinker, S., & Bloom, P. (1990). Natural language and natural selection. *Behavioral and Brain Sciences, 13*(4), 707–784.

Pollitt, E. (1994). Poverty and child development: Relevance of research in developing countries to the United States. *Child Development, 65*(2), 283–295.

Pouw, W. T. J. L., van Gog, T., & Paas, F. (2014). An embedded and embodied cognition review of instructional manipulatives. *Educational Psychology Review, 26,* 51–72. doi:10.1007/s10648-014-9255-5

Proctor, B., Semega, J. L., & Kollar, M. A. (2016). *Income and poverty in the United States: 2015* (U.S. Census Bureau, Report Number: P60-256).

Retrieved from https://www.census.gov/library/publications/2016/demo/p60-256.html

Pronin, E., Jacobs, E., & Wegner, D. M. (2008). Psychological effects of thought acceleration. *Emotion*, 8(5), 597–612. https://doi.org/10.1037/a0013268

Provine, R. R. (2000). *Laughter: A scientific investigation*. New York, NY: Viking.

Pugh, K., Mencl, W., Jenner, A., Katz, L., Frost, S., Lee, J., Shaywitz, S., & Shaywitz, B. (2000). Functional neuroimaging studies of reading and reading disability (Developmental Dyslexia). *Mental retardation and developmental disabilities research reviews*, 6,207–213.10.1002/1098-2779(2000)6:3<207::AID-MRDD8>3.0.CO;2-P.

Ramos, B. P., Arnsten, A. F. (2007). Adrenergic pharmacology and cognition: Focus on the prefrontal cortex. *Pharmacology & Therapeutics*, 113, 523–536. doi.org:10.1016/j.pharmthera.2006.11.006

Rao, H., Betancourt, L., Giannetta, J., Brodsky, N., Korczykowski, M., Avants, B., Gee, J., Wang, D. J., Hurt, H., Detre, J., & Farah, M. (2010). Early parental care is important for hippocampal maturation: Evidence from brain morphology in humans. *NeuroImage*, 49, 1144–1150.

Rauscher, F. H., Shaw, G. L., & Ky, K. N. (1995). Listening to Mozart enhances spatial temporal reasoning: Towards a neurophysiological basis. *Neuroscience Letters*, 185, 44–47.

Raver, C., & Blair, C. (2016). Neuroscientific insights: Attention, working memory, and inhibitory control. *Future of Children, 26*, 95–118.

Reardon, S. F. (2011). The widening academic achievement gap between the rich and the poor: New evidence and possible explanations. In R. Murnane, & G. Duncan (Eds.), *Whither opportunity? Rising inequality and the uncertain life chances of low-income children* (pp. 91–116). New York, NY: Russell Sage Foundation.

Reardon, S. F., Valentino, R. A., & Shores, K. A. (2012). Patterns of literacy among U.S. students. *The Future of Children, 22*(2), 17–37. https://doi.org/10.1353/foc.2012.0015

Reeve, J. (2009). Why teachers adopt a controlling motivating style toward students and how they can become more autonomy supportive. *Educational Psychologist*, 44(3), 159–175.

Reeves, T. C., Herrington, J., & Oliver, R. (2004). A development research agenda for online collaborative learning. *Educational Technology Research and Development*, 52(4), 53.

Reinke, W. M., Herman, K. C., & Stormont, M. (2013). Classroom-level positive behavior supports in schools implementing SW-PBIS: Identifying areas for enhancement. *Journal of Positive Behavior Interventions*, 15(1), 39–50.

Reyes, M. R., Brackett, M. A., Rivers, S. E., White, M., & Salovey, P. (2012). Classroom emotional climate, student engagement, and academic achievement. *Journal of Educational Psychology*, 104(3), 700.

Ribera, T., BrckaLorenz, A., Cole, E. R., & Laird, T. F. N. (2012, April). *Examining the importance of teaching clarity: Findings from the faculty survey of student engagement*. Paper presented at the Annual Meeting of the American Educational Research Association. April 13–17, 2012, Vancouver, BC, Canada.

Ribner, A. D., Willoughby, M. T., & Blair, C. B. (2017). Executive function buffers the association between early math and later academic skills. *Frontiers in Psychology*, 8, 869. doi:10.3389/fpsyg.2017.00869

Rimm-Kaufman, S. E., Baroody, A., Larsen, R., Curby, T. W., & Abry, T. (2015). To what extent do teacher–student interaction quality and student gender contribute to fifth graders' engagement in mathematics learning? *Journal of Educational Psychology*, 107(1), 170–185. http://dx.doi.org/10.1037/a0037252

Rimm-Kaufman, S. E., Curby, T., Grimm, K., Nathanson, L., & Brock, L. (2009).The contribution of children's self-regulation and classroom quality to children's adaptive behaviors in the kindergarten classroom. *Developmental Psychology*, 45(4), 958–972.

Rizzolatti, G., & Arbib, M. A. (1998). Language within our grasp. *Trends in Neuroscience*, 21, 188–194.

Rizzolatti, G., Cattaneo, L., Fabbri-Destro, M., & Rozzi, S. (2014). Cortical mechanisms underlying the organization of goal-directed actions and mirror neuron-based action understanding. *Physiological Reviews*, 94, 655–706.

Rizzolatti, G., & Craighero, L. (2004). The mirror-neuron system. *Annual Review Neuroscience, 27*,

169–192. doi:10.1146/annurev.neuro.27.070203.144230. PMID: 15217330.

Roden, I., Grube, D., Bongard, S., & Kreutz, G. (2014). Does music training enhance working memory performance? Findings from a quasi-experimental longitudinal study. *Psychology of Music*, *42*(2), 284–298. https://doi.org/10.1177/0305735612471239

Rohner, R. P., & Britner, P. A. (2002). Worldwide mental health correlates of parental acceptance-rejection: Review of cross-cultural and intracultural evidence. *Cross-Cultural Research*, *36*(1), 16–47. https://doi.org/10.1177/106939710203600102

Romeo, R. R., Christodoulou, J. A., Halverson, K., Murtagh, J., Cyr, A. B., Schimmel, C., Chang, P., Hook, P. E., & Gabrieli, J. D. (2017). Socioeconomic status and reading disability: Neuroanatomy and plasticity in response to intervention. *Cerebral Cortex*, *28*, 2297–2312.

Roorda, D. L., Koomen, H. M., Spilt, J. L., & Oort, F. J. (2011). The influence of affective teacher–student relationships on students' school engagement and achievement: A meta-analytic approach. *Review of Educational Research*, *81*(4), 493–529.

Rosenberg, M. (1986). *Conceiving the self* (Reprint Edition). Melbourne, FL: Krieger.

Rosenshine, B. (2012). Principles of instruction: Research-based strategies that all teachers should know. *American Educator*, *36*(1), 12.

Rosenthal, T. L., & Zimmerman, B. J. (1978). *Social learning and cognition*. New York, NY: Academic Press.

Rowe, M. L., & Goldin-Meadow, S. (2009). Differences in early gesture explain SES disparities in child vocabulary size at school entry. *Science*, *323*(5916), 951–953. doi:10.1126/science.1167025

Rudorf, S., & Hare, T. (2014, November). Interactions between dorsolateral and ventromedial prefrontal cortex underlie context-dependent stimulus valuation in goal-directed choice. *Journal of Neuroscience*, *34*(48), 15988–15996.

Rueda, M. R., Rothbart, M. K., McCandliss, B. D., Saccomanno, L., & Posner, M. I. (2005). Training, maturation, and genetic influences on the development of executive attention. *Proceedings of the National Academy of Sciences of USA*, *102* 41, 14931–14936.

Sabin, J. A., Nosek, B. A., Greenwald, A. G., & Rivara, F. P. (2009). Physician's implicit and explicit attitudes about Race by MD race, ethnicity and gender. *Journal of Health Care for the Poor and Underserved*, *20*, 896.

Sachs, M., Kaplan, J., Der Sarkissian, A., & Habibi, A. (2017). Increased engagement of the cognitive control network associated with music training in children during an FMRI Stroop Task. *PLoS One*, *12*, e0187254. doi:10.1371/journal.pone.0187254

Sala, G., & Gobet, F. (2017b). When the music's over. Does music skill transfer to children's and young adolescents' cognitive and academic skills? A meta-analysis. *Educational Research Review 20*, 55–67. doi:10.1016/j.edurev.2016.11.005

Sanchez, H. (2003). *The mentor's guide to promoting resiliency*. Bloomington, IN: Xlibris.

Sanchez, H. (2008). *A brain-based approach to closing the achievement gap*. Bloomington, IN: Xlibris.

Sanchez, H. (2010). *School climate assessment data* (Unpublished, n.d.). Resiliency Inc., Durham, NC.

Sangrigoli, S., Pallier, C., Argenti, A.-M., Ventureyra, V. A. G., & de Schonen, S. (2005). Reversibility of the other-race effect in face recognition during childhood. *Psychological Science*, *16*, 440–444.

Sarsour, K., Sheridan, M. M., Jutte, D. P., Nuru-Jeter, A., Hinshaw, S., & Boyce, W. T. (2011). Family socioeconomic status and child executive functions: The roles of language, home environment, and single parenthood. *Journal of the International Neuropsychological Society: JINS*, *17*(1), 120–132.

Schacter, D. L., Gilbert, D. T., & Wenger, D. M. (2009). *Psychology*. New York, NY: Worth.

Schellenberg, E. G. (2004). Music lessons enhance IQ. *Psychological Science*, *15*, 511–514.

Schellenberg, E. G. (2006). Long-term positive associations between music lessons and IQ. *Journal of Educational Psychology*, *98*, 457–468.

Shield, M., & Dole, S. (2013). Assessing the potential of mathematics textbooks to promote deep learning. *Educational Studies in Mathematics*, *82*(2), 183–199.

Schiff, M., & Lewontin, R. (1986). *Education and class*. Oxford, England: Clarendon Press.

Schiller, C. E., Meltzer-Brody, S., & Rubinow, D. R. (2015). The role of reproductive hormones in postpartum depression. *CNS Spectrums*, *20*(1), 48–59. https://doi.org/10.1017/S1092852914000480

Schlaug, G., Jäncke, L., Huang, Y., Staiger, J. F., & Steinmetz, H. (1995a). Increased corpus callosum size in musicians. *Neuropsychologia, 33,* 1047–1055.

Schlaug, G., Jäncke, L., Huang, Y., & Steinmetz, H. (1995b). In vivo evidence of structural brain asymmetry in musicians. *Science, 267,* 699–671.

Schlesinger, A. (2007). Folly's antidote. *The New York Times.* ProQuest, p. A19.

Schnall, S., Haidt, J., Clore, G. L., & Jordan, A. H. (2008). Disgust as embodied moral judgment. *Personality & Social Psychology Bulletin, 34*(8), 1096–1109. https://doi.org/10.1177/01461672 08317771

Schneider, P., Scherg, H. G., Dosch, H. J., Specht, Gutschalk, A., & Rupp, A. (2002). Morphology of Heschl's gyrus reflects enhanced activation in the auditory cortex of musicians. *Nature Neuroscience, 5,* 688–694.

Schon, D. A. (1987). *Educating the reflective practitioner. Toward a new design for teaching and learning in the professions* (The Jossey-Bass Higher Education Series). San Francisco, CA: Jossey-Bass.

Schunk, D. H. (2001). Social cognitive theory and self-regulated learning. In B. J. Zimmerman & D. H. Schunk (Eds.), *Self-regulated learning and academic achievement: Theoretical perspectives* (p. 125–151). Mahwah, NJ: Lawrence Erlbaum.

Schunk, D. H., & Ertmer, P. A. (2000). Self-regulation and academic learning: Self-efficacy enhancing interventions. In M. Boekaerts, P. R. Pintrich, & M. Zeidner (Eds.), *Handbook of self-regulation* (pp. 631–649). New York, NY: Academic Press. https://doi.org/10.1016/B978-012109890-2/50048-2

Schunk, Dale & Zimmerman, Barry. (1997). Social origin of self-regulatory competence. *Educational Psychologist 32.* 195–208. 10.1207/s15326985ep3204_1

Schupp, H. T., Flaisch, T., Stockburger, J., & Junghöfer, M. (2006). Emotion and attention: Event-related brain potential studies. *Progress in Brain Research, 156,* 31–51.

Schwartz, S. E. O., Rhodes, J. E., Spencer, R., & Grossman, J. B. (2013). Youth initiated mentoring: Investigating a new approach to working with vulnerable adolescents. *American Journal of Community Psychology, 52,* 155–169.

Schweder, R. (2009). *The child: An encyclopedic companion* (pp. 1–3). Chicago, IL: University of Chicago Press.

Seidel, T., & Shavelson, R. J. (2007). Teaching effectiveness research in the past decade: The role of theory and research design in disentangling meta-analysis results. *Review of Educational Research, 77*(4), 454–499.

Sentencing Project, The. (2010). *U.S. racial disparity.* Washington, DC: Author.

Shapiro, S., Lyons, K., Miller, R. C., Butler, B., Vieten, C., & Zelazo, P. (2015). Contemplation in the classroom: A new direction for improving childhood education. *Educational Psychology Review, 27,* 1–30.

Sharpe, T., Brown, M., & Crider, K. (1995). The effects of a sportsmanship curriculum intervention on generalized positive social behavior of urban elementary school students. *Journal of Applied Behavior Analysis, 28*(4), 401–416.

Shaywitz, B. A., Shaywitz, S. E., Pugh, K. R., Mencl, W. E., Fulbright, R. K., Skudlarski, P., Constable, R. T., Marchione, K. E., Fletcher, J. M., Lyon, G. R., & Gore, J. C. (2002). Disruption of posterior brain systems for reading in children with developmental dyslexia. *Biological Psychiatry, 52*(2), 101–110. https://doi.org/10.1016/s0006-3223(02)01365-3

Shaywitz, S. E., & Shaywitz, B. A. (2005). Dyslexia (specific reading disability). *Biological Psychiatry, 57*(11), 1301–1309. https://doi.org/10.1016/j.biopsych.2005.01.043

Shaywitz, S., Shaywitz, B., Pugh, K., Fulbright, R., Constable, R., Mencl, W., Shankweiler, D., Liberman, A.,Skudlarski, P., Fletcher, J., Katz, L., Marchione, K., Lacadie, C., Gatenby, C., & Gore, J. (1998). Functional disruption in the organization of the brain for reading in dyslexia. *Proceedings of the National Academy of Sciences of the USA, 95,* 2636–2641. 10.1073/pnas.95.5.2636

Shonkoff, J. P. & Garner, A. (2012). The Committee on Psychosocial Aspects of Child and Family Health, Committee on Early Childhood, Adoption, and Dependent Care, and Section on Developmental and Behavioral Pediatrics, and Siegel, B. S., Dobbins, M. I., Earls, M. F., Garner, A. S., McGuinn, L., Pascoe, J., & Wood, D. L. The lifelong effects of early childhood adversity and toxic stress. *Pediatrics, 129*(1).

Shute, V. J. (2008). Focus on formative feedback. *Review of Educational Research, 78*(1), 153–189.

Sikora, J., Evans, M. D. R., & Kelley, J. (2018). Scholarly culture: How books in adolescence enhance adult literacy, numeracy and technology skills in 31 societies. *Social Science Research*. 10.1016/j.ssresearch.2018.10.003.

Sisk, V. F., Burgoyne, A. P., Sun, J., Butler, J. L., & Macnamara, B. N. (2018). To what extent and under which circumstances are growth mind-sets important to academic achievement? Two meta-analyses. *Psychological Science, 29*(4), 549–571.

Skiba, R. J., Horner, R. H., Chung, C. G., Rausch, M., May, S. L., & Tobin, T. (2011). Race is not neutral: A national investigation of African American and Latino disproportionality in school discipline. *School Psychology Review, 40*, 85–107.

Skinner, E. A., & Pitzer, J. R. (2012). Developmental dynamics of student engagement, coping, and everyday resilience. In S. L. Christenson, A. L. Reschly, & C. Wylie (Eds.), *Handbook of research on student engagement* (pp. 21–44). New York, NY: Spring Science+Business Media.

Smith, F., & Smith, M. (2018). Decoding dynamic implicit and explicit representations of facial expressions of emotion from EEG [Abstract]. bioRxiv (preprint server). doi: https://doi.org/10.1101/453654

Smith, F. W., & Rossit, S. (2018). Identifying and detecting facial expressions of emotion in peripheral vision. *PLoS One, 13*(5): e0197160. https://doi.org/10.1371/journal.pone.0197160

Solomon, D., Battistich, V., Watson, M., Schaps, E., & Lewis, C. (2000). A six-district study of educational change: Direct and mediated effects of the Child Development Project. *Social Psychology of Education, 4*(1), 3–51.

Son, S. H., & Morrison, F. J. (2010). The nature and impact of changes in home learning environment on development of language and academic skills in preschool children. *Developmental Psychology, 46*, 1103–1118.

Sousa, D. A., (2011). *How the brain learns* (4th ed.), Thousand Oaks, CA: Corwin.

Southern Poverty Law Center. Easy money, impossible debt: How predatory lending traps Alabama's poor (2013, February), p. 7. Retrieved from https://www.splcenter.org/20130227/easy-money-impossible-debt-how-predatory-lending-traps-alabama%E2%80%99s-poor

Sowell, E. R., Peterson, B. S., Thompson, P. M., Welcome, S. E., Henkenius, A. L., & Toga, A. W. (2003). Mapping cortical change across the human life span. *Nature Neuroscience, 6*(3), 309–315.

Spreckelmeyer, K. N., Kutas, M., Urbach, T., Altenmüller, E., & Münte, T. F. (2009). Neural processing of vocal emotion and identity. *Brain and Cognition, 69*(1), 121–126. 10.1016/j.bandc.2008.06.003.

Srivastava, K., & Das, R. C. (2016). Empathy: Process of adaptation and change, is it trainable? *Industrial Psychiatry Journal, 25*(1), 1–3. doi:10.4103/0972-6748.196055

Stanley, D., Sokol-Hessner, P., Banaji, M. R., & Phelps, E. A. (2011). Implicit race attitudes predict trustworthiness judgments and economic trust decisions. *Proceedings of the National Academy of Science, 108*, 7710–7715.

Stanley, D., & Sokol-Hessner, P., Fareri, D., Perino, M., Delgado, M., Banaji, M., & Phelps, E. (2012). Race and reputation: Perceived racial group trustworthiness influences the neural correlates of trust decisions. *Philosophical Transactions of the Royal Society of London. Series B: Biological Sciences, 367*, 744–753. 10.1098/rstb.2011.0300

Stephens, N. M., Fryberg, S. A., & Markus, H. R. (2012). It's your choice: How the middle-class model of independence disadvantages working-class Americans. In S. T. Fiske & H. R. Markus (Eds.), *Facing social class: How societal rank influences interaction* (p. 87–106). New York, NY: Russell Sage Foundation.

Storch, S., & Whitehurst, G. J. (2001). The role of family and home in the literacy development of children from low-income backgrounds. *New Directions for Child and Adolesccent Development*, (92), 53–72.

Strøm, I. F., Thoresen, S., Wentzel-Larsen, T., & Dyb, G. (2013). Violence, bullying and academic achievement: A study of 15-year-old adolescents and their school environment. *Child Abuse & Neglect, 37*(4), 243–251. https://doi.org/10.1016/j.chiabu.2012.10.010

Strong, M., Gargani, J., & Hacifazlioğlu, Ö. (2011). Do we know a successful teacher when we see one? Experiments in the identification of effective teachers. *Journal of Teacher Education*, *62*(4), 367–382.

Stuss, D. T., & Benson, D. F. (1983). *Advances in neuropsychology and behavioral neurology: Vol.1. Neuropsychology of human emotion* (pp. 111–140). New York: NY: Guilford Press.

Swartz, J., Hariri, A., & Williamson, D. (2017). An epigenetic mechanism links socioeconomic status to changes in depression-related brain function in high-risk adolescents. *Molecular Psychiatry*, *22*, 209–214.

Sylvester, R. (2003). *A biological brain in a cultural classroom* (2nd ed.). Thousand Oaks, CA: Sage.

Tamis-LeMonda, C., Bornstein, M., & Baumwell, L. (2001). Maternal responsiveness and children's achievement of language milestones. *Child Development*, *72*(3), 748–767. Retrieved February 21, 2020, from www.jstor.org/stable/1132453

Tang, Y., Ma, Y., Wang, J., Fan, Y., Feng, S., Lu, Q., Yu, Q., Sui, D., Rothbart, M. K., Fan, M., & Posner, M. I. (2007). Short-term meditation training improves attention and self-regulation. *Proceedings of the National Academy of Sciences of the USA*, *104*(43), 17152–17156.

Taylor, B. M., Pearson, P. D., Peterson, D. S., & Rodriguez, M. C. (2003). Reading growth in high-poverty classrooms: The influence of teacher practices that encourage cognitive engagement in literacy learning. *The Elementary School Journal*, *104*(1), 3–28.

Taylor, S. E., Repetti, R. L., & Seeman, T. (1997). Health psychology: What is an unhealthy environment and how does it get under the skin? *Annual Review of Psychology*, *48*, 411–447. https://doi.org/10.1146/annurev.psych.48.1.411

Temple, E., Deutsch, G., Poldrack, R., Miller, S., Tallal, P., Merzenich, M., Gabrieli, J. (2003). Neural deficits in children with dyslexia ameliorated by behavioral remediation: Evidence from functional MRI. *Proceedings of the National Academy of Sciences of the USA*, *100*, 2860-5. 10.1073/pnas.0030098100.

Tharp, R. G., & Gallimore, R. (1988). *Rousing minds to life: Teaching, learning, and schooling in social context*. New York, NY: Cambridge University Press.

Thierry, G., Pegna, A. J., Dodds, C., Roberts, M., Basan, S., & Downing, P. (2006). An event-related potential component sensitive to images of the human body. *NeuroImage*, *32*, 871–879.

Tishman, S., Jay, E., & Perkins, D. N. (1993). Teaching thinking dispositions: From transmission to enculturation. *Theory into Practice*, *32*(3), 147–153.

Toch, T. (2003). *High Schools on a Human Scale*. Boston, MA: Beacon Press.

Todd, A. R., Thiem, K. C., & Neel, R. (2016). Does seeing faces of young Black boys facilitate the identification of threatening stimuli? *Psychological Science*, *27*, 384–393. doi:10.1177/095679761 5624492

Tomalski, P., Moore, D. G., Ribeiro, H., Axelsson, E., Murphy, E., Karmiloff-Smith, A., Johnson, M. H., & Kushnerenko, E. (2013). Socioeconomic status and functional brain development: Associations in early infancy. *Developmental Science*, *16*(5), 676–87.

Tottenham, N., Hare, T. A., Millner, A. J., Gilhooly, T., Zevin, J. D., & Casey, B. J. (2011). Elevated amygdala response to faces following early deprivation. *Developmental Science*, *14*(2), 190–204.

Trainor, L. J., Shahin, A. J., & Roberts, L. E. (2009). Understanding the benefits of musical training. *Annals of the New York Academy of Sciences. 1169*, 133–142. doi:10.1111/j.1749-6632.2009.04589.x

Trzesniewski, K. H., Donnellan, M. B., Moffitt, T. E., Robins, R. W., Poulton, R., & Caspi, A. (2006). Low self-esteem during adolescence predicts poor health, criminal behavior, and limited economic prospects during adulthood. *Developmental Psychology*, *42*(2), 381–390. https://doi.org/10.1037/0012-1649.42.2.381

Turkeltaub, P. E., Eden, G. F., Jones, K. M., & Zeffiro, T. A. (2002). Meta-analysis of the functional neuroanatomy of single-word reading: Method and validation. *NeuroImage*, *16*(3, Pt. 1), 765–780. https://doi.org/10.1006/nimg.2002.1131

Uehara, E. S., Chalmers, D., Jenkins, E. J., & Shakoor, B. H. (1996). African American youth encounters with violence: Results from the community mental health council violence screening project. *Journal of Black Studies*, *26*(6), 768–781. https://doi.org/10.1177/002193479602600607

University of California–Los Angeles. (2007, May 4). Why autistic children do not imitate or empathize: It could be a dysfunctional mirror-neuron system. *ScienceDaily*. Retrieved October 13, 2020, from www.sciencedaily.com/releases/2007/05/070504121241.htm

U.S. Bureau of Labor Statistics [Bureau of Labor Statistics]. (2018, May). *Occupational employment and wages*. Retrieved from https://wweallw.bls.gov/oes/2018/may/oes111011.htm

U.S. Census Bureau. (2017, September). *Income and poverty in the United States*. Retrieved from https://www.census.gov/library/publications/2018/demo/p60-263.html

U. S. Department of Education [U.S. DOE], National Center for Education Statistics [NCES], Common Core of Data (CCD). (2012), *Public Elementary/Secondary School Universe Survey, 2010–11*. See Digest of Education Statistics 2012, table 112.

U.S. Department of Education [U.S. DOE], National Center for Education Statistics [NCES], Common Core of Data (CCD), (2016a). *Public Elementary/Secondary School Universe Survey, 2014–15*. See Digest of Education Statistics.

U.S. Department of Education [U.S. DOE], Office of Civil Rights [OCR]. (2016b, June). 2013–2014 Civil rights data collection: Key data highlights on equity and opportunity gaps in our nation's public schools. Retrieved from http://www2.ed.gov/about/offices/list/ocr/docs/crdc-2013-14.html

Uvnäs-Moberg K. (1997). Oxytocin linked antistress effects: The relaxation and growth response. *Acta physiologica Scandinavica, Supplementum, 640*, 38–42.

Uys, E. L. (2003). Riding the rails: Teenagers on the move during the Great Depression. New York, NY: Routledge.

Valenstein, E., Bowers, D., Verfaellie, M., Watson., R., Day, A., & Heilman K. M. (1987). Retrosplenial amnesia. *Brain, 110*(163), 1–1636.

Van de Riet., Wim A. C., Grèzes., J., & de Gelder, B. (2009). Specific and common brain regions involved in the perception of faces and bodies and the representation of their emotional expressions. *Social Neuroscience, 4*(2), 101–120. doi:10.1080/17470910701865367

Vellutiino, F. R., Fletcher, J. M., Snowling, M. J., & Scanlon, D. M. (2004). Specific reading disability (dyslexia): What have we learned in the past four decades? *Journal of Child Psychology and Psychiatry and Allied Disciplines, 45*(1), 2–40. https://doi.org/10.1046/j.0021-9630.2003.00305.x

Vericker, T. C., Macomber, J. E., & Golden, O. A. (2010). *Infants of depressed mothers living in poverty: Opportunities to identify and serve* [Brief 1, August 2010]. Washington, DC: The Urban Institute.

Viding, E., Sebastian, C., Dadds, M., Lockwood, P., Cecil, C., De Brito, S., & McCrory, E. (2012). Amygdala response to preattentive masked fear in children with conduct problems: The role of callous-unemotional traits. *The American Journal of Psychiatry, 169*, 1109–1116. 10.1176/appi.ajp.2012.12020191

Vorhauser-Smith, S. (2011). The neuroscience of talent management. *Employment Relations Today, 38*, 17–22. 10.1002/ert.20327

Vygotsky, L. S. (1978). *Mind in society*. Cambridge, MA: Harvard University.

Walker, P. M., Silvert, L., Hewstone, M., & Nobre, A. C. (2008). Social contact and other-race face processing in the human brain. *Social Cognitive and Affective Neuroscience, 3*, 16–25.

Wang, Y., Chung, M. K., Dentico, D., Lutz, A., & Davidson, R. J. (2017). Does self-compassion facilitate resilience to stigma? A school-based study of sexual and gender minority youth. *Mindfulness*, 1–11.

Weaver, K., Garcia, S. M., Schwarz, N., & Miller, D. T. (2007). Inferring the popularity of an opinion from its familiarity: A repetitive voice can sound like a chorus. *Journal of Personality and Social Psychology, 92*(5), 821–833. https://doi.org/10.1037/0022-3514.92.5.821

Weisbuch, M., Pauker, K., & Ambady, N. (2009). The subtle transmission of race bias via televised nonverbal behavior. *Science, 326*, 1711–1714. doi:10.1126/science.1178358

Weng, H. Y., Fox, A. S., Shackman, A. J., Stodola, D. E., Caldwell, J. Z., Olson, M. C., Rogers, G. M., & Davidson, R. J. (2013). Compassion training alters altruism and neural responses to suffering. *Psychological Science, 24*(7), 1171–1180.

Werner, E. E. (1989). High-risk children in young adulthood: A longitudinal study from birth to 32 years. *The American Journal of Orthopsychiatry, 59*(1), 72–81.

Werner, E. E. (2005). What can we learn about resilience from large-scale longitudinal studies? In S. Goldstein & R. Brooks (Eds.), *Handbook of resilience in children* (pp. 91–106). New York, NY: Kluwer Academic.

West, R. L., Bagwell, D. K., & Dark-Freudeman, A. (2005). Memory and goal setting: The response of older and younger adults to positive and objective feedback. *Psychology and Aging, 20*(2), 195–201. https://doi.org/10.1037/0882-7974.20.2.195

Werner, E. E., & Smith, R. S. (2001). *Journeys from childhood to midlife: Risk, resilience, and recovery.* New York, NY: Cornell University Press.

Wharton-McDonald, R., Pressley, M., & Hampston, J. M. (1998). Outstanding literacy instruction in first grade: Teacher practices and student achievement. *Elementary School Journal, 99*, 101–128.

White, S., Marsh, A. A., Fowler, K. A., Schechter, J., Adalio, C., Pope, K., Sinclair, S., Pine, D., & Blair, R. (2012). Reduced amygdala response in youths with disruptive behavior disorders and psychopathic traits: Decreased emotional response versus increased top-down attention to nonemotional features. *The American Journal of Psychiatry, 169*(7), 750–8.

Wigfield, A., Gladstone, J. N., & Turci, L. (2016). Beyond cognition: Reading motivation and reading comprehension. *Child Development Perspectives, 10*(3), 190–195.

Wild, L. G., Flisher, A., Bhana, A., & Lombard, C. (2004). Associations among adolescent risk behaviours and self-esteem in six domains. *Journal of Child Psychology and Psychiatry and Allied Disciplines, 45*(8), 14541467.

Wilen, W. W., & Clegg, A. A. (1986). Effective questions and questioning: A research review. *Theory & Research in Social Education, 14*(2), 153–161. doi10.1080/00933104.1986.10505518

Wilkinson, N. D. (2019). Changing mindsets. *Nature Reviews Cancer, 19*, 539–539.

Williams, K. E., Barrett, M. S., Welch, G. F., Abad, V., & Broughton, M. (2015). Associations between early shared music activities in the home and later child outcomes: Findings from the longitudinal study of Australian children. *Early Childhood Research Quarterly, 31*, 113–124. doi: 10.1016/j.ecresq.2015.01.004

Wills, T. A., & Cleary, S. D. (1996). How are social support effects mediated? A test with parental support and adolescent substance use. *Journal of Personality and Social Psychology, 71*(5), 937–952. https://doi.org/10.1037/0022-3514.71.5.937

Wills, T., & Dishion, T. (2004). Temperament and adolescent substance use: A transactional analysis of emerging self-control. *Journal of Clinical Child & Adolescent Psychology, 33*, 69–81.

Wolfgang, C., Stannard, L., & Jones, I. (2001). Block play performance among preschoolers as a predictor of later school achievement in mathematics. *Journal of Research in Childhood Education, 15*, 173–180. 10.1080/02568540109594958

Wood, W., & Neal, D. T. (2007). A new look at habits and the habit-goal interface. *Psychological Review, 114*(4), 843–863. https://doi.org/10.1037/0033-295X.114.4.843

Woolfolk, A., 2014. Educational psychology: Active learning edition (12th ed.). San Francisco, CA: Pearson Education.

Wyman, L., Crum, R. M., & Celentano, D. (2012). Depressed mood and cause-specific mortality: A 40-year general community assessment. *Annals of Epidemiology, 22*(9), 638–643. https://doi.org/10.1016/j.annepidem.2012.06.102

Xu, J., Kemeny, S., Park, G. H., Frattali, C., & Braun, A. (2005). Language in context: Emergent features of word, sentence, and narrative comprehension. *NeuroImage, 25*, 1002–1015.

Young, A., Beitchman, J., Johnson, C., Douglas, L., Atkinson, L., Escobar, M., & Wilson, B. (2002). Young adult academic outcomes in a longitudinal sample of speech/language impaired and control children. *Journal of Child Psychology and Psychiatry and Allied Disciplines, 43*, 635–645. 10.1111/1469-7610.00052

Yurgelun-Todd, D. (2007). Emotional and cognitive changes during adolescence. *Current Opinion in Neurobiology, 17*, 251–257. 10.1016/j.conb.2007.03.009

Zak, P. J., Kurzban, R., Ahmadi, S., Swerdloff, R. S., Park, J. W., Efremidze, L., Redwine, K. E., Morgan, K., & Matzner, W. (2009). Testosterone administration decreases generosity in the ultimatum game. *PloS One, 4*(12), e8330.

Zak, P., Kurzban, R., & Matzner, W. (2005). Oxytocin is associated with human trustworthiness.

Hormones and Behavior, *48*(5), 522–527. doi: 10.1016/j.yhbeh.2005.07.009. PMID 16109416

Zampierin, Sara. (2013). *Easy money, impossible debt: How predatory lending traps Alabama's poor*. Southern Poverty Law Center. Retrieved from www.splcenter.org/20130227/easy-money-impossible-debt-how-predatory-lending-traps-alabama%E2%80%99s-poor

Zatorre, R. J., Perry, D. W., Beckett, C. A., Westbury, C. F., & Evans, A. C. (1998). Functional anatomy of musical processing in listeners with absolute pitch and relative pitch. *Proceedings of the National Academy of Sciences*, *95*, 3172–3177.

Zelazo, P. D., & Müller, U. (2010). Executive function in typical and atypical development. In U. Goswami (Ed.), *The Wiley-Blackwell handbook of childhood cognitive development* (2nd ed., pp. 574–603). Hoboken, NJ: Wiley-Blackwell. doi:10.1002/9781444325485.ch22

Zins, J. E., & Ponti, C. R. (1990). Strategies to facilitate the implementation, organization, and operation of system-wide consultation programs. *Journal of Educational & Psychological Consultation*, *1*(3), 205–218. https://doi.org/10.1207/s1532768xjepc0103_1

Index

A SAGE Publishing Company

CORWIN HAS ONE MISSION: to enhance education through intentional professional learning.

We build long-term relationships with our authors, educators, clients, and associations who partner with us to develop and continuously improve the best evidence-based practices that establish and support lifelong learning.

Keep learning...

Also from Horacio Sanchez

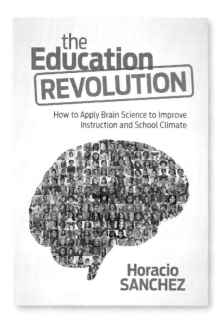

BESTSELLER!

THE EDUCATION REVOLUTION

How to Apply Brain Science to Improve Instruction and School Climate

Brain research has the power to revolutionize education, but it can be difficult for educators to implement innovative strategies without the proper knowledge or resources. *The Education Revolution* bridges the gap between neuroscience, psychology, and educational practice to deliver what educators need: concrete applications of current research that they can use in their schools. Readers will find

- Teaching strategies based on the latest brain research

- Scientifically sound, solution-focused practices to address the root of negative behaviors

- Strategies for counteracting the negative impact of technology on the brain

- Model lessons for teachers that demonstrate how to implement the given strategies

Available for consulting!

Horacio Sanchez is a highly sought-after speaker and educational consultant, helping schools learn to apply neuroscience to improve educational outcomes. He presents diverse topics, such as overcoming the impact of poverty, improving school climate, engaging in brain-based instruction, and addressing issues related to implicit bias. He is recognized as one of the nation's leading authorities on resiliency and applied brain science.

Visit **www.resiliencyinc.com** for information about consulting.

Made in United States
Orlando, FL
07 February 2024